D1565191

ABRAHAM LINCOLN.

The
Assassination
of
Abraham Lincoln

Flight, Pursuit, Capture, and Punishment
of the Conspirators

BY

Osborn H. Oldroyd

AUTHOR OF "A SOLDIER'S STORY OF THE SEIGE OF VICKSBURG"
EDITOR AND COMPILER, "WORDS OF LINCOLN"

WITH AN INTRODUCTION BY

T. M. Harris

LATE BRIGADIER-GENERAL U. S. V., AND MAJOR-GENERAL BY BREVET,
A MEMBER OF THE COMMISSION

HERITAGE BOOKS
2007

HERITAGE BOOKS
AN IMPRINT OF HERITAGE BOOKS, INC.

Books, CDs, and more—Worldwide

For our listing of thousands of titles see our website
at
www.HeritageBooks.com

A Facsimile Reprint
Published 2007 by
HERITAGE BOOKS, INC.
Publishing Division
65 East Main Street
Westminster, Maryland 21157-5026

Originally published

Washington, D.C.
O. H. Oldroyd
1901

International Standard Book Number: 978-1-55613-360-2

PREFACE.

PRESIDENTS, kings, and emperors have not unfrequently become the innocent victims of private animosity, ambitious rivalry, treasonable conspiracy, and even ignorant, misguided patriotism. Dark, indeed, is the history of assassinations. But in its long and cruel records no crime has ever paralleled in atrocity the murder of Abraham Lincoln by John Wilkes Booth, whose name will forever stand out conspicuously on the roll of infamy as that of the arch-assassin.

Rome mourned the tragic end of Cæsar; France wept over the downfall, exile, and death of Napoleon; the Netherlands were inconsolable at the loss of the illustrious Prince of Orange; but no people of ancient or modern times ever felt a more profound sorrow over the death of their " foremost man," or ever paid to his memory a more sincere and universal tribute of veneration, love, and tears, than did the American nation on the occasion of the cruel, wanton assassination of their beloved President. Shocking to the civilized world as was his sudden taking off, the name of Abraham Lincoln has risen to shine as a star of the first magnitude in the galaxy of History's most influential characters, never to be eclipsed by the fame of a greater or a better man. William the Silent fell when his country could illy spare him, and his last words were, " Oh, my God, have mercy on this poor people! "

President Lincoln died in the hour of his country's

triumph, and could he have spoken after the assassin fired upon him, doubtless his kindly words would have been: "Forgive them, they know not what they do." It is but fair to state that men are not wanting who claim the assassination of President Lincoln was the result of a Roman Catholic conspiracy; or that the leaders of the Confederacy planned it. For one, I cannot believe that the Roman Catholic Church ever sanctioned that heinous crime. There were Roman Catholics among the conspirators, but it would be unjust to confound the innocent and the guilty; history cannot hold the Roman Catholic hierarchy responsible for this assassination. This is evident from the fact that the Pope hastened with unusual zeal to deliver up John H. Surratt, a fugitive in his dominions, the moment he heard that he was suspected of having participated in the crime. There was no extradition treaty with the Papal States at the time, but the crime with which Surratt was charged was so diabolical that the Pope and Cardinal Antonelli ordered the suspect's arrest without waiting for a formal demand from the Government of the United States. But whatever light the author of this book may be able or unable to throw upon this phase of the subject, he is confident that he is in possession of facts relating to the general subject that will be of interest to the reader.

During the last forty years I have made a very extensive collection of books, papers, medals, medallions, statuary, original photographs, autograph letters and documents, furniture from the old homestead in Springfield, Ill., and numerous other valuable articles relating to Lincoln. To many persons who have visited this collection I have made the promise that I would some day compile for future reference an authentic history of the assassination of President Lincoln, and the flight, pursuit, capture, and punishment of the conspirators. In turning back the leaves of history to that page on which is recorded that awful incident of April 14, 1865, I simply wish to give a faithful record of the plot, not only to destroy a noble human life, but the life of the nation and the life of liberty. Picture Mr. Lincoln, if you will, sitting in the private box of a theater, a *victor*. He is there in relaxation from the terrible strain that he had experienced in carrying the nation's burden for four long years. The very triumph that had come to him in the surrender of the Confederate army awakens no emotions in his heart save those of forgiveness and charity. The assassin's bullet pierced his brain at the moment when the South most needed his wise counsels. He would have been magnanimous to the foe. It would have pleased him better to pardon than to punish. He would have overcome his and his country's enemies and transformed them into friends.

The many accounts of the assassination of Abraham Lincoln that have been written make me hesitate to offer still another; but having lived for ten years under the roof that once sheltered him in Springfield, Ill., and eight years later in the house in which he died, and having met so many persons during the past thirty-six years who either assisted in the escape of the conspirators or took some official part in their capture, trial, and punishment, rare opportunities have been offered me for gathering much true and valuable historical data on this subject.

It is to be hoped that this work will answer the hundreds of questions that have been asked concerning the man and the accomplices of the man who destroyed the precious life of the good and great President, as many of the reports published at the time, and many of the stories since told, have misled the people. As first impressions are the most lasting, the object of this book is to correct those first false impressions. The many questions that are asked by the younger generation who visit the " Old-royd Lincoln Memorial Collection " in the house in which the President died, convince me that they do not possess the true history of that sad event, though eager to gain a knowledge of the facts.

To satisfy that desire, I present this book to the public, with the hope that the work, which has been performed with faithfulness, care, and " malice toward none," will meet its approval. A careful investigation of all the facts and circumstances connected with the assassination, as given by competent authority, tends to show that all the persons who were tried were actually engaged in the conspiracy to kidnap or murder the President. Had the military court reached out a little farther in its investigations, I believe it would have implicated many persons holding positions of power and authority in the service of the Confederate Government.

Whether Booth was the hired agent of a movement organized in Canada to murder the President, and approved at Richmond, I am unable to say, but we do know that the representatives of the Southern Confederacy, who abused the privilege of hospitality while in Canada, made that neutral point a basis of operation against the United States, by organizing plots to burn Northern cities. Many went to Canada to sneakingly operate in the rear, too cowardly to stand in the front of the battle with the brave men they deserted.

There were many persons throughout the country who talked disloyalty, sympathized with the spirit of murder, expressed treasonable words, and said Mr. Lincoln ought to be killed, and they would like to shoot him or furnish

the means for his removal. While these persons did not
actually perpetrate the deed, their language, spirit, and
influence helped to a very great extent to swell the surg-
ing tide of conspiracy which culminated at Ford's
Theater. They unquestionably shared the responsibility
for the crime.

As authority for many statements regarding the evidence given at the trial, reference has been had to Pit-
man's report, and for valuable information freely given
by officers of the Government and others the author is
deeply indebted.

OSBORN H. OLDROYD.

WASHINGTON, D. C.,
October, 1901.

CONTENTS.

CHAPTER I.

CHAPTER II.

CHAPTER III.

DEATH OF THE PRESIDENT, AND THE TAKING OF THE OATH OF OFFICE OF HIS SUCCESSOR.

CHAPTER IV.

OTHER ATTEMPTS AT ASSASSINATION EVENING OF APRIL 14, 1865.

CHAPTER V.

THE FLIGHT AND CAPTURE OF BOOTH AND HEROLD, AND CONFINEMENT OF THEIR ASSOCIATES—BIOGRAPHIES AND STATEMENTS.

ILLUSTRATIONS.

The eighty-two half-tone illustrations are from original photographs and drawings in the "Oldroyd Lincoln Memorial Collection," in the house where Lincoln died, Washington, D. C., and over half of them published for the first time.

xiii

INTRODUCTION.

WHEN the great soul of Abraham Lincoln took its flight on the morning of the 15th of April, 1865, his War Secretary, Edwin M. Stanton, who had sat by his bedside all the night with a heart almost bursting with grief, quietly arose and said, " Now he belongs to the ages."

Never was this more truly predicated of any man. Among all the great men of earth whose names are written on the imperishable rolls of fame none ever had a greater commission given him by his Creator, none a more important mission to the world, and so he was endowed by his Maker with all the great qualities of mind and heart that fitted him for his mighty task, and enabled him to bring it to a successful issue. His mission to the world has its only parallel in that of Moses. Abraham Lincoln belongs not only to his country, but to the world and to the ages. He was in the broadest sense a philanthropist. His story will never pall. Men will never tire of reading of Lincoln. From his humble birth in a log cabin in Kentucky, on to the end, his life is full of interest.

This book treats of his last days and of his sad taking off. Although it contains facts only, carefully gathered up, yet these facts are of so much interest, and of such a character, that it will have the interest of a novel, and insure it a great popularity. The very name of Lincoln, when pronounced in an audible voice, has a sweetness to the ear, and the story of his last days on earth and of his death by the hand of a vile miscreant will always be read with the deepest interest. The facts recorded in this book have been gathered with the greatest care, and will be found both new and interesting.

T. M. HARRIS.

THE ASSASSINATION OF ABRAHAM LINCOLN.

CHAPTER I.

REJOICING AT THE CLOSE OF THE REBELLION, AND
SCENES AT THE WHITE HOUSE.

APRIL 14, 1861, the American flag was hauled down
from Fort Sumter amid the rockings of the Rebellion,
and, after four years of war on a scale of astonishing
vastness, it was again hoisted over the crumbled battle-
ments, April 14, 1865, and throughout the land loyal
hearts felt a thrill of exultation at the thought that right-
eousness had finally triumphed on the very spot where
the first open onslaught upon the Union was made. That
very day President Lincoln was full of life and hope,
laboring with a cheerful heart for the public welfare; and
the dark clouds of rebellion, which during his whole
administration had lowered above, were just beginning
to lift and give assurance that the stars were shining beyond. In such an hour of hope and joy the fatal blow
of the assassin was struck. The President had returned
to Washington in the *River Queen* the evening of April 9,
in safety, from a trip to the front, which included a visit
to Richmond, on the 4th of April, the day after its
evacuation, with the full confidence that the blood of the
nation would soon stop flowing, and that the remaining
years of his Presidency would be years of comparative

THE WHITE HOUSE.

quietude. The capital of the Southern Confederacy, fortified with the utmost care and skill, defended with an army equal in courage and skill to our own, fell, and, without pomp or military escort, the President entered it and walked the streets from which the Southern army had fled forever. Then came on the 9th the surrender of the Napoleon of the Southern army, and the breeze from the South land wafted to the North the first breath of returning peace, which brought forth great rejoicing. President Lincoln laid aside the sword of battle, and in return stretched out in his hand the olive branch, and his great heart went out in sympathy for the defeated.

General Grant arrived at Washington on the 13th, for the purpose of making proper arrangements for the disbanding of a portion of the immense army in the field. Robert T. Lincoln, who was on his staff, accompanied him. In January, 1865, he was attached to the staff of

General Grant, with the rank of captain, at the special request of the President, and the appointment pleased Mr. Lincoln very much. Robert breakfasted at the White House on the morning of the 14th, and the President listened with much interest to the details of the campaign that had just terminated. The Cabinet held a meeting at eleven o'clock, at which General Grant was present. This was the last time the President met with his Cabinet, and it was a most important and satisfactory meeting. The restoration of that portion of country lately in rebellion was discussed, and with one voice it was agreed to restore them to their old place in the sisterhood of States. In the afternoon the President had a pleasant interview with Governor Richard Oglesby and Senator Richard Yates of Illinois, and other prominent persons. He wrote—probably his last letter—on this date to General James H. Van Alen of New York, who had asked Mr. Lincoln not to expose his life unnecessarily, as he had done at Richmond, and assuring him of the earnest desire of all of his countrymen to close the war he had so successfully conducted. " I intend," wrote Lincoln, " to adopt the advice of my friends, and use precaution. I thank you for the assurance you give me that I shall be supported by conservative men like yourself in the efforts I may make to restore the Union, so as to make it, to use your own language, a union of hearts and hands as well as of States." Hon. Schuyler Colfax was one of the early callers upon the President that day. He contemplated visiting the mining regions of the West. Mr. Lincoln conversed with him for an hour, saying: " I want you to take a message from me to the miners whom you visit. I have very large ideas of the mineral wealth of our nation. I believe it practically inexhaustible. It exists all over the Western country, from the

Rocky Mountains to the Pacific, and its development has scarcely commenced. During the war, when we were adding a couple of millions of dollars every day to our national debt, I did not care about encouraging the increase in the volume of our precious metal. We had the country to save first. But now that the rebellion is overthrown, and we know pretty nearly the amount of our national debt, the more gold and silver we mine makes the payment of that debt so much the easier. Now, I am going to encourage that in every possible way. We shall have hundreds of thousands of disbanded soldiers, and many have feared that their return home in such great numbers might paralyze industry by furnishing suddenly a greater supply of labor than there will be a demand for. I am going to try to attract them to the hidden wealth of our mountain ranges, where there is room enough for all. Immigration, which even the war has not stopped, will land upon our shores hundreds of thousands more per year from overcrowded Europe. I intend to point them to the gold and silver that waits for them in the West. Tell the miners, from me, that I shall promote their interests to the utmost of my ability, because their prosperity is the prosperity of the nation; and we shall prove, in a very few years, that we are, indeed, the treasury of the world."

During the afternoon the President and Mrs. Lincoln took quite an extended drive through the city, and during the time he was in a cheerful mood, talking of the troubles of the past and the long looked-for pleasures of the future, when they would be again settled at Springfield, Ill. Mr. Lincoln was extremely happy in the events of the day which closed his mortal career.

President Lincoln and Mr. Colfax sat together in a room at the White House at 8 o'clock P. M., engaged in earnest conversation, when Mrs. Lincoln entered to remind the President that it was time to go to the theater. General and Mrs. Grant had left the city that evening; and Mrs. Lincoln, learning of their departure, extended an invitation to Major Henry R. Rathbone and Miss Clara Harris to accompany them, which was accepted.

Mr. Lincoln gave Mr. George Ashmun, who had called to see him just as he was leaving for the theater, a card to admit himself and friend early the next morning. This was the last bit of writing that the President's hand ever traced.

To Mr. Colfax his last words were: " Do not forget to tell the people in the mining regions, as you pass through them, what I told you this morning about the developments when peace comes, and I will telegraph you at San Francisco." It was ten minutes after eight o'clock when Mr. and Mrs. Lincoln entered their carriage, arriving at the residence of Senator Harris, corner of Fifteenth and H streets, the present site of the Columbian University, ten minutes later, calling for Major Rathbone and Miss Harris, and reaching the theater at half-past eight o'clock.

Through a great desire to see General Grant, who was advertised in the *Evening Star* to attend the theater with the President, many persons purchased tickets for that occasion. The President was a familiar figure to many, consequently his presence did not create quite the desire to see him as did that of the man who caused the curtain to drop upon the closing scene of the great civil war drama. General and Mrs. Grant, however, left Washington for Burlington, N. J., at six o'clock on the evening of the 14th, to visit their children; but upon learning of the assassination of the President, General Grant returned to Washington, leaving Burlington at the same hour on the morning of the 15th. His sudden departure from the capital undoubtedly defeated one of the plans of the conspirators, and spared the country the horror of a double tragedy.

From the moment the President entered the theater he saw nothing to indicate that he was not as secure as any one of the audience around him, and no one in that vast assembly dreamed that there was any murderous agency lurking there. The brilliant lights shone upon the happy face of the President, and the sweet music and ringing cheers of the audience were the joyous evidences of a preserved Union and a new national life.

Lincoln, followed by the huzzas of the whole theater rising and cheering, stopped in the door of that fatal box, and returned the acclamations with his benignant bow and smile!

CHAPTER II.

THE night of April 14, 1865, was to witness the culmination of a conspiracy which had its inception at the time of the first inauguration of President Lincoln. John Wilkes Booth, an actor, was now its foremost local leader and figure. But, of all this, more anon.

Now let us step down to Ford's Theater on Tenth Street N. W., between E and F, then owned by John T. Ford. The building is a plain brick structure, three stories high, seventy-one feet front and one hundred feet deep. At the beginning of the war it was converted into a theater, having previously been a Baptist church, but was never used as a theater after the assassination. The company attempted to open the theater some time afterward, with the " Octoroon," as advertised on the play bill, but the Government prohibited its further use as a theater, and, upon legal proceedings being threatened, the following bill was passed by Congress: " For the purchase of the property in Washington City known as Ford's Theater, for the deposit and safe-keeping of documentary papers relating to the soldiers of the Army of the United States, and the Museum of the Medical and Surgical Departments of the Army, one hundred thousand dollars." When the Government took possession of it, the interior was torn out, converting it into three floors, and it was first used for the Medical Museum. It is used at the present time by the Record and Pension Division of the War Department. June 9, 1893, the day

FORD'S THEATER.

Door No. 1 was the entrance to the gallery.

No. 2, President and Mrs. Lincoln and Booth entered.

No. 3 and 4 were open in mild weather, but in April were closed as means of entrance, and only used for exits after the performance.

No. 5 was used for exit only, as the stairway leading to the dress circle was located there.

Across the lobby from the point where the two ladies are walking on the sidewalk was an iron railing where the doorkeeper took the tickets for both down- (orchestra and dress circle) and upstairs (dress circle). Mr. Lincoln and Booth, to get to the private box after going in No. 2 door, went along the lower lobby northwardly, then up the stairway, then along the upper lobby southwardly, and down the aisle easterly to the private box. The box office was located between the doors No. 1 and 2, marked F. It had a ticket window facing north for the best parts of the house and facing south for the gallery; also a window facing east, looking into the auditorium.

A was a restaurant; B a reception room, with a door leading into dress circle, from which some of the furniture was removed to the private box for that occasion. C was H. Clay Ford's sleeping room. D was a saloon.

NOTE.—The author is indebted to H. Clay Ford for this description of the theater.

that Edwin Booth was buried at Boston, the three floors
collapsed during repairs of the building, pouring into
the basement over a hundred men, chairs, desks, file-
cases, etc., killing twenty-two men and injuring sixty-

LAURA KEENE.

Laura Keene played *Florence Trenchard* in "Our American Cousin" at
Ford's Theater on the night of the assassination.

eight.   There is no trace of the interior of the theater
left, it having been remodeled for the use of the Government.

The play on the boards at Ford's Theater upon the

night of the 14th of April, 1865, was " Our American Cousin," by Tom Taylor. Laura Keene was the star, she having performed in this play over one thousand

PLAY BILL USED AT FORD'S THEATER ON THE NIGHT OF THE ASSASSINATION.

nights, and this was to have been her last night and benefit. As a reminiscence it may be recalled that a number of the delegates, the evening of the close of the Republican Convention at Chicago, May, 1860, attended this play with Laura Keene in the cast at McVicker's Theater. The portrait of Lincoln was displayed on canvas at the time, as the nominee of the convention.

The mail delivery of the morning of April 14 had brought to Ford's Theater several letters for John Wilkes Booth. It was his custom to have his mail addressed to him there. At half-past eleven he leisurely walked up to the theater, after a late breakfast at the National Hotel, and pleasantly saluted a group of young men standing in front, several of them being connected with the theater. He took the letters that were handed him, seating himself on one of the door sills to carefully peruse them, after which he placed them in his pocket, and entered into conversation with those surrounding him. The surrender of Lee's army was the all-absorbing topic in those days, and Harry Ford, knowing Booth's feelings toward the South, said, in a joking manner: " John, the President has the State box to-night, and is coming with General Grant to see the play, and possibly General Lee will also be with them." He started at this, and said immediately: " Never! Lee would not let himself be used as Romans used their captives, and be paraded." Ford's reply was: " Oh, no! I was only joking."

From that moment Booth's manner underwent an entire change; he became quiet and abstracted, as if some dark thought was in his brain, and very soon left the crowd, going down Tenth Street, and walked hurriedly up E Street to the Kirkwood House, now the Raleigh, corner Twelfth Street and Pennsylvania Avenue. This was the first knowledge that Booth had of the intended visit of the President to the theater that evening.

Mr. James R. Ford, business manager of the theater, was in the box office when the messenger came from the White House at half-past ten o'clock on the morning of the 14th to secure a box for the President, Mrs. Lincoln, and General and Mrs. Grant. The two latter had accepted that morning an invitation from the President to accompany him and Mrs. Lincoln to the theater. The President had been previously invited to the theater that night, but they had no knowledge there of his intended visit until the reception of the message at half-past ten o'clock that day.

Mr. Henry Clay Ford superintended the decorations of the President's box. He secured two flags, which he looped up, and placed a silk one that he borrowed from the Treasury Department in the center. He had some of the furniture taken out of the box, a sofa and high-backed chair brought from the stage, and a rocking-chair brought from his sleeping room and placed in the box. The rocking-chair had not been in the box during the season until that night; it was placed nearest the audience, and was to be occupied by the President. Ed-

THE DAMASK-BACK ROCKING-CHAIR

In which the President was sitting when shot. It was placed in the box
that night for the first time in over a year.

ward Spangler, who assisted in preparing the box for the Presidential party, it is believed bored the hole in the door, loosened the screws to the latches, and prepared the piece of wood with which to bar the door through which Booth entered.

The notice that the President and General Grant would be at the theater was written by Mr. James R. Ford, and sent to the *Evening Star*, which appeared about two o'clock.

When Booth reached the Kirkwood House he wrote the following on a card:

For Mr. ANDREW JOHNSON:
Don't wish to disturb you; are you at home?
J. W. BOOTH.

The card was sent to the room of Vice-President Andrew Johnson, but he not being in, the messenger returned the note to the office of the hotel, where it was supposed to have been placed in the Vice-President's box; but, instead, it was put in the box adjoining— that of his private secretary. The object of this note is not known, but the theories are that Booth wanted to obtain a view of the Vice-President's room, by which he could direct Atzerodt; or expected to receive an invitation from him to call, which would cast suspicion upon Mr. Johnson, and probably implicate him in the assassination of the President.

After his visit to the hotel Booth emerged into the busy throng on the sidewalk, and was lost sight of. The afternoon no doubt was spent in planning with the other members of the conspiracy, and arranging their share in the intended assassinations. He was seen on horseback late in the afternoon, inquiring for David Herold, whom he needed very much, for he was to have been his escort through southern Maryland.

Mr. James W. Pumphrey, now living, who kept a livery stable on C Street, in the rear of the National Hotel, gives the details of Booth's visit to his stable: "He came to my stable about one o'clock on the 14th of April, 1865, and engaged a saddle horse, which he said he wanted about four or half-past four o'clock of that day. He had been in the habit of riding a sorrel horse, and he came to get it, but that horse was engaged, and I gave him instead a small bay mare, about fourteen hands high. He asked me to give him a tie rein with which to hitch the horse, but I told him she was in the habit of breaking the bridle, and not to hitch her; but he insisted on having one, for he said he wanted to tie her while he stopped at a restaurant to get a drink. I told him to get a boy at the restaurant to hold her. He said he could not get a boy. He then said, ' I am going to Grover's Theater [National] to write a letter, and there is no use of tying her there, as there is a stable in the back part of the alley, and I will put her there.' He then asked me where was the best place to take a ride. I told him: ' You have been around here some time and ought to be familiar with the drives.' He said, ' How is Crystal Springs?' 'A very good place,' I said, ' but it is rather early for it.' ' Well,' said he, ' I will go there after I get though writing a letter at Grover's Theater.' He rode off, and I never saw Booth or my horse since."

Booth put the horse in his stable in the rear of Ford's Theater, and afterward was seen by his friends, and to them he seemed lively, chatting in a familiar way and taking a social glass with them in their accustomed haunts. To all of these he appeared light-hearted, but there is no doubt that he suffered great anxiety through that afternoon, for the great responsibility of the successful murder of the President, the perfecting of the plans in all the little details to insure not only his own success and escape, but that of his assistants, was his; but for all that, he presented a bold front when meeting his friends, and kept to himself his awful secret.

When Booth handed his key to the clerk of the National Hotel on the evening of the assassination, he asked him: "Are you going down to Ford's Theater to-night?" The clerk answered, "No." Booth replied by saying: "You ought to go; there is to be some splendid acting there to-night."

A few minutes after nine o'clock Booth led his horse from his stable to the back door of the theater. The stable was on the south side of the alley, and about one hundred and fifty feet from the rear of the theater.

James L. Mattox, property man at the theater, seemed to have been Booth's agent, for he rented the stable from Mrs. Davis in December, 1864, and Booth always gave him the rent to be paid to Mrs. Davis. When Booth sold his horse and buggy, he still retained the stable, and so it was available to shelter his hired horse that day. When he reached the rear of the theater he called out, "Ned!" and Spangler appeared. Booth asked him if he would help him, and Spangler said, "Yes." Booth stepped in the back door of the building, went under the stage to the opposite side, and out of the side door to the front.

As soon as Booth disappeared Spangler called for Joseph Burroughs, *alias* "Peanuts," and turned the horse over to him, saying: "Hold it, and if there is anything wrong, lay the blame on me." So the boy held the horse. Spangler and Burroughs were in charge of Booth's stable, and had cared for his horse and buggy. Burroughs' duties at the theater were to carry bills and stand at the stage door at night to keep out intruders and strangers. Harry Ford during the afternoon ordered Burroughs to assist Spangler to take out the partition of the box, and while there Spangler said: "Damn the President and General Grant!" Burroughs replied: "What are you damning the man for—a man that has never done harm to you?" Spangler retorted: "He ought to be cursed, when he got so many men killed."

Booth was seen sauntering up and down the pavement, and at ten minutes past ten he stepped into an adjoining saloon on the south side and called for brandy. This would blunt his sensibilities, steady his nerves, and make him feel like a hero, ready to rid the country of a tyrant and immortalize his name. After paying for his drink he walked out and entered the theater lobby, asking Mr. John E. Buckingham, the night doorkeeper, the time, after which he ascended the stairs and passed around the dress circle to the door leading into the President's box. Booth had free access to the theater by all the entrances, just as one of the employees. When he reached the door of the passageway leading to the box, he stopped and, probably to avoid attracting attention, made a leisurely survey of the house, and possibly waiting for the progress of the play to a situation when the stage would be more nearly clear for his intended purpose. Thus, he bided his time, and he had time enough.

It has been said that before Booth went into the President's box he handed his card to an attendant of the President who was on guard, but this assertion is not supported by any testimony that was made public during the trial. After entering the passageway he took a bar of wood that had been prepared for the purpose during the afternoon, and placed one end of it in an indentation in the wall and the other against the door, making it impossible for anyone to enter from without. The stick or bar was three feet six inches long. The mortise in the plaster looked as though it had been recently made, and had the appearance of having been done with a knife.

There were two doors leading into the box from the

passage, and the box was divided by a partition, one door entering each compartment. When the President attended the theater the partition was removed, making the box into one. These two doors were generally locked when the President occupied the box; but upon this occasion they were not, and no one connected with the theater could ever explain why they were left in that condition on that night. Upon examination after the assassination the screws of the locks to both doors were found to be loosened, so that, if they had been locked, a very little push would have opened them. The farthest door from the audience had a hole bored in it—probably for the accommodation of the assassin, to look through in order to get a view of the position of the President. Upon a careful examination of the hole the next day, it had the appearance of being bored with a gimlet, and then reamed round the edge with a knife. In several places it was scratched down, as if the knife had slipped.

The door being unlocked, Booth sneaked in behind the President, and, at twenty minutes past ten o'clock, fired a bullet into the brain that had so recently acted with such magnanimity toward the nation's enemies. The assassin called this man a tyrant before he fired the fatal bullet.

> " The songs of joy ran o'er the land like fire,
>   All hearts exultant leaped with wild delight;
> We saw the dawn of Peace gild every spire,
>   And with thanksgiving hailed the holy sight.

> " But in an instant all the joy was gone!
>   Gloom clothed the earth, and darkness filled the skies
> The assassin had shot down the gentlest man
>   That ever ruled a nation's destinies."

All eyes in the audience were turned to the stage, intent upon the closing of the second scene in the third act of the play, and did not realize what was happening in the President's box. The instant the report of the pistol was heard, Major Rathbone sprang up and grappled Booth, but was thrust aside, receiving several slashes of the assassin's knife in his arm. Rathbone made

BOOTH IN THE ACT OF LEAPING OUT OF THE BOX TO THE STAGE, AFTER SHOOTING THE PRESIDENT.

His spur caught in the flag that was draped in front of the box.

the second attempt to grasp him, but was too late, for Booth laid his right hand upon the railing and vaulted out upon the stage. He had dropped his Derringer in the box during the scuffle, but retained the knife in his right hand. As his legs passed between the folds of the flag decorating the box, his spur, which he still wore upon his heel, caught in the flag. Falling on his knee, he put forth both hands to help himself to recover an erect posi-

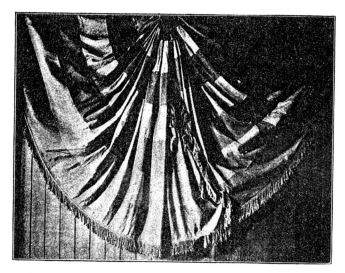

THE FLAG, DRAPED IN THE PRESIDENT'S BOX, IN WHICH BOOTH
CAUGHT HIS SPUR.

tion, which he did with the rapidity of an athlete. He
alighted in a crouching position, like one who had
brought his body down to break the shock of the fall.
Cæsar *saw* Brutus stab. Lincoln never saw, thank God!
his death shot, or knew what or who did the deed.

The leap from the President's box upon the stage was
not a difficult one for Booth to make, for he had made
similar leaps, which he had introduced into the play of
" Macbeth." There was no necessity for a rehearsal, as
he had the reputation of being a great gymnast, and he
probably would have made a perfect leap had it not been
for the flag. The distance from the box to the stage was
nine feet, and the inanimate flag became animate in its
vengeance upon the assassin, and, turning him from his
true course, he fell upon the stage, breaking the fibula
bone of his left leg.

The following is the testimony of William Withers, Jr., leader of the orchestra at the theater that evening: " I was leader of the orchestra at the time, and as the President was to witness the performance, I thought that as befitting the occasion I would compose a song, which I did. It was entitled, ' Honor to Our Soldiers,' and dedicated to the President:

> " ' Honor to our soldiers,
>   Our nation's greatest pride,
> Who, 'neath our starry banner's folds,
>   Have fought and bled and died ;
> They're nature's noblest handiwork—
>   No king as proud as they;
> God bless the heroes of the land,
>   And cheer them on their way.' *

This was to be sung between two of the acts by a quartet I had engaged, and the entire company, who were to be attired in the American colors.

" After the first act J. P. Wright, the stage manager, sent me word he would be unable to have the special song sung at that time, but would try to have it rendered between the second and third acts. A similar message was sent me at the close of the second act, and I became somewhat exercised.

" When the President entered the theater, I signaled for ' Hail to the Chief.' The audience caught sight of him, and, rising as a body, they cheered again and again. As the President entered the box he turned smilingly to the audience and bowed.

" A few minutes after ten o'clock I started to go upon the stage, when I saw Booth in the balcony,. walking down the aisle in the direction of the President's box.

* Words by H. B. Phillips; music composed and arranged by Professor William Withers, Jr.

I did not think strange of this, as Booth was a frequent visitor to the building, and his appearance at this time created no suspicion whatever. He was seemingly attentive toward the acting, for the curtain had again gone up.

" I encountered a scene shifter, Spangler, whose office I afterward learned was to turn out the lights in the theater as soon as the shot was fired. He obstructed my passage, and remarked: 'What do you want here?' In reply I told him it was none of his business! Mr. Wright appearing, Spangler left his position on the stage alongside the box in which was the apparatus for illuminating the theater. I closed the lid of the box, and sat upon it to talk to the manager, unconscious that I was spoiling the plan of the conspirators as to turning out all the lights!

" Mr. Wright told me the song would be sung at the close of the performance, and Laura Keene had sent word to the President requesting him to stay and hear it. I was just about to return to the orchestra when the crack of a revolver startled me. All was quiet instantly. I saw a man jump from the President's box on to the stage. He ran directly toward the aisle leading to the back door. This course brought him right in my pathway. He had a dagger in his hand, and he waved it threateningly. He slashed at me, and the knife cut through my coat, vest, and underclothing. He struck again, the point of the weapon penetrating the back of my neck, and the blow brought me to the floor. I recognized him as J. Wilkes Booth, and watched him make his exit into the alley."

Booth was hot with cruelty, and as he grasped the reins from the patient, simple boy, Joseph Burroughs, he felled him to the pavement with the butt of his knife.

He was enacting tragedy from the President's box to the rear of the theater.

There has been much difference of opinion relative to the Latin words, " Sic semper tyrannis " (" Thus always with tyrants "), the motto of Virginia, as quoted by Booth. Some persons who were present at the time maintain that Booth used them in the box, while others positively claim that he made use of the words while on the stage. Booth in his diary says that he uttered them before he fired the shot. How false and foolish were the words of the murderer—as words were never more falsely exclaimed nor more unjustly applied than these!

Major Rathbone gives a clear and authentic statement of the scene in the box:

BOOTH CROSSING THE STAGE AFTER LEAPING FROM THE BOX.

"When the party entered the box, a cushioned arm-chair (rocking-chair) was standing farthest from the stage and nearest the audience. This was also the nearest point to the door by which the box is entered. The President seated himself in this chair, and, except that he once left the chair for the purpose of putting on his

SPUR WORN BY BOOTH.

When he leaped from the box to the stage it caught in the flag, which caused him to fall and break his leg.

overcoat, remained so seated until he was shot. Mrs. Lincoln was seated in a chair between the President and the pillar in the center of the box.

"At the opposite end of the box, that nearest the stage, were two chairs. In one of these, standing in the corner, Miss Harris was seated. At her left hand, and along the wall running from that end of the box to the rear, stood a small sofa. At the end of this sofa, next to Miss Harris, I was seated. The distance between the sofa and the President was about seven or eight feet. The distance between where the President sat and the door was about four or five feet.

"When the second scene of the third act was being performed, I was intently observing the proceedings upon the stage, with my back toward the door, when I heard the discharge of a pistol behind me, and, looking around, saw, through the smoke, a man between the door and the President. I instantly sprang toward him and seized him. He wrested himself from my grasp and made a violent thrust at my breast with a large knife. I parried the blow by striking it up, and received a wound several inches deep in my left arm between the elbow and the shoulder. The orifice of the wound was about an inch and a half in length, and extended upward toward the shoulder several inches.

"The man rushed to the front of the box, and I endeavored to seize him again, but only caught his clothes as he was leaping over the railing of the box. As he went over upon the stage I cried with a loud voice, 'Stop that man!' I then turned to the President. His position was not changed. His head was slightly bent forward and his eyes were closed. I saw that he was unconscious, and, supposing him mortally wounded, rushed to the door for the purpose of calling medical aid. On reaching the outer door of the passageway I found it barred by a piece of plank, one end of which was secured in the wall and the other rested against the door. This wedge or bar was about four feet from the floor. Persons upon the outside were beating against the door for the purpose of entering. When the bar was removed and the door was opened, several persons representing themselves to be surgeons entered."

The audience seemed stunned for an instant, no one realizing what had happened. It was all the work of a moment. The people were intent upon the stage, waiting for the appearance of some favorite. Even when the report of a pistol was heard and the assassin's leap seen from the box to the stage, there were many who thought it all a part of the programme.

BOOTH'S ESCAPE FROM THE REAR OF THE THEATER.

The boy was holding Booth's horse until he made his appearance followed by Major Joseph B. Stewart.

The screams of Mrs. Lincoln first disclosed to the audience the fact that the President was shot. Then the excitement was of the wildest nature. The people surged to and fro in frantic excitement, not knowing what to do or where to go, but under the influence of a few cool heads the audience was quieted and the theater vacated for the last time.

Booth had visited Grover's Theater on the day before the assassination, and asked Mr. C. D. Hess, the manager, "Do you intend to," or "Are you going to invite the President?" Mr. Hess replied, " Yes; that reminds me; I must send that invitation." Mr. Hess intended to send his invitation to Mrs. Lincoln, but had neglected to do so until reminded of it by Booth's call. The invitation was sent, and little " Tad " (Thomas) was present, representing the White House. When he heard from the stage the announcement of the assassination of his father, he shrieked and sobbed in a heart-rending manner. He was immediately taken to the White House.

Joseph B. Stewart, an attorney-at-law residing in Washington, was sitting in the front seat of the orchestra, on the right-hand side. When he heard the report of a pistol he was startled, and in looking up saw a man leap from the President's box. At the same instant he jumped on the stage, ran across, following the man as he disappeared at the left-hand entrance. Mr. Stewart called out, " Stop that man! " several times. When he neared the back door it slammed shut, and, it being dark, he put his hand on the wrong side of it, after which he caught the knob on the other side and opened it, stepping out just in time to see the man mounting a horse, which soon carried its rider out on F Street.

Harry Hawk, as *Asa Trenchard*, held the stage at the moment Mr. Lincoln was shot. The second scene of the third act was drawing to a close. In a personal interview with Mr. Hawk he described the scene upon the stage: "Mrs. Muzzey, in the rôle of *Mrs. Mountchesington*, having just discovered that *Asa Trenchard*—my part— was not the man of wealth she supposed, had turned angrily to her daughter *Georgina*, the part taken by May Hart, saying: ' Go to your room; you may go to your room at once! ' Then, turning to me, she said: ' Sir, it is plain to be seen you are not accustomed to manners of good society.' Then she turned haughtily and made her exit on the left, leaving me alone, and looking after her. My lines were: ' Society, eh? Well, I guess I know enough to turn you inside out, old woman, you darned old sockdologing man-trap! ' I was looking up at the President's box as I repeated the lines, and the words had barely left my lips and the shouts of laughter were ringing, when the shot sounded through the house."

The last words that President Lincoln ever heard were probably those that fell from the lips of Harry Hawk.

The assassin's view, in his flight, of the murdered Lincoln. The tree under which the victim stands contains numerous portraits of him.

CHAPTER III.

THE first shock of the tragedy had hardly abated when
there was an almost spontaneous call for and impulse to
render aid to the President, especially by the medical
profession present.

Dr. Charles Taft gives his recollections of that eventful night in a letter to the author, dated March 1, 1900:
" I was in the theater when Mr. Lincoln was shot, and
was in uniform. When a call for a surgeon was made,
I fought my way to the stage and was lifted up into the
box by the people underneath. Two army paymasters
had already entered the box from the dress circle, and
had ordered the President's carriage, to take him to the
White House. As soon as I had located the wound, just
behind the left ear, I countermanded that order, and directed that the President be removed to the nearest bed.
He would not have lived to reach home, because the jolt-
ing over the [then] cobblestone pavement would have
brought on fatal hemorrhage. In leaving the theater I
took charge of the head, others the rest of the body, and
several men preceded us and tore up the chairs from their
fastenings to the floor. Major Rathbone, with another
gentleman, assisted Mrs. Lincoln. On reaching the street
I saw a man standing on the porch of a house opposite, the door open behind, showing a lighted hall. To
that house I directed my steps, and was pleased to find
a neat bedroom at the end of the hall, without going up-

stairs. The single bed was pulled out from the corner of the room, and the dying President laid upon it, diagonally, his extreme length not admitting of any other position. I then administered a small glass of brandy and water, and it was swallowed without much difficulty.

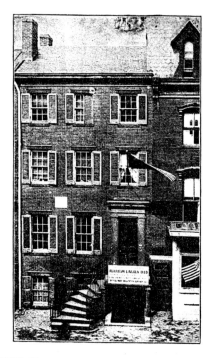

THE HOUSE IN WHICH LINCOLN DIED, 516 TENTH STREET.
WASHINGTON, D. C.

Was the property of William Petersen at the time of the assassination It was sold to Louis Schade, and by him to the Government, in 1897, to be preserved as a memorial to the martyred President. It is now occupied by O. H. Oldroyd and his family, who have on exhibition the "Oldroyd Lincoln Memorial Collection."

Twenty minutes afterward I gave him another teaspoonful, but it was not swallowed. To the whole anterior surface of the body, from neck to ankles, sinapism was applied, with the hope of restoring vitality, but not the smallest sign of consciousness was shown by the patient from the moment I saw him in the box until his death. Dr. Robert King Stone, the family physician, and Surgeon-General Joseph K. Barnes had in the meantime probed the wound, and had pronounced it mortal. While the oozing of the blood and brain tissue was free the respiration was less labored; and, to keep the head from rolling over on the pillow and obstructing the discharge, I stood at the head of the bed and supported the President's head, keeping the wound free from coagula. I remained in that position nearly all night, being at times relieved by Surgeon Charles H. Crane."

All through the long, weary night the watchers stood by the couch of the dying President. He was unconscious every moment from the time the bullet crashed into his brain until the dawn of day, when the tide of life ebbed out.

About seven o'clock in the morning Dr. Stone announced that death was at hand, and at twenty-two minutes past seven the pulse ceased beating. Secretary Stanton approached the bed and uttered, in low voice: "*Now he belongs to the ages.*" Rev. Phineas D. Gurley, the President's pastor, dropped upon his knees by the bedside and uttered a fervent prayer. Never was a supplication wafted to Heaven under more solemn circumstances. Dr. Gurley went to the front parlor, where he prayed with Mrs. Lincoln. At its conclusion, he, with Robert Lincoln, assisted her to the death chamber.

The end of a great life had come just as the end of the nation's struggle was at hand. Victory after victory had gladdened the ears of the loyal people, and they began, for the first time, to see the dawning of an abiding peace.

At the very moment when all was joy and exultation, when the President's heart beat strong and his hand was outstretched to the repentant returning to their homes, the demon struck his terrible blow. It was upon the anniversary of two great events; one was Good Friday, the anniversary of the day upon which the Saviour was crucified; and the other the anniversary of the day when the national flag was taken down from Fort Sumter in 1861.

The record of Lincoln's acts and the results of his principles will constitute an everlasting monument of his greatness. He needs no other eulogy; no brighter page can be written for him. But how sad his taking off! In truth, as the iron-hearted Stanton had said, at the last passing of this life, " Now he belongs to the ages! "

Dr. Ezra W. Abbott has kindly furnished me with the minutes that he kept of the condition of the President through the night:

11 o'clock. Pulse 41.

11.05 o'clock.   Pulse 45, and growing weaker.

11.10 o'clock.   Pulse 45.

11.15 o'clock.   Pulse 42.

11.20 o'clock.   Pulse 45; respiration 27 to 29.

11.25 o'clock.   Pulse 42.

11.32 o'clock.   Pulse 48, and full.

11.40 o'clock.   Pulse 45.

11.45 o'clock.   Pulse 45; respiration 22.

12 o'clock.   Pulse 48; respiration 22.

12.15 o'clock.   Pulse 48; respiration 21; ecchymosis of both eyes.

12.30 o'clock.   Pulse 54.

12.32 o'clock.   Pulse 60.

12.35 o'clock.   Pulse 66.

DEATHBED OF LINCOLN.

Secretary Welles, Secretary Stanton, Surgeon-General Barnes, William Dennison, Charles Sumner, Robert Lincoln, General Halleck, John Hay, General Meigs.

12.40 o'clock. Pulse 69, right eye much swollen, and ecchymosed.

12.45 o'clock. Pulse 70; respiration 27.

12.55 o'clock. Pulse 80; struggling motion of arms.

1 o'clock. Pulse 86; respiration 30.

1.30 o'clock. Pulse 95; appearing easier.

1.45 o'clock. Pulse 86; very quiet; respiration irregular; Mrs. Lincoln present.

2.10 o'clock. Mrs. Lincoln, with Robert Lincoln, retired to an adjoining room.

2.30 o'clock. Pulse 54; President very quiet; respiration 28.

2.52 o'clock. Pulse 48; respiration 30.

3 o'clock. Visited again by Mrs. Lincoln.

3.25 o'clock. Respiration 24, and regular.

3.35 o'clock. Prayer by Rev. Dr. Gurley.

4 o'clock. Respiration 26, and regular.

4.15 o'clock. Pulse 60; respiration 25.

5.50 o'clock. Respiration 28, regular, sleeping.

6 o'clock. Pulse failing; respiration 28.

6.30 o'clock. Still failing, and labored breathing.

7 o'clock. Symptoms of immediate dissolution.

7.22 o'clock. Death.

The house to which the President was carried from the theater was No. 453 Tenth Street (now 516), between E and F streets, and owned at the time by William Petersen, a tailor. The house is a plain four-story brick, built in 1849. The room in which the President died is on the first story above the basement, at the end of a hall, from which rises a stairway. The room measures nine by seventeen feet. The bed on which he lay was a low walnut four-poster. The walls were hung with a photograph taken from a lithograph of Rosa Bonheur's " Horse Fair," an engraved copy of Herring's " Village

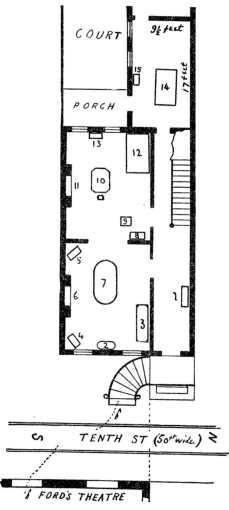

DIAGRAM OF THE SECOND STORY OF THE HOUSE IN WHICH LINCOLN DIED.

Mrs. Lincoln occupied the front parlor, making frequent visits to the bedside of the President.
1. Hat-rack in hall. 2. Table. 3. Sofa, occupied by Mrs. Lincoln. 4 and 5. What-nots. 6. Fireplace. 7. Center table.

Back parlor.

8. Washstand. 9. Table at which Secretary Stanton wrote his dispatches. 10. Table and chair occupied by Corporal James Tanner as stenographer during the preliminary examinations of the witnesses. 11. Fireplace. 12. Bed, not made up. 13. Bureau.
14. Bed on which the President died. 15. Table.

Blacksmith," and two smaller ones of " The Stable " and " Barn Yard," by the same artist. The room had been occupied for some time by William T. Clark, a soldier belonging to Company D, 13th Massachusetts Infantry, and detailed in the Quartermaster's Department.

As a number of persons have claimed the occupancy of the room at the time, I give a copy of a letter Mr. Clark wrote to his sister, Mrs. H. Estes Wright of Boston, Mass., which now hangs in the room. His wife, still living in Boston, Mass., received many loving epistles from him while a tenant of this historic house.

WASHINGTON, D. C., Wednesday, April 19, 1865.
DEAR SISTER IDA :

To-day the funeral of Mr. Lincoln takes place. The streets are being crowded at this early hour (9 A. M.), and the procession will probably not move for three hours.

The past few days have been of intense excitement; arrests are numerously made—if any party is heard to utter secesh sentiments. The time has come when persons cannot say what they please, for the people are awfully indignant. Hundreds daily call at the house to gain admission to my room. I was engaged nearly all Sunday with one of Frank Leslie's special artists, aiding him in making a complete drawing of the last moments of Mr. Lincoln, as I know the position of everyone present. He succeeded in executing a fine sketch, which will appear in their paper. He wished to mention the names of all pictures in the room, particularly the photograph of yourself, Clara, and Nannie; but I told him he must not do that, as they were members of my family, and I did not wish them to be made so public. He also urged me to give him my picture, or at least allow him to take my sketch, but I could not see that either. Everybody has a great desire to obtain some memento from my room, so that whoever comes in has to be closely watched for fear they will steal something. I have a lock of Mr. Lincoln's hair, which I have had neatly framed ; also a piece of linen with a portion of his brain. The pillow and case upon which he lay when he died, and nearly all his wearing apparel, I intend to send to Robert Lincoln as soon as the funeral is over, as I consider him the most justly entitled to them. The same mattress is on my bed, and the same coverlid covers me nightly that covered him while dying. Enclosed you will find a piece of lace that Mrs. Lincoln wore on her head during the evening and was dropped by her while entering my room to see her dying husband; it is worth keeping for its historical value. The cushion worked by Clara, and the cushion by you, you little dreamed would be so historically connected with such an event. Love to father, mother, and Clara. Don't forget you have a brother, and send me a longer note soor.

I will write again soon.

Your affec. brother,

WILLIE.

Charles Sumner remained by the bedside all night, and he and General W. H. Halleck left the house a few minutes after the President's death, in the latter's carriage, and drove to the Kirkwood House, where General Halleck first notified the Vice-President of the President's death.

William Reith, John C. Weaver, Eli Morey, David Frantz, John Richardson, and Antonio Bregazzi were detailed by General Daniel H. Rucker, Quartermaster, to report to the Petersen house on the morning of the death, and at nine o'clock they placed the body of the President in a temporary coffin, wrapped it with the American flag, and carried it to the hearse. The squad of soldiers with a guard of cavalry, followed by General C. C. Augur and other military officers on foot, formed the procession, which moved up Tenth Street to G, thence west to the White House, where the body was carried in by the soldiers. Every loyal man felt that he had suffered a personal bereavement, and as the sad news spread throughout the city the rain began to softly fall, as if the heavens were weeping for the nation's loss.

After the death of the President, on Saturday morning,

Attorney-General James Speed waited upon Andrew
Johnson, Vice-President, and officially informed him of
the death of President Lincoln, and asked that an early

WILLIAM T. CLARK,

A soldier of Company D, 13th Massachusetts Infantry, who occupied the
room in which President Lincoln died.

hour might be appointed for his inauguration as Lincoln's
successor. A communication was handed him signed by
all the members of the Cabinet, except Secretary Seward,
notifying him that, by the death of President Lincoln,
the office of President had devolved, under the Constitution, upon him, and that the emergency of the Government demanded that he should immediately qualify according to the requirements of the Constitution and
enter upon the duties of President of the United States.
Mr. Johnson requested that the ceremonies take place at
his rooms in the Kirkwood House,

At eleven o'clock (15th) Chief Justice Salmon P. Chase proceeded to the Kirkwood House, accompanied by the members of the Cabinet and several United States senators, and administered the oath of office under more solemn and impressive circumstances than ever before in the history of our country.

After receiving the oath, and being declared President of the United States, Mr. Johnson made a few feeling remarks, acknowledging his incompetency to perform duties so important and responsible as those which had been so unexpectedly thrown upon him, also stating that he had been almost overwhelmed by the announcement of the sad event which had so recently occurred. At the conclusion of his remarks the President received the kind wishes of those present. Mr. Johnson retained the Cabinet of Mr. Lincoln, asking them to go on and discharge their respective duties in the same manner as before the deplorable event that had changed the head of the Government, the wheels of which were not stopped for a moment; and this sudden change of administration, taking place at a time of a great national calamity, ought to teach the world a lesson as to the permanency and character of our republican form of government. On Friday night President Lincoln was assassinated; on Saturday morning Vice-President Johnson grasped the reins of government as they fell from the dying hand of his predecessor.

The autopsy was performed under the direction of Surgeon-General Barnes, assisted by Doctors Stone, Curtis, Woodward, Crane, and Taft, in the presence of President Johnson, General Augur, and General Rucker.

The face of the President presented a deep black appearance around both eyes. The fatal wound was on the left side of the head, behind, in a line with, and three inches from the left ear. The course of the ball was diagonally forward toward the right eye, crossing the brain in an oblique manner, and lodging a few inches behind that eye. In the track of the wound were found fragments of bone that had been driven forward by the ball, which was embedded in the anterior lobe of the left hemisphere of the brain. The orbital plates of both eyes were the seat of a comminuted fracture, and the eyes were filled with extravasated blood. The serious injury of the orbital plates was due to the *contre-coup*—the result of the intense shock of so large a projectile fired so closely to the head. The ball was evidently a Derringer hand-cast, from which the neck had been clipped. A shaving of lead had been removed by the skull, which was found in the orifice of the wound. The first fragment of bone was found two and a half inches within the brain; the second and larger fragment about four inches from the orifice of the wound, which was about one inch in diameter. The ball lay still farther in advance. The autopsy fully confirmed the opinion of the surgeons on the night of the assassination, that the wound was mortal.

CHAPTER IV.

OTHER ATTEMPTS AT ASSASSINATION EVENING OF APRIL 14, 1865.

THE assassination of President Lincoln was but a part of the scheme of the conspirators to entirely destroy the executive branch of the Government. Lewis Payne (his real name was Lewis Thornton Powell) boarded at the Herndon House, corner Ninth and F streets, where the Loan and Trust Building now stands, for two weeks, leaving there on the afternoon of April 14. He paid his bill at four o'clock, and requested dinner before the regular time, and it was served to him. Very little is known of his whereabouts from that time until 10 P. M., when he rang the bell of the Seward mansion, which stood on the ground now occupied by the Lafayette Opera House. When the door was opened by the colored doorkeeper, Payne stepped in, holding a little package in his hand, saying that he had some medicine for Secretary Seward, sent by Dr. Verdi, which he was directed to deliver in person and give instructions how it was to be taken. The doorkeeper informed him that he could not see Mr. Seward, but he repeated the words, saying he must see him. He talked very roughly for several minutes against the protest of the doorkeeper, who said he had positive orders to admit *no one* to the sick-chamber. The door-keeper finally weakened, thinking perhaps he was sent by Dr. Verdi, and let him ascend the stairs. When at the top, he met Mr. Frederick Seward, a son of the Secretary's, to whom he told the object of his visit, but Mr.

Seward told him that he could not see his father; that he was asleep, but to give him the medicine and he would take it to him. That would not do; he must see Mr. Seward; and then Mr. Frederick Seward said: " I am the proprietor here, and his son; if you cannot leave your message with me, you cannot leave it at all."

THE BLAINE HOUSE.

The house in which Secretary William H. Seward was living when Payne made the attempt to assassinate him. The Hon. James G. Blaine died in this house. It was a club-house at the time of the Sickles-Key difficulty, and near here Key was killed.

Payne started downstairs, and, after taking a few steps, suddenly turned around and struck Mr. Frederick Seward, felling him to the floor. Sergeant George F. Robinson, acting as attendant nurse to Mr. Seward, was in an adjoining room, and on hearing the noise in the hall opened the door, where he found Payne close up to it. As soon as the door was opened, he struck Robinson in the forehead with a knife, knocking him partially down, and pressed past him to the bed of Mr. Seward, where he leaned over it and struck him three times in the neck with his dagger.

Mr. Seward had been out riding shortly before the fatal day, and had been thrown from his carriage with great violence, breaking an arm and fracturing his jaw. The physician had fixed up a steel mask or frame to hold the broken bones in place while setting. The assassin's dagger cut his face from the right cheek down to the neck, and but for this steel bandage, which deflected two of the stabs, the assassin might have accomplished his purpose. The carriage disaster was after this night almost considered a blessing in disguise. Frederick Seward suffered intensely from a fracture of the cranium. The nurse attempted to haul Payne off the bed, when he turned and attacked him the second time. During this scuffle Major Augustus H. Seward, son of Secretary Seward, entered the room and clinched Payne, and between the two they succeeded in getting him to the door, when he broke away and ran downstairs and outdoors. The colored doorkeeper ran after the police or guards when Frederick Seward was knocked down, and returned and reported that he saw the man riding a horse and followed him to I Street, where he was lost sight of.

In some way Payne's horse got away from him, for a little after one o'clock on the morning of the 15th, Lieutenant John F. Toffey, on going to the Lincoln Hospital, East Capitol and Fifteenth streets, where he was on duty, found a dark bay horse, with saddle and bridle on, standing at Lincoln Branch Barracks. The horse no doubt came in on a sort of byroad that led to Camp Barry, which turned north from the Branch Barracks toward the Bladensburg road. The sweat pouring from the animal had made a regular puddle on the ground. A sentinel at the hospital had stopped the horse. Lieutenant Toffey and Captain Lansing of the 13th New York Cavalry took the horse to the headquarters of the picket at the Old Capitol Prison, and from there to General E. O. C. Ord's headquarters. After reaching there, they discovered that the horse was blind of one eye, which identified it as the one Booth purchased in November, 1864, from Squire George Gardiner.

Many persons wonder why Payne did not shoot Mr. Seward, as he had a revolver in his hand. But it was disabled when he struck the Secretary's son, as the pin of the revolver bent very slightly, but sufficiently to prevent the chamber from turning. Every chamber was loaded, but the hammer could not be raised. Payne no doubt thought that the three stabs he had given the Secretary had killed him.

George A. Atzerodt spent the two weeks previous to the assassination at the Pennsylvania House, 307 C Street N. W., and returning one night after a round of drinking with some young men, he said: "I am pretty near broke, though I have friends enough to give me as much money as will keep me all my life. I am going away one of these days, but I will return with as much gold as will keep me all my lifetime."

On a leaf of the register of the Kirkwood House the name of G. A. Atzerodt was written, on the morning of April 14, about eight o'clock, and Room 126 was assigned him. He paid one day's board in advance, but did not occupy the bed that night, although he deposited in the room his numerous effects, among which was a coat, found hanging on the wall, in which was a bank-book of J. Wilkes Booth, showing a credit of $455 with the Ontario Bank, Montreal, October 27, 1864, and also a map of Virginia, and some handkerchiefs with various initials. Underneath the pillow was found a revolver, loaded and capped. This room was on the floor above the room then occupied by Vice-President Johnson, and in coming down from Room 126, to reach the office of the hotel, a person would pass Mr. Johnson's door.

Mr. John Fletcher was foreman of Allison Naylor's livery stable on E Street, between Thirteen-and-a-half and Fourteenth streets N. W. He said that on the 3d of April Atzerodt, in company with another man, called at the stable with two horses. Atzerodt's horse was a dark brown, and blind of one eye. Atzerodt's friend said that he was going to Philadelphia, and would leave the sale of his horse to Atzerodt. The horses remained at the stable until the 12th, when Atzerodt sold the one belonging to his friend to Thompson, the stage contractor, and took his own away. At 1 o'clock P. M., on the 14th, David E. Herold and Atzerodt went to the stable with a dark bay mare. Atzerodt said he had sold his horse and had bought this mare. He told Mr. Fletcher to put it in the stable. This bay mare is evidently the same one that Atzerodt hired about noon of the same day at the stable of Keleher & Pywell, Eighth Street, between D and E streets N. W., and returned it near midnight.

Herold engaged a horse, which he ordered to be kept for him, and he would call for it at four o'clock. At a quarter past four he called at the stable and asked how much the charge would be for the hire of the horse. He was told the price was five dollars. He then asked for a reduction of the price to four, but Mr. Fletcher told him he could not have it for any less.

Herold called for a particular horse, he being acquainted with it. He was very particular in the selection of a saddle and bridle, and picked out a double-reined bridle, and objection was made to the stirrups being covered with leather, he preferring the English steel stirrups. Before he left he asked how late he could stay out, and Mr. Fletcher told him he could stay out no later than eight or nine o'clock. Near ten o'clock that night Atzerodt went to the stable for his horse. In returning from an adjoining saloon to the stable Atzerodt remarked to Mr. Fletcher that if "this thing happens to-night, you will hear of a present," or "get a present." Not much attention was paid to this remark, as Mr. Fletcher thought that he was a little intoxicated and somewhat excited. As Atzerodt mounted the mare Fletcher remarked that he would not like to ride that mare through the city in the night, for she looked skittish. "Well," said Atzerodt, "she's good upon a retreat." Mr. Fletcher said: "Your acquaintance is staying out very late with our horse." "Oh," said he, "he'll be back after a while." Atzerodt then left, and Mr. Fletcher watched him until he passed Thirteen-and-a-half Street and saw him go into the Kirkwood House. He soon came out, and, mounting his horse, rode along D Street and turned up Tenth.

Having a suspicion that Herold was going to take the horse away, Mr. Fletcher walked up to Willard's Hotel, where he saw Herold riding the roan horse. He was coming down apparently from the Treasury. He was passing Fourteenth Street, and the horse was pulling to get to the stable, as he was very well acquainted with the place, and no doubt thought he had been out late enough. Mr. Fletcher hallooed at Herold: " You get off that horse now; you have had it long enough!" but he put spurs to it, and went as fast as the horse could go up Fourteenth Street, turning east on F. Herold made no reply, although he knew Mr. Fletcher, as the gas-light shone in his face. The horse was a fast one, his pace being a single-foot rack, but would trot with a loose rein.

Fletcher returned to his stable, saddled a horse, and started in pursuit, tracking Herold to the bridge over the Eastern Branch, leading to Uniontown (now Anacostia). He would have been permitted to cross, but not to return, as he would be compelled to have the password. This he could not get, so he gave up the chase and returned to the stable. Mr. Allison Naylor was at his home, and consequently was not aware of what was going on at his stable until the following morning.

Atzerodt made no attempt upon the life of Vice-President Johnson, although he had been assigned by Booth to perform that act, but probably through cowardice he failed to make the attempt. He was seen at different times during the night of the 14th. About half-past eleven o'clock he got on a car at the corner of Pennsylvania Avenue and Sixth Street, and on the same car was Washington Briscoe, an acquaintance, who asked him if he had heard the news of the assassination. Atzerodt said he had, and immediately asked his friend if he could sleep in his store with him, but the privilege was denied him. When the car neared the Navy Yard, he again asked, and, when getting off the car, asked for the third time.

Briscoe's store was in the Navy Yard, and he positively refused Atzerodt's pleadings for shelter. Atzerodt then said he would go back to the Pennsylvania House. He had appeared on horseback at that hotel between ten and eleven o'clock, and asked James Walker, a colored man working at the hotel, to hold his horse while he went in to the bar. After spending a few minutes in there he came out, mounted his horse, and rode off. He again appeared about two o'clock on the morning of the 15th, this time on foot, and applied for a room, when he tendered Mr. Greenwalt a five-dollar bill in payment for his room, and the change was returned to him. He started for his room, when he was reminded by Mr. Greenwalt that he had not registered. He said: " Do you want my name? " He hesitated some, but stepped back and registered. He had never previously hesitated to register the numerous times that he had stopped there. He had a short sleep, if he slept at all, for he left the hotel between five and six in the morning, and the next we hear of him is in Georgetown, about 8 o'clock A. M., when he entered Matthews & Co.'s store, 49 High Street, and asked the loan of ten dollars, offering to give his revolver for security, saying that he would bring the money back the following week. The money was given him, as the clerk considered the revolver well worth the amount asked.

He was next located at the country residence of Hezekiah Metz, who resided in Montgomery County, Maryland, about twenty-two miles northwest of Washington, where he arrived between 10 and 11 A. M., Sunday, the 16th. He dined with the family, and remained there several hours. Mr. Metz inquired about the news, and in the conversation said that he understood that General Grant had been shot. Atzerodt replied that " if the man that was to follow him had done so, it was likely to be so." He said that a man was to have gotten on the same train that General Grant did, thus disclosing very clearly that one of the conspirators was assigned the task of killing General Grant. Atzerodt knew that General Grant had left Washington on the evening of the assassination.

Atzerodt passed in this neighborhood by the name of Andrew Attwood. From Mr. Metz he went to the home of his cousin, Hartman Richter, near Middleburg, in Montgomery County, Maryland, which place he reached between three and four o'clock on Sunday afternoon. He remained there, occupying his time by walking about and occasionally working in the garden, until Thursday, the 20th, when he was arrested by Sergeant Z. W. Gemmill, of Captain S. Townsend's company, 1st Delaware Cavalry. Sergeant Gemmill was sent with a detail of six men, and reached the house of a Mr. James W. Purdon, and pressed him in as a guide to Mr. Richter's. When the sergeant knocked at the door Mr. Richter inquired who it was, and the sergeant invited him out to see. He was then asked if there was a man by the name of Attwood in the house, and he said, No, there was no one there—that he had been there, but had gone to Frederick, or to that neighborhood. The sergeant told him he would go in and search the house, whereupon Richter said that his cousin was upstairs in bed. His wife then spoke up, and said that as for that, there were three men there. Richter got a light, and the sergeant, taking two men with him, went upstairs, where he found Atzerodt lying on the front of the bed. The sergeant asked him his name, and he gave one that was not understood—probably a fictitious one. He was ordered to get up and dress, and he was taken to a Mr. Leaman, a loyal man, who knew him. Atzerodt made no further denial, nor did he inquire why he was arrested. The sergeant asked him if he had anything to do with the assassination, and he said he had not. He afterward confessed to J. S. McPhail, provost-marshal-general of the State of Maryland, that he threw away his bowie-knife above the Herndon House, corner F and Ninth streets. A colored man subsequently picked it up on the south side of F Street, between Eighth and Ninth, where Atzerodt said he threw it.

O'Laughlin, Booth, Surratt, Arnold, and Atzerodt were all interested in an oil speculation, as they frequently said. They at least made it appear so, that they might better excuse their frequent meetings held in Washington. Booth stopped at the National Hotel, and when the parties living out of the city came in, they lost but little time until they called upon him. Among the rendezvous of these persons in Washington were the Lichau Restaurant, connected with Rullman's Hotel, 456 Pennsylvania Avenue; the Lichau Hotel, 34 Louisiana Avenue, next door to the Canterbury Music Hall; the Pennsylvania House, kept by John Greenwalt, and the Herndon House, corner Ninth and F streets.

O'Laughlin and Arnold lodged for several weeks, in February, 1865, at Mrs. Mary Van Tyne's lodging house, 420 D Street N. W. While here Booth frequently called upon them, but they did not stay much of the time in their rooms, and occasionally they were out all night. They told Mrs. Van Tyne that they were in the oil business. The following telegrams savor a little of *oil* transactions:

WASHINGTON, D. C., March 27, 1865.
To M. O'LAUGHLIN, Esq., 57 North Exeter Street, Baltimore, Md.:
    Get word to Sam. Come on, with or without him, Wednesday morning. We sell that day sure. Don't fail.
J. WILKES BOOTH.

The " Sam " mentioned has reference to Samuel Arnold.

Booth telegraphed O'Laughlin March 13, 1865:

Don't fear to neglect your business; you had better come at once.

On April 13, the day before the assassination, O'Laughlin, in company with three companions, arrived in Washington from Baltimore about five o'clock in the afternoon. From the depot they sauntered up Pennsylvania Avenue, stopping at Rullman's for a drink, and from there they went the rounds of the various saloons. O'Laughlin and Mr. Early, one of the party, went to the National Hotel, and O'Laughlin, excusing himself, went into the hotel, and after inquiring at the desk came out, and the two walked back and joined their party. These companions tried to prove that O'Laughlin was with them until two o'clock on the morning of the 14th, when they registered and retired at the Metropolitan Hotel. James B. Henderson, one of the party, said that O'Laughlin was not out of his sight after their arrival until they retired, except for a few minutes between five and six o'clock, shortly after their arrival, when O'Laughlin said he had been to see Booth at the National Hotel. Henderson also said that O'Laughlin went to the hotel the next morning to see Booth.

The illuminations which had preceded the evening of the 13th were continued, and the capital was in a blaze. The public buildings were magnificently illuminated, and bands of music were stationed at various places. The President's mansion and the War and Navy Departments were especially brilliant. The people expressed their joy and happiness that the hour of danger had passed and the nation stood redeemed. After the illumination at the

War Department was over, a band of music and a large crowd proceeded to the residence of Secretary Stanton, 320 K Street N. W., and serenaded him, and also General Grant, who was present. About ten o'clock David Stanton saw O'Laughlin pass in the door of the Secretary's house and take a position on one side of the hall. He asked O'Laughlin what his business was, who asked where the Secretary was, and was told that he was standing on the steps. He remained there some minutes, when he was requested by David Stanton to go out, which he did. O'Laughlin could see General Grant in the brilliantly lighted parlors from where he stood in the hall. While the band was playing in front of the house, General and Mrs. Grant, the Secretary, General Barnes and his wife, with some other guests, appeared upon the front steps, as the crowd was calling for General Grant. Major Kilburn Knox was one of the party, and as he walked down to the lower step O'Laughlin said to him: "Is Stanton in?" The major said: "I suppose you mean the Secretary?" "Yes," he said; "I am a lawyer in town; I know him very well." Mr. John C. Hatter was standing on the steps listening to the music, when O'Laughlin approached him and asked if General Grant was in, saying he wished to see him, but was told that this was no occasion to see him; that if he remained in front of the house he could see the general when he came out.

There is but little doubt that one if not both of these distinguished men were to become the victims of his violence, although his visit to the house was the night before the assassination.

Mr. Bernard T. Early, one of the men who came to Washington with O'Laughlin, said that on Friday morning about nine o'clock they had breakfast at Welcker's

Restaurant, 322 Pennsylvania Avenue,* and then they walked up the avenue. When passing the National Hotel, O'Laughlin stopped and went in and up to Booth's room. His companions waited for him three-quarters of an hour, and as he didn't come out they went away without him; but O'Laughlin joined them later. The party spent the day of the assassination in drinking pretty freely and visiting places of resort.

O'Laughlin was at the Lichau House about eleven o'clock Friday night, and went out a few minutes later with John H. Fuller, a friend, who took him to the Franklin House, Eighth and D streets N. W., where they remained all night. On Saturday afternoon the whole party returned to Baltimore on the three o'clock train.

Upon their arrival in Baltimore, and while going to his home, O'Laughlin met his brother-in-law, who told him that some parties had been there that morning looking for him. O'Laughlin went into the house to see his mother, but only remained with her a few minutes, when he came out and said to Mr. Early: " I will not stay here all night, for fear I will be arrested. If I am, it will kill my mother." He went to the house of a friend by the name of Bailey, on High Street, where he was arrested on Monday the 17th by William Wallace. Mr. Wallace asked him why he was there instead of at his boarding place. He said that when he arrived in town Saturday he was told that the officers had been looking for him, and that he went away to a friend of his on Saturday and Sunday. When he was arrested he seemed to understand what it was for, and did not ask any questions about it.

*The numbers of the houses at that time do not correspond with those at present.

Edward Spangler was employed as a stage hand, frequently misrepresented as a stage carpenter, of the theater. He was to assist in shoving the scenery in its place as the necessity of the play required. These were his duties at night, but during the day he was to assist in doing the rough carpenter work incidental to plays to be produced. He had been in the employ of John T. Ford at the theater for four years, at intervals, and the two last years continuously. He was always regarded as a very good-natured, kind, willing man. At times he drank to excess, which had a tendency to make him vicious and unfit him for work. He seldom drank to excess about the theater, as his duty of shifting the scenes required his presence upon the stage constantly.

Spangler seemed to have a great admiration for J. Wilkes Booth. Booth's peculiar fascinating manner appealed to the lower class of people, such as Spangler belonged to. Spangler was a man without self-respect. He took his meals at a boarding-house on the corner of Seventh and G streets, and rarely slept in a bed; he usually slept in the theater. As he was considered a very harmless man by the company around the theater, he was often the subject of sport and fun. During the awful scene at the theater Spangler appears to have been Booth's right-hand man. He was called out of the theater to hold Booth's horse, but, as his presence was needed upon the stage, he called a boy by the name of Joseph Burroughs and told him to hold the horse, Spangler returning to his place on the stage. It is understood, and without much doubt, that Spangler prepared the bar which Booth placed in the wall and against the door, to prevent entrance to the box from the audience. Spangler had been a sort of general servant to Booth, taking care of his horse and stable, and doing his errands. The evidence at the trial strongly implicated him in aiding Booth to make his escape from the theater after the murder.

Samuel Arnold first met Booth at Barnum's Hotel, Baltimore. The first part of September, 1864, Booth sent for him, and the two had not met since 1852, when they were both schoolmates at St. Timothy's Hall. The two were engaged in conversation upon their former school days while they sipped their wine and smoked cigars that Booth had ordered. They were interrupted by a knock at the door. When opened, Michael O'Laughlin stepped in, and after an introduction to Arnold the trio sipped and smoked. It was here that Booth ventured his proposition to kidnap the President. Booth seemed positive that it could be successfully accomplished, and after fully understanding the politics and feelings of Arnold and O'Laughlin, Booth invited them to join him in the conspiracy. He assured them that it could be accomplished between Washington and the Soldiers' Home, three miles north of the city, as Lincoln frequently went out there unguarded.

The first plan was to capture and carry the President to Richmond, and for his exchange produce the exchange of all the Southern prisoners in Federal prisons, or other concessions favorable to the South. Booth in his fascinating manner painted the chances of success in such glowing colors that the two readily consented to join him. Booth made another trip to Baltimore, after which he went to New York, Boston, and Canada, and was to return in a month, but did not again visit Arnold and O'Laughlin until January, 1865. Upon this visit he had with him a trunk containing two guns, cartridges, revolvers, knives, and a pair of handcuffs to shackle the President. The weapons were to be used to de-

fend themselves in case they were pursued. He gave
the pistols, knives, and handcuffs to O'Laughlin and
Arnold to take to Washington. Booth himself went
to Washington, and the two men soon followed in
a buggy that Booth had purchased in Baltimore.
Upon their arrival in the capital they happened to
meet Booth on the street, when they alighted, took
a drink, and Booth hinted to them of the theater plan,
saying he would wait until they put the horse and buggy
away, and then tell them more fully of the project.
At the first interview in Baltimore Booth told them that,
if they did not succeed at the Soldiers' Home, the
chances were good at the theater. The three went to
Ford's Theater that night, and Booth explained to them
the different back entrances, and how feasible the plan
was. He had rented a stable in the rear of the theater,
having bought two horses down the country. Booth's
first theater plan was for Arnold to rush in the box and
seize the President, while Booth and Atzerodt were to follow, handcuff him, and lower him to the stage, while another was to catch and hold him till those in the box got
down. The lights were then to be put out, and the exit
to the rear of the theater made, John H. Surratt with
a number of armed men to be on the other side of the
Eastern Branch to facilitate escape through Surrattsville
and thence to Port Tobacco River in Charles County,
Maryland, where a boat was to be in waiting to take the
captive across the river and on to Port Royal, which is
on the direct line to Richmond. This boat had been
in readiness in a concealed spot for months, waiting for
the arrival of the President.

Another plot was to abduct the President and secrete
him in what is known as the Van Ness House, on
Seventeenth Street, near the Potomac River, until a

suitable occasion presented itself, when he would nave been taken to Richmond, or some safe place in the South, only to be released when the price of the independence of the South was paid.

Mr. Lincoln frequently visited Secretary Stanton's office at the War Department, adjoining the White House, during the night, to learn the news from the front, especially on the eve of an expected battle or after it had occurred. It was during one of these unaccompanied midnight excursions that his capture was contemplated.

The Van Ness house was built in 1820, near the old homestead of David Burns, a Scotchman whose plantation embraced a large portion of Washington City. It was a large brick house, two stories and a half high. The partition walls all ran to the same depth, terminating as cellar walls. The cellars made by these walls were used for various purposes. One of them had a trapdoor going down through the floor, and it was in one of these secret vaults that the conspirators expected to confine the President until they were able to have gotten him across the Potomac. While all these preparations were going on, Dr. Samuel Mudd and a number of gentlemen living in the vicinity of Bryantown, Piscataway, Port Tobacco, and Pope's Creek were waiting execution of the plot, ready to faithfully perform their part in securing the safe transport of the President to the Virginia side of the Potomac River.

From the testimony of Weichmann we cannot discredit the fact that about the 20th of March the conspirators were foiled in an attempt upon the life of the President. Mrs. Mary E. Surratt, in great excitement and weeping, said that her son John had gone away not to return, when about three hours subsequently, in the afternoon of the same day, he reappeared, rushing in a state of frenzy into the room in his mother's house, armed, proclaiming that his prospects were blasted and his hopes gone. Lewis Payne soon came into the same room, also armed and under great excitement, and was immediately followed by Booth, with his riding-whip in his hand, who walked rapidly across the floor from side to side, so much excited that for some time he did not notice the presence of Weichmann. Observing him, the parties withdrew, upon a suggestion from Booth, to an upper room, and there had a private interview. From all that transpired on that occasion it is apparent that when these parties left Mrs. Surratt's house that day, booted and spurred, it was with the full purpose of completing some act essential to the final execution of the work of assassination; but for some unknown cause their well-laid plans failed.

The President's murder had become a topic of common conversation among the Confederates in Canada, and it was also talked about throughout the camps in and around Richmond, and even in Washington City, which no doubt encouraged these men to capture the President, dead or alive.

Arnold seemed to have weakened, for he hesitated about committing murder, and even withdrew from the plan of kidnaping the President, for at a meeting held in February, 1865, at the Lichau House, Pennsylvania. Avenue N. W., he refused to aid the plot, and declared that he would have nothing to do with the conspiracy. At this meeting Booth, O'Laughlin, Atzerodt, Surratt, and several others were present. Booth got very angry when Arnold said that if the thing was not done that week, while he was there, he would withdraw. Booth said that he ought to be shot for expressing himself in that way. Arnold replied that two could play at that

game. The following letter, written from Hookstown,
Md., six miles from Baltimore, the home of his brother,
explains itself. His parents were at that time residing in
Baltimore.

HOOKSTOWN, BALTO'. Co., March 27, 1865.

DEAR JOHN:
  Was business so important that you could not remain in
Balto. till I saw you? I came in as soon as I could, but found
you had gone to W——n. I called also to see Mike, but learned
from his mother he had gone out with you, and had not returned. I concluded, therefore, he had gone with you. How
inconsiderate you have been! When I left you, you stated we
would meet in a month or so. Therefore I made application for
employment, an answer to which I shall receive during the
week. I told my parents I had ceased with you. Can I then,
under existing circumstances, come as you requested? You
know full well that the Go——t suspicions something is going
on there; therefore the undertaking is becoming more compli-
cated. Why not, for the present, desist for various reasons?
which, if you look into, you can readily see without my making
any mention thereof to you. Nor anyone can censure me for
my present course. You have been its cause, for how can I
now come after telling them I had left you? Suspicion rests on
me now, from my whole family, and even parties in the country.
I will be compelled to leave home, anyhow, and how soon I care
not.
  None, no, not one, were more in a favor of the enterprise
than myself, and to-day would be there had you not done as
you have—by this, I mean, manner of proceeding. I am, as
you well know, in need. I am, you may say, in rags, whereas
to-day I ought to be well clothed. I do not feel right stalking
about without means, and more from appearance a beggar.
I feel my independence; but even all this would and was
forgotten, for I was one with you. Time more propitious
will arrive yet. Do not do act rashly or in haste. I would
prefer your first query, "Go and see how it will be taken at
R——d," and ere long I shall be better prepared to again be
with you. I dislike writing; would sooner verbally make known
my views, yet you know writing causes me thus to proceed.

Do not in anger peruse this, weigh all I have said, and as a rational man and a *friend*, you cannot censure or upbraid my conduct. I sincerely trust this, nor naught else that shall or may occur, will ever be an obstacle to obliterate our former friendship and attachment. Write me to Balto., as I expect to be in about Wednesday or Thursday, or, if you can possibly come on, I will Tuesday meet you in Balto. at B——. Ever I subscribe myself,

Your friend,

SAM.

About the first of March, 1865, Arnold applied to John W. Wharton, who kept a sutler's store outside of the fortifications at Fortress Monroe, for a clerkship. Mr. Wharton was from Baltimore, and it was through a letter from Arnold's father that he gave him a position as clerk, which commenced on the 2d of April, the day after his arrival at Fortress Monroe. He continued in that position until the 17th of April, when he was arrested by Voltaire Randall and Eaton G. Horner. When arrested, Arnold made a confession, making a statement and giving the names of certain men connected with a plan for the abduction of President Lincoln. He was asked if he ever corresponded with Booth. At first he denied the truth, but on mentioning the letter mailed at Hookstown, that had been found in Booth's trunk, he admitted that he wrote that letter. His carpet sack was examined at the time of his arrest, and in it was found some letters, papers, clothing, a revolver, and some cartridges. The revolver was loaded. He was taken to Baltimore, thence to Washington.

The doorbell of Mrs. Surratt's house, 541 (now 604) H Street N. W., was rung by Major H. W. Smith, in company with other officers, about eleven o'clock Monday night, the 17th. When the bell rang, Mrs. Surratt appeared at the window and said: " Is that you, Mr.

Kirby?" The reply was that it was not Mr. Kirby, and to open the door. She opened the door, and was asked: "Are you Mrs. Surratt?" She said: "I am the widow of John H. Surratt." The officer added, "And the mother of John H. Surratt, Jr.?" She replied: "I am." Major Smith said: "I come to arrest you and all in your house, and take you for examination to General Augur's headquarters." No inquiry whatever was made as to the cause of the arrest. Mr. R. C. Morgan, in the service of the War Department, made his appearance at the Surratt house a few minutes later, sent under orders to superintend the seizure of papers and the arrest of the inmates. While the officers were in the house a knock and ring were heard at the door, and Mr. Morgan and Captain Wermerskirch stepped forward and opened the door, and Lewis Payne stepped in with a pickax over his shoulder, dressed in a gray coat and vest and black trousers. As he had left his hat in the house of Secretary Seward, he had made one out of the sleeve of a shirt or the leg of a drawers, pulling it over his head like a turban. He said he wished to see Mrs. Surratt, and when asked what he came that time of night for, he replied he came to dig a gutter, as Mrs. Surratt had sent for him in the morning. When asked where he boarded, he said he had no boarding-house, that he was a poor man, who got his living with the pick. Mr. Morgan asked him why he came at that hour of the night to go to work. He said he simply called to find out what time he should go to work in the morning. When asked if he had any previous acquaintance with Mrs. Surratt, he answered, " No," but said that she knew he was working around the neighborhood and was a poor man, and came to him. He gave his age as twenty, and was from Fauquier County, Virginia, and pulled out an oath of allegiance, and on it was, " Lewis

MRS. SURRATT'S HOUSE, 604 H STREET N. W., WASHINGTON, D.

This house is a three-story brick. Basement, containing two rooms, is on a level with the pavement. The front one was used as a dining-room and the other as a kitchen. Second story front room was used as a parlor, and the back one by Mrs. Surratt as a bedroom. There are three rooms in the third story, and two large and one small one in the attic.

Payne, Fauquier Co., Va." Mrs. Surratt was asked whether she knew him, and she declared in the presence of Payne, holding up her hands: " Before God, I have never seen that man before; I have not hired him; I do not know anything about him." Mrs. Surratt said to Mr. Morgan: " I am so glad you officers came here to-night, for this man came here with a pickax to kill us." From Mrs. Surratt's house Payne was taken to the provost-marshal's office. Mrs. Surratt was informed that the carriage was ready to take her to the provost-marshal's office, and she, with her daughter Annie, Miss Honora Fitzpatrick, and Miss Olivia Jenkins (the latter two boarded at the house), were driven away.

Dr. Samuel Mudd was arrested at his home, Friday the 21st, by Lieutenant Alexander Lovett, and taken to Washington. The main points charged against Dr. Mudd were that he was personally acquainted with Booth before the murder, and had been seen in company with him and some of the assassins upon several occasions, and that he set Booth's broken leg, knowing that it was he, though positively denying it to the detectives.

John H. Surratt, Jr., made his escape, leaving Washington the night of the murder or the following morning, going direct to Canada, as proven beyond a doubt at the trial.

CHAPTER V.

MAJOR A. C. RICHARDS, Superintendent of the Metropolitan Police, who was in Ford's Theater when the President was shot, being satisfied that Booth was the perpetrator of the deed and had taken flight across the Navy Yard bridge, was ready to pursue the assassin as soon as the Government would furnish the horses; but owing to red tape, *to which our Government is so prone*, the posse could not leave Washington till twelve hours after the shooting. A tapering peninsula stretches down through southern Maryland to Leonardstown, and over this course nearly two thousand soldiers on horses galloped the day after the assassination, bent on avenging the murder of their Commander-in-Chief. The road passed through a section of the Western Shore of Maryland that possessed but very few loyal citizens.

A detective party, consisting of Lee, D'Angelis, Callahan, Hoey, Bostwick, Harrover, Bevins, and McHenry, under the personal command of Major James R. O'Beirne, embarked on a steamer at Washington for Chapel Point, on Tuesday the 18th, reaching that point in the night, and immediately started for Port Tobacco, four miles distant. Here they heard that Herold had visited the place three weeks before, and told his friends that he intended fleeing the country. Atzerodt had been in the town just prior to the murder. He had been living with a widow, who admitted to Major O'Beirne she loved him, and refused to betray him, although she hinted that he had committed some terrible crime. Here Major O'Beirne met Major John M. Waite, of the 8th Illinois Cavalry, who had pushed on south to Leonardstown Monday night. Major O'Beirne believed that the fugitive had either pushed on for the Potomac or taken to the swamps. The officers determined to follow him to the one and to explore the other. Fourteen hundred cavalry were collected here, seven hundred men of the 8th Illinois Cavalry, six hundred of the 22d Colored Troops, and one hundred men of the 16th New York Cavalry. This force dismounted and swept the swamps. Major O'Beirne's description of this section is dismal indeed. He said: " The swamps tributary to the various branches of the Wicomico River, of which the chief feeder is Allen's Creek, bear various names, such as Jordan's Swamp, Atchall's Swamp, and Scrub Swamp. These are dense growths of dogwood, gum, and beech, planted in sluices of water and bog. Frequent deep ponds dot this wilderness place, with here and there a stretch of dry soil, but no human being inhabits the malarious expanse; even a hunted murderer would shrink from hiding there. Serpents and slimy lizards are the only living denizens. Not even the hunted negro dared to fathom the treacherous clay, nor make himself a fellow of the slimy reptiles which reign absolute in this terrible solitude." Around this dismal place the soldiers made a thorough search for the President's assassins, but no trace of them could anywhere be found. Major O'Beirne started for Leonardstown with his detective force, inquiring at the farmhouses. Meeting a colored man, he was given by him sufficient information to warrant the belief that Booth had crossed the river. On Saturday night the major with his detectives crossed the Potomac to Boone's farm, where the fugitives were supposed to have landed. The party was tired out, and all stopped for the night except Major O'Beirne and one man, who pushed on all night to King George's Court-House, and next day, Sunday, returned to Chapel Point, where he telegraphed his information and asked permission to pursue and catch the assassins before they reached Port Royal. This the Department refused. We can but think that after getting so close to them he ought to have followed the trail and captured them without waiting further orders. The party returned on the boat to Washington, reporting their expedition and information gained, after which Colonel Lafayette C. Baker decided upon a course, writing a note to Major-General W. S. Hancock, then in command of the Department of the Potomac, requesting him to send a detachment of twenty-five cavalry, under charge of a competent, discreet, and reliable officer, to report immediately.

About 2 P. M. of the 24th Lieutenant Edward Doherty and twenty-six men of the 16th New York Cavalry reported to Colonel L. C. Baker at his office on Pennsylvania Avenue, opposite Willard's Hotel. Colonel Baker put the command in charge of Lieutenant-Colonel Everton J. Conger of Ohio, and Lieutenant L. B. Baker, his cousin, of New York, and the expedition left the Sixth Street wharf on board the steamer *John S. Ide* about four o'clock, arriving at Belle Plain, now "Brick House landing," on the border of Stafford County, Virginia, at ten o'clock. Belle Plain is the nearest landing to Fredericksburg, seventy miles from Washington, and located on Potomac Creek. After the steamer tied up to the wharf the cavalry disembarked and galloped off in the darkness, with Conger and Baker riding ahead, across the country, reaching Port Conway between three and four o'clock the next afternoon, the 25th. Here they refreshed themselves and fed their horses. While resting here Lieutenant Baker engaged in conversation with a William Rollins, living near the ferry, who, after looking at the photographs of Booth and Herold, recognized them as the party who crossed the ferry the day before, except that Booth had no mustache. Rollins informed Lieutenant Baker that Booth and Herold wanted to be taken to Bowling Green, sixteen miles distant, and that they started with three Confederate officers on horseback. Lieutenant Baker took Rollins along as a guide, and, at his own request, he was arrested in order to avert suspicion. The expedition was ferried over the river, and started hungry, sleepy, and tired for Bowling Green, reaching the place between eleven and twelve o'clock at night. It was learned that one of the Confederates, Captain Jett, was stopping here at the hotel owned by Henry Galdman, whose daughter was Jett's sweetheart. The building was surrounded and Colonel Conger and the two officers entered it, found their way to Jett's room, and arrested him. Jett was very much alarmed, and seemed to know what the intruders wanted. When he found himself in the hands of the officers, he asked for a private conference, which was held for a few minutes, when his horse was ordered, the bugle sounded, and back the party started, over the same route they had come, for Garrett's farm—a distance of thirteen miles.

At 2 o'clock A. M., April 26, the deathlike stillness of the night was broken by the approach of the horsemen as they entered and surrounded Garrett's old farmhouse.

HOME OF RICHARD HENRY GARRETT.
Near Port Royal, Va., where Booth made his last stop.

If anyone had attempted to escape, a ring of fire would have encircled the house, for every man had his carbine poised. After a pause, Lieutenant Baker rapped at the kitchen door, calling loudly, when an old gentleman, owner of the farm, Richard Henry Garrett, dressed in his night-clothes, made his appearance. Baker roughly seized him by the throat with one hand and with the other held a pistol to his head. The old man was very much frightened at seeing so many horses and men near his house, and being so roughly handled. He could scarcely give an intelligent answer to Lieutenant Baker's questions as to where the men were that stayed with him. He was ordered to get a candle, and the old gentleman did so as quickly as possible, when Lieutenant Baker again asked him where the men were. "They are gone," he said. "We haven't got them in the house.

I assure you that they are gone." At this time a young
man, Jack Garrett, appeared very suddenly upon the
scene, saying: " Father, we had better tell the truth about
the matter. Those men whom you seek, gentlemen, are
in the tobacco house, I know. They went there to
sleep." A guard was left with Mr. Garrett, and when
the cavalry reached the barn they were dismounted, the
horses sent to the rear, and the men were stationed
around the barn, about thirty feet from it on three sides,
the front side being left clear. The barn contained in
one corner a lot of furniture covered with hay. The
building stood about one hundred yards from the house.
The guards were stationed about ten yards distant from
the building, with four of them at the door. The door
was locked with a padlock, and, while the key was being
secured, a rustling noise could be heard inside. Lieutenant Baker notified the parties within that he had a
proposal to make; that a son of the man whose hospitality they had enjoyed would enter, and they should give
up their arms or the building would be fired.

Lieutenant Baker gave me a verbal account some
years before he died of what happened, and it varied but
little from his report made after reaching Washington.
There was no reply to Baker's proposal, so he unlocked
the door and pushed the boy in. He wore the uniform of
a Confederate soldier, had faced the cannon's mouth and
charged the Yankee soldiers, but this was more like death
than anything that he had met before. Young Garrett
appealed in low tones for their surrender, but Booth
replied, " —— you! get out of here; you have betrayed
me." The boy did not tarry long, for the door was
opened and he was let out. The officers were in full
view of and exposed to a possible shot from Booth and
Herold, for the candle, still burning, shone through the

cracks of the barn; but, it being dark inside, the fugitives could not be seen. When the soldiers observed this, the officers removed the candle; but those surrounding the building still exhibited considerable uneasiness, and, when this was noticed, Baker repeated his demands for a surrender. "You must surrender inside there! Give up your arms and appear; there is no chance for escape. We give you five minutes to make up your mind." "Who are you, and what do you want with us?" came out in a bold voice that could be heard by everyone around, even to the house. Baker replied: "We want you to deliver up your arms and become our prisoners." "But who are you?" hallooed the same voice. "That makes no difference; we know who you are, and we want you. We have fifty men, armed with carbines and pistols. You cannot escape." After quite a pause Booth said: "Captain, this is a hard case, I swear. Perhaps I am being taken by my own friends." Booth then asked for time to consider, and it was granted.

What fearful and anxious moments those were to Booth! What a part he was enacting in the last scene of the great play of his life! His immediate audience was small in numbers, but the people of a nation were watching the scene with throbbing hearts. He must have thought of the plaudits received so many times from appreciative audiences, while the memory of a mother and brothers flashed upon him. No one will ever know what really passed through his mind during those few moments of reprieve.

The time being up, Lieutenant Baker said: "Well, we have waited long enough. Surrender your arms and come out, or we'll fire the barn." Booth answered, "I am but a cripple, a one-legged man. Withdraw your forces one hundred yards from the door, and I will go out. Give me a chance for my life, captain, for I will never be taken alive." " We did not come here to fight, but to capture you, and if you do not come out I will fire the barn." A sigh could be heard from the inside, when Booth said: " Well, my brave boys, you can prepare a stretcher for me!" The first conversation between Booth and Herold was then heard, when Booth said: " You're a —— coward, and mean to leave me in my distress; but go, go! I don't want you to stay—I won't have you stay!" Then he shouted: " There's a man inside who wants to surrender!" " Let him come out, if he will bring his arms." A rattle at the door was heard, and a voice saying: " Let me out; open the door; I want to surrender." " Hand out your arms then." " I have no arms." " You are the man who carried the carbine yesterday; hand it out!" In a whining voice he replied, " I haven't got any." Booth cried out, " He has not any arms; they are mine, and I have kept them." " Well, he carried the carbine, and must bring it out." " On the word and honor of a gentleman, he has no arms with him. They are mine, and I have got them." Herold was pleading at the door to be let out, when he was told to put out his hands, and the door was opened just far enough for his two arms to protrude, when handcuffs were placed upon them and he was quickly jerked out. He was immediately given into the hands of a squad of cavalrymen. He positively and constantly claimed that he was innocent, but was made to cease his talking. Booth now made a last appeal for a chance for his life. " Draw off your men, and I will fight them singly. I could have killed half a dozen of your men to-night; but I believe you to be brave men, and would not murder you. Give a lame man a show."

Too late! Before he had uttered the last sentence

Colonel Conger made a rope of straw, set it on fire, thrust it inside on top of a little pile of hay in the corner, and a sheet of flame and smoke soon leaped up from the rear of the building. The barn was so brilliantly lighted that an inventory could have been taken of the farm implements and furniture that were within. There, in the middle of the building, Booth was seen standing erect, one arm over his crutch, assisting the other in holding his carbine. As the blaze came toward him he stepped nearer the door. The flames inside only concealed from his view those outside. He peered at the cracks of the building as if to get a shot at someone outside, but the opportunity did not come to him.

An unexpected shot came from a pistol in the steady hand of Sergeant Corbett, and Booth sank down limp upon the barn floor, when the door was opened and the soldiers rushed in and dragged him out. He

BOOTH STANDING IN THE BARN WHILE IT IS BURNING.

was laid on the grass for a few minutes, then carried to the front porch of the house. He was apparently dead, but after some water had been dashed in his face he revived somewhat, and was noticed to move

THE OFFICERS AND SOLDIERS DRAGGING BTOOH OUT OF THE BURNING
BARN AFTER HE WAS SHOT.

his lips, when an officer put his ear down to his face and heard him say: " Tell my mother——" There was a pause of nearly a minute before he could get sufficient vitality to say what he wanted to, but he began again: " Tell my mother I died for my country, and "—the voice sank into a whisper, so that the officers were compelled to bend down in order to hear his finishing words—" I did what I thought was best." He could say no more. His arms lay by his side, and, not being able to move them, he asked that they be raised so that he could see his hands. The officers raised them up; he looked at them, and as they were laid down he said, very faintly, "Useless, useless!" These were his last words.

He received the fatal shot at fifteen minutes past three on the morning of the 26th of April, and, after lingering two hours and a quarter in terrible agony, died, just as the morning sun brilliantly lighted up the awful scene. From the time he shot the President until he died in the very State whose motto he had disgraced, he had not a moment's peace or comfort.

While lying on the porch of the stranger who had befriended him he had time for reflection. High medical authority says it was a living, active mind within a helpless, paralyzed body, accompanied by most excruciating, agonizing pain that a human being can be subject to. From the moment the ball struck him he was helpless, with a mind clear in intense suffering—a living witness of his own just punishment for his atrocious deed. Could the end of such a life be more painful, more dreadful, of more appalling?

Physically Booth from the crown of his head to the sole of his foot was without blemish. As seen on the streets—his symmetrical form of faultless height and proportions; his dark flashing eye; his marble forehead, crowned by a head of curling black hair; a youth of agility and graceful enough for a statue of Apollo—he was the handsomest man in Washington, and the graces sat on him externally in strange contrast to those of his victim. Behind the footlights and among the flashy settings of the stage he was admired by an enthusiastic audience, evidencing how much wickedness may lurk under the most beautiful form.

Sergeant Boston Corbett wrote me an account of his shooting Booth: "When the fire approached Booth,

standing in the middle of the barn, he stepped toward
the door, and I supposed that he was going to fight his
way out.   I was told by one of the men that he pointed
his carbine at me.   My mind was upon his movements all

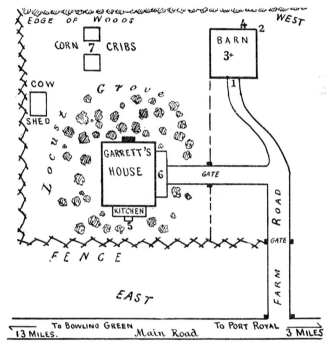

PLAN OF GARRETT'S PLACE.

1. Door of barn through which Booth was brought.
2. Corner of barn which was fired.
3. Where Booth stood.
4. Where Boston Corbett stood.
5. Door of kitchen of house where Baker met Garrett.
6. Front porch, on which Booth died.
7. Corn cribs, where the two Garrett boys slept.

the time, and I was afraid that he would shoot someone,
as he said he could have shot half a dozen soldiers.   I
became convinced that it was time for me to shoot, and

I took a steady aim on my arm with my revolver and, through a large crack in the barn, shot him. When he was brought out, I found that the wound was made in the neck, back of the ear, and came out a little higher up on the other side of the head."

There was no vehicle about the Garrett farm that could be used for the transportation of Booth's body, so an officer and several soldiers went out a quarter of a mile toward Bowling Green road, and pressed into service an old ambulance owned by a colored man by the name of Edward Freeman. This ambulance had seen service upon many a battlefield, for it was in a dilapidated condition at the time. Booth's body was sewed up in an army blanket, lashed to a board, and put in the ambulance, and the procession started, crossing the Rappahannock at Port Royal on the same boat over which Booth and the soldiers had crossed but a few days before. All went well until, about halfway between the ferry and the boat at Belle Plain, eighteen miles distant, the old ambulance broke down. There was no time or inclination to stop for repairs, so a new vehicle was pressed into service, and the journey continued, Edward Freeman returning home with his horses, leaving the old ambulance, dripping for the last time with human blood, to decay by the roadside. Belle Plain was reached, and the boat started on its return to Washington. Lieutenant-Colonel Conger reached Washington by an overland route about 5 P. M. on the 26th, immediately informing Colonel Baker of the capture. The two then went to the house of Secretary Stanton and informed him. The Secretary directed Colonel Baker to take a tug and go to Alexandria and meet the steamer that was bringing the body up. The steamer *Ide* reached Alexandria at 10.40 on the 26th, and Herold and the body of Booth were transferred to the tug on which Baker went down. The officer of the monitor *Montauk* stated that at 1.45 A. M., 27th, a tug came alongside, on board of which was Colonel Baker, the detective, with a dead body, said to be that of J. Wilkes Booth. Said body was placed on board for safekeeping. Herold was put in double irons and placed in the hold of the vessel. The body of Booth was taken out of the blanket in which it had been securely wrapped before leaving Garrett's farm, and placed on deck in charge of a guard. Commodore J. B. Montgomery, commandant at the Navy Yard, sent a message to the Secretary of the Navy (Gideon Welles) April 27:

> David E. Herold, prisoner, and the remains of Wilkes Booth were delivered here at 1.45 this morning. The body of Booth is changing rapidly. What disposition shall be made of it? It is now on board the iron-clad *Montauk*.

On the 27th an order was issued by the Secretary of the Navy to the commandant of the Navy Yard permitting Surgeon-General Barnes and his assistant, accompanied by Judge-Advocate-General Holt, Hon. John A. Bingham, Major Eckhert, William G. Moore, clerk of the War Department, Colonel L. C. Baker, Lieutenant Baker, Lieutenant-Colonel Conger, Charles Dawson, J. L. Smith, Mr. Gardner, photographer, and an assistant, T. H. O'Sullivan, to go on board the *Montauk* and see the body of John Wilkes Booth. The Secretary ordered as follows:

> Immediately after the Surgeon-General has made his autopsy, you will have the body placed in a strong box and deliver it to the charge of Colonel Baker, the box being carefully sealed.

In order that the body should be identified beyond a doubt, Dr. J. F. May, a physician of Washington, who had

POST-MORTEM ON BOOTH'S BODY ON THE MONITOR "MONTAUK."

some two years before removed a tumor from Booth's neck, readily found the scar. His body was fully identified by his initials on his arm in India ink, and by the personal recognitions of those who knew him intimately. Surgeon-General Barnes, with an assistant, cut from Booth's neck a section of the spine through which the ball passed, and this was the only mutilation of the body that occurred. On the 27th Colonel Baker received instructions from the Secretary of War to make a secret burial of Booth. At 2.45 the same day Colonel Baker quietly took the body away, leaving the officers at the Navy Yard astonished at its sudden departure. The commandant called for an explanation from the marine officer, but he only reported that the body was so suddenly and unexpectedly removed to the boat which conveyed it away that he had no opportunity of reporting before the work was accomplished. He said: "This unusual transaction deprived me of the opportunity of inclosing the body in a box prepared for it, as ordered by

THE MONITOR "SAUGUS."

A number of the conspirators after arrest were confined on board the monitor as it lay at anchor in the Eastern Branch, in front of the Navy Yard.

the Department. The box is now on board the *Montauk*, and ready for delivery when called for." Colonel Baker, with the assistance of Lieutenant L. B. Baker and sailors to row the boat, took the body down the Eastern Branch, and around to the landing on the west side of the Arsenal grounds, into the old penitentiary. The lower ground-floor cells of that building were filled with fixed ammunition, stored there by the Ordnance Department. One of the largest of these cells was cleared of ammunition, a large flat stone lifted from its place, and a grave dug, the body being placed in a pine gun box. It was then lowered in and the grave filled up, the stone replaced, and the body rested, known to but a few persons, until February, 1869, when President Andrew Johnson gave Edwin Booth permission to have it removed to Baltimore.

When Mrs. Surratt was arrested she was taken to the Old Capitol Prison, and during her stay there was permitted to associate with other prisoners confined there for various offenses against the Government. She was finally transferred to one of the monitors, where she was placed in close confinement, with the other conspirators. A lady prisoner at Old Capitol gives the following account of Mrs. Surratt's departure: " One of the officers entered the prison and said: ' Mrs. Surratt, you are wanted. You will put on your bonnet and cloak, if you please, and follow me.' Mrs. Surratt arose silently, but tremblingly, and going to her own room arrayed herself as directed. She returned in a few moments, her daughter Annie clinging to her, and begging to be allowed to accompany her, which request was refused. Mrs. Surratt kissed each one of us, and when she came to me, she threw her arms around my neck, and said in an agitated voice: ' Pray for me, pray for me.' "

April 18 Lewis Payne was delivered at the Navy Yard and placed on board the monitor *Saugus*, in double irons, and, on the day following, Samuel Arnold was put on board the same vessel. On the 20th Atzerodt and his brother-in-law, Hartmann Richter, were placed on board at 11 P. M., but, upon the receipt of a request from the Secretary of War, Atzerodt was separated from his brother-in-law and put on board the *Montauk*. Ned Spangler was taken from the Old Capitol Prison on the 24th and placed on the monitor. At 10.30 P. M. of the 29th of April the commandant of the Navy Yard delivered all the prisoners to General Hancock. While they were on the monitors the Secretary of War ordered for better security against conversation, "and they shall have a canvas bag put on the head of each, and tied around the neck, with a hole for proper breathing and eating, but not seeing," and that Payne be secured to prevent self-destruction. An order was also issued prohibiting any person holding communication with the prisoners confined on the boats without a pass signed jointly by the Secretary of War and Secretary of the Navy.

The credit of the capture of Booth and Herold was given to Colonel Baker's force by the Secretary of War. As the War Department had offered large rewards for the capture of the assassins, many of those engaged in the search made demands for a portion of it. A commission was appointed by the Secretary of War, composed of General J. Holt, Judge-Advocate-General, and Adjutant-General E. D. Townsend, to whom were referred all the applications, statements, affidavits, and papers forwarded by those making claims. Some persons who were merely engaged in the search, and could not show a particle of testimony, put in for a large slice of the reward. Three months were spent in making the examination of persons and papers, when the Secretary

War Department. Washington. April 20. 1865.

$100,000 REWARD!

THE MURDERER

Of our late beloved President. ABRAHAM LINCOLN,

IS STILL AT LARGE.

$50,000 REWARD!

will be paid by this Department for his apprehension, in addition to any reward offered by Municipal Authorities or State Executives,

$25,000 REWARD!

will be paid for the apprehension of JOHN H. SURRATT, one of Booth's accomplices.

$25,000 REWARD!

will be paid for the apprehension of DANIEL C HARROLD, another of Booth's accomplices.

LIBERAL REWARDS will be paid for any information that shall conduce to the arrest of either of the above-named criminals, or their accomplices.

All persons harboring or secreting the said persons, or either of them, or aiding or assisting their concealment or escape, will be treated as accomplices in the murder of the President and the attempted assassination of the Secretary of State, and shall be subject to trial before a Military Commission and the punishment of DEATH.

Let the stain of innocent blood be removed from the land by the arrest and punishment of the murderers.

All good citizens are exhorted to aid public justice on this occasion. Every man should consider his own conscience charged with this solemn duty, and rest neither night nor day until it be accomplished.

EDWIN M. STANTON, Secretary of War.

DESCRIPTIONS.—BOOTH is 5 feet 7 or 8 inches high, slender build, high forehead, black hair black eyes, and wears a heavy black moustache. JOHN H. SURRATT is about 5 feet 9 inches. Hair rather thin and dark, eyes rather light; no beard. Would weigh 145 or 150 pounds. Complexion rather pale and clear with color to his cheeks. Wore light clothes of fine quality. Shoulders square; check bones rather prominent; chin narrow; ears projecting at the top. forehead rather low and square, but broad. Parts his hair on the right side, neck rather long. His lips are firmly set. A slim man. DANIEL C HARROLD is 22 years of age, 5 feet 6 or 7 inches high, rather broad shouldered, otherwise light built; dark hair, little (if any) moustache, dark eyes weighs about 140 pounds.

GEO. F NESBITT & CO. Printers and Stationers, cor. Pearl and Pine Streets, N. Y.

REWARD BILL FOR THE APPREHENSION OF BOOTH, SURRATT, AND HEROLD.

of War limited the time of filing claims to January, 1866. After that date another three months were spent, when the commission finally made their report, giving the entire credit of the capture to Colonel Baker's force and

allowing him a small portion of the reward; but, owing
to so much dissatisfaction expressed among the appli-
cants, the whole matter was referred to Congress, and
from there to the Committee on Claims. That committee, being very busy, referred the whole matter to the
Hon. George W. Hotchkiss of New York. Another
long delay occurred, when the Committee on Claims reported as follows:

The Committee further report that the expeditions which
resulted in the capture of Booth and Herold were planned and
directed by Colonel Lafayette C. Baker, then a detective
officer in the War Department, the forces consisting of Lieutenant-Colonel Everton J. Conger, Lieutenant Luther B. Baker,
then in the detective service, Lieutenant Edward P. Doherty,
and twenty-six privates and non-commissioned officers of the
16th New York Cavalry. And the Committee further report
that Major James R. O'Beirne, then provost-marshal of the
District of Columbia, General H. H. Wells, then under General
C. C. Augur's command, Captain George Cottingham, and
Alexander Lovett, detectives, and Samuel H. Beckwith, a telegraph operator at Chapel Point, rendered important service leading to the arrest of Booth and Herold, and the committee regard
them as coming within the terms of the offer of the reward.
The committee do not regard the capture of Booth and Herold
as purely military service, and do not feel bound to award compensation to mere rank, without regard to the extent and merit
of the service performed, but look to the rank and position of
the officers engaged in such service as evidence of the opportunity afforded them, and the duty imposed upon them to exer-
cise greater care, skill, and diligence than persons in a sub-
ordinate position. And the committee further report, after
careful consideration of the evidence presented to them of the
service of the respective parties engaged in the capture of
Booth and Herold, in their opinion the sum of seventy-five
thousand dollars reward for the capture of Booth and Herold
should be distributed as follows.

The report of this committee was still unsatisfactory
to a majority of those claiming rewards. The amount

to the credit of Colonel Baker and Colonel Conger was $17,500 each. So much dissatisfaction prevailed that the report was submitted to Congress, and the lobbyists and interested parties went to work with the members of Congress. The final result of the action of that body was the disapproval of the report of the Committee on Claims, substituting the following sums:

E. J. Conger, detective,	$15,000.00
Lafayette C. Baker, detective,	3,750.00
Luther B. Baker, detective,	3,000.00
Lieutenant Edward P. Doherty, in command of the cavalry,	5,250.00
James R. O'Beirne, detective,	2,000.00
H. H. Wells, George Cottingham, Alexander Lovett, each $1,000,	3,000.00
Sergeant Boston Corbett, Sergeant Andrew Wendell, Corporal Charles Zimmer, Corporal Michael Uniac, Corporal John Winter, Corporal Herman Newgarten, Corporal John Walz, Corporal Oliver Lonpay, Corporal Michael Hormsbey, Privates John Myers, John Ryan, William Byrne, Philip Hoyt, Martin Kelley, Henry Putnam, Frank McDaniel, Lewis Savage, Abraham Genay, Emery Parady, David Baker, William McQuade, John Millington, Frederick Dietz, John H. Singer, Carl Steinbrugge, and Joseph Zisgen, each $1,653.85	43,000.00
	$75,000.00

Amount paid for the capture of Atzerodt:

Major E. R. Artman, 213th Pennsylvania Infantry,	$1,250.00
Sergeant Z. W. Gemmill, 1st Delaware Cavalry,	3,598.54
Christopher Ross, David H. Baker, Albert Bender, Samuel J. Williams, George W. Young, James Longacre, privates 1st Delaware Cavalry, and James W. Purdman, citizen, each $2,878.78,	20,151.46
	$25,000.00

Paid to the captors of Payne:

Major H. W. Smith, ...	$1,000.00
Richard C. Morgan, Eli Devore, Charles H. Rosch,	
Thomas Sampson, W. M. Wermerskirch, detective,	
each $500.00, ...	2,500.00
J. H. Kimball, citizen, ...	500.co
P. M. Clark, citizen, ...	500.00
Susan Jackson, colored, ...	250.00
Mary Ann Griffin, ...	250.00
	$5,000.00

John Wilkes Booth was born on " The Farm," near Baltimore, in 1838. His father, Junius Brutus Booth, was born near London, England, in 1796, and became a famous actor, meeting with long and triumphant successes upon the English and American stage. He died in 1852, leaving four sons, Junius Brutus, Edwin, John Wilkes, and Joseph. The three oldest were actors, and the youngest, Joseph, tried the stage, but failed. There were also five daughters. John Wilkes displayed much affection for his mother and sisters, but they had no influence over him, as he was wayward, headstrong, and disobedient. He was not fond of the pent-up life of the schoolhouse, but, instead, loved the enthusiasm of hunting, fishing, and outdoor sports; especially was he fond of the stable, where he learned to be a graceful horseman. While quite young he became a lover of the stage, but the beginning of his career upon it was not assuring of success. He lacked enterprise, and did not study his parts, so that when he appeared upon the stage he blundered continually, and was frequently hissed while playing in Philadelphia. At the age of twenty-two he had the reputation at first of having no promise, but after many trials showed some talent and merited some applause. He made his first appearance in 1855 in " Richard III." at the St. Charles Theater in Baltimore, and in the fall of 1857 appeared under the name of

JOHN WILKES BOOTH.

Wilkes at the Arch Street Theater in Philadelphia, where he played stock parts during the entire season. The name of Wilkes was given him by his father in honor of an old Baltimore friend, Jim Wilkes. Booth next became a member of the Richmond (Va.) Theater, improved, and became a favorite with the Southerners. He was very fond of the Southern people, and at the breaking out of the rebellion sympathized with them and espoused their cause.

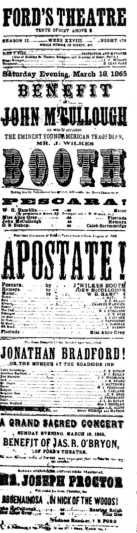

PLAY BILL
of Ford's Theater, March 18, 1865, when J. Wilkes Booth played for the benefit of John McCullough. This was the last appearance of Booth on the stage until the night of April 14.

In 1859 he was in a new rôle. At Richmond he enlisted in a company of militia, and with his company stood guard around the scaffold, at Charlestown, W. Va., on which the old white-haired John Brown was hanged. During the season of 1860 and 1861 we find him engaged still farther South, playing chiefly at Montgomery, and Columbus, Ga. While he favored the Southern cause, he did not fancy conscription into the Southern army, so escaped North. Unlike his brother Edwin and many others of the profession, he was unwilling to start at the foot of the ladder and work his way up by hard work, but wanted to make fame at one bound. However, he finally made a success of the profession, and from eight dollars a week he got half the gross proceeds of many performances. His favorite acting was tragedy. He was, by a long period of training, especially fitted to become a graceful and dramatic murderer. His models were great criminals, and he studied their lives, their schemes, their attitude in the commission of crime, until in his acting upon the mimic stage he had become accomplished. Familiarity with all these things made his task comparatively easy, and inspired him with the spirit of fanaticism, inciting him to kill the President. It has been said that he excelled in the part of *Richard III*. Did he not remember the tent scene?

> ' My conscience hath a thousand several tongues,
> And every tongue brings in a several tale,
> And every tale condemns me for a villain.
> Perjury, perjury in the highest degree,
> Murder, stern murder, in the direst degree;
> All several sins, all used in each degree,
> Throng to the bar, crying all—Guilty! guilty!
> I shall despair. There is no creature loves me;
> And, if I die, no soul will pity me."

Upon several occasions he remarked: "What a glorious opportunity there is for a man to immortalize himself by killing Lincoln," and often quoted these lines:

> " The ambitious youth who fired the Ephesian dome
> Outlives in fame the pious fool who reared it."

He had played a number of times at Ford's Theater, and was of course well acquainted with its entrances and exits, which accounts for the ease with which he escaped. When Booth played the part of *Pescara* in the " Apostate," at Ford's Theater on March 18, 1865, the last night he ever performed upon the stage, there were in the audience John H. Surratt, Herold, Atzerodt, and John T. Holahan, who boarded at Mrs. Surratt's. Booth supplied these four with complimentary tickets.

McKee Rankin tells an interesting incident that happened a short time before the assassination: " John Wilkes Booth was in Boston shortly before the assassination. At that time I was acting at the Howard Athenæum, then a leading theater, and I met Booth one day at the Tremont House. He was very despondent, and said he was going south. He packed his theatrical wardrobe, of which he was very proud, and shipped it for safety to Montreal on a little blockade runner. Then he bade us good-by, and left Boston. On the very night he shot Lincoln that little blockade runner was wrecked. The wardrobe was finally taken from the wreck and was in the custody of the admiralty court for a long time. Then my brother George purchased it at public sale, and presented it to me."

John McCullough, the actor, once related an incident showing that Booth was constantly working upon his plans for abducting the President. He said: " Booth was undoubtedly a little insane in the direction of the capture of President Lincoln. I never was a horseback rider, but Booth had a wandering mind and love of physical excitement, and against my will he got me on a horse one day. Instead of taking me to the pleasant places around Washington, he rode into byroads up along the Eastern Branch; and he would show me some uninteresting place and say: ' Now, Johnny, if a fellow was in a tight fix he could slip right out here, do you see?' ' Well,' said I, ' when I leave Washington I shall leave on the cars; I am all raw now with riding this old horse. For God's sake, take me back to the hotel.' I have no doubt," continued the actor, " that he was then working out his long-intended scheme of seizing Lincoln's person and carrying him through lower Maryland into the rebel lines. At another time I came over from New York suddenly, and being in the habit of going right into Booth's room without knocking, I turned the knob and pushed straight in. At the first wink I saw Booth sitting behind a table, on which was a map, a knife, and a pistol. He had gauntlets on his hands, spurs on his boots, and a military hat of a slouch character on his head. As the door opened he seized that knife and came for me. Said I, ' John, what in the name of sense is the matter with you—are you crazy?' He heard my voice and arrested himself, and placed his hands before his eyes like a man dissipating a dream, and then said: ' Why, Johnny, how are you?' When I heard that it was he who killed Lincoln, I thought that he had been at the time I describe ready to carry out his purpose. It was at the time of Lincoln's second inauguration."

The diary taken from Booth's pocket when captured in Garrett's barn contains a few interesting notes, among which are the following:

April 14, Friday, the Ides.—Until to-day nothing was ever thought of sacrificing to our country's wrongs. For six months we had worked to capture, but our cause being almost lost, something decisive and great must be done. But its failure was owing to others, who did not strike for their country with a heart. I struck boldly, and not as the papers say. I walked with a firm step through a thousand of his friends; was stopped, but pushed on. A colonel was at his side. I shouted " Sic semper" before I fired. In jumping broke my leg. I passed all his pickets; rode thirty-six miles that night with the bone of my leg tearing the flesh at every jump. I can never report it. Though we hated to kill, our country owed all her troubles to him, and God simply made me the instrument of his punishment. The country is not what it was. This forced Union is not what I have loved. I care not what becomes of me. I have no desire to outlive my country. The night before the deed I wrote a long article and left it for one of the editors of the *National Intelli- gencer*, in which I fully set forth our reasons for our proceed- ings. He or the South.

Friday, 21.—After being hunted like a dog through swamps and woods, and last night being chased by gunboats till I was forced to return, wet, cold, and starving, with every man's hand against me, I am here in despair. And why? For doing what Brutus was honored for—what made William Tell a hero; and yet I, for striking down an even greater tyrant than they ever knew, am looked upon as a common cutthroat. My act was

purer than either of theirs.   One hoped to be great himself; the
other had not only his country's, but his own, wrongs to avenge.
I hoped for no gain; I knew no private wrong.   I struck for my
country, and her alone.   A people ground beneath this tyranny
prayed for this end, and yet now see the cold hands they extend
to me!   God cannot pardon me if I have done wrong; yet I
cannot see any wrong, except in serving a degenerate people.
The little, the very little, I left behind to clear my name the
Government will not allow to be printed.   So ends all!   For
my country I have given up all that makes life sweet and holy
—to-night misfortune upon my family, and am sure there is no
pardon for me in the heavens, since man condemns me so.   I
have only heard of what has been done (except what I did myself), and it fills me with horror.   God, try and forgive me and
bless my mother.   To-night I will once more try the river, with
the intention to cross; though I have a greater desire and almost
a mind to return to Washington, and in a measure clear my
name, which I feel I can do.

I do not repent the blow I struck.   I may before my God, but
not to man.   I think I have done well, though I am abandoned,
with the curse of Cain upon me, when, if the world knew my
heart, that one blow would have made me great, though I did
desire no greatness.   To-night I try once more to escape these
bloodhounds.   Who, who, can read his fate!   God's will be
done.   I have too great a care to die like a criminal.   Oh! may
He spare me that, and let me die bravely.   I bless the entire
world.   I have never hated nor wronged anyone.   This last
was not a wrong, unless God deems it so, and it is with Him to
damn or bless me.   And for this brave boy, Herold, here with
me, who often prays (yes, before and since) with a true and
sincere heart, was it crime in him?   If so, why can he pray
the same?   I do not wish to shed a drop of blood, but I must
fight the course.   'Tis all that's left me.

Although speculations and theories as to the motives
of Booth in assassinating President Lincoln will never
come to an end or settlement, it is the author's opinion
that it was solely to immortalize himself.   Money could
not have hired him to do such an act, but the picture of
a famous name appeared before him, and he could not

resist the temptation to grasp it. The original scheme of kidnaping, whether of his own origin or that of others, was to abduct Lincoln, take him South, and hold him until the supposed ills of the Confederacy had been righted. The various plots having failed, and now that the cause of secession was lost, he became desperate. The opportunity for fame for himself and revenge for the South was ebbing away, and when the last opportunity presented itself, he grasped it with the eagerness of the " ambitious youth who fired the Ephesian dome."

The loyalty to the Union of Edwin Booth, his brother, was never questioned. Judge J. W. Edmonds, who knew Booth well, wrote him a letter during the period that cast a shadow over his family name, and said: " All who know you as well as I do will bear testimony to your unwavering loyalty, and accord you their heartfelt sympathy in suffering so peculiar to yourself, and flowing so fatally from causes which you could not control, and in which you had no participation. I have been long aware of your high regard for the lamented Lincoln, and I know you will share deeply with every loyal heart in the intense sorrow which his sudden death has so universally created." Edwin Booth replied in a feeling manner, in which he said: " Your letter so fully expresses the inmost sentiment of my heart that I can only say, God bless you." Edwin Booth was modest, and he had no desire to show off, or to make himself conspicuous in a crowd, yet he appreciated the applause of the public so far as it bore testimony to his success. He was sincere in his aversion to flattery. His brother John Wilkes was exactly the reverse of this. He was more handsome than Edwin, and possessed a romantic style, being ever desirous of public notoriety. This was best proven by the remark at the dinner table at

Garrett's the last day that Booth spent in life. Miss Garrett said she thought the assassin of the President was well paid for it, and he replied: " It is my opinion he wasn't paid a cent, but did it for notoriety's sake."

Edwin had been playing an engagement at the Boston Theater, and was to have taken his farewell on the afternoon of the day the President died. When the terrible intelligence of the murder of the President by his brother was conveyed to him, he was prostrated by the great affliction and could not keep the engagement. Edwin Booth's closest friends refrained from speaking to him in after years of the awful deed that his brother committed, and Harry Hawk, who played upon Ford's stage that night, for twenty-nine years refused all entreaty to tell the story, in consideration of the feelings of his dear friend. Edwin Booth never played in Washington after that sad event, although he would have received a hearty reception.

Junius Brutus Booth came near falling a sacrifice for his brother's crime. He was billed to play in Cincinnati, and arrived at the Burnet House on the evening when his brother shot Lincoln. Emil Benlier, then a clerk at the hotel, describes the exciting event:

" Booth came downstairs the morning after the assassination, and after breakfast was on the point of going out to take a stroll. I had just heard, a few minutes before, that the people were in a tumult, and had torn down his bills all over the city. He came up to the desk, and as he did so I informed him that I thought it would be best for him not to go out in the streets. He looked at me in amazement, and asked what I meant. ' Haven't you heard the news?' said I. He replied that he had not. I didn't like to say any more, and he walked off, looking greatly puzzled. Going to a friend who was standing near, he asked in rather an excited manner what that young man meant by talking that way, and wanted to know if I wasn't crazy. The man told him no, that I was the clerk. More mystified than ever, he returned and demanded my reason for the remark. I saw that he was ignorant of the tragedy, and reluctantly informed him that his brother had killed the President. He was the most horrified man that I ever saw, and for the moment he was overcome by the shock. I suggested to him that it would be better for him to go to his room, and he did so, being accompanied by one or two of his friends. He had scarcely gone upstairs before the room he left was filled with people. The mob was fully five hundred in number, and wanted to find Booth. They were perfectly furious, and it was with the greatest difficulty that we checked them by the story that their intended victim had left the house. They would have hanged him in a minute if they could have laid hands upon him, so great was their rage. After leaving they returned almost immediately, but by this time we had removed Booth from his room to that of a friend. The mob watched the house so closely that it was four or five days before he had a chance to leave. We finally smuggled him away, however."

He was arrested at a later date when visiting Philadelphia, taken to Washington and confined in the Old Capitol Prison for some weeks, and then released.*

Major Rathbone was the son of Mrs. Rathbone of Albany, N. Y., by her first husband, and Clara Harris was the daughter of Ira Harris, United States Senator

* On November 25, 1864, a performance was given in New York, the three brothers appearing together in "Julius Cæsar," Edwin playing *Brutus*, Junius Brutus playing *Cassius*, and John Wilkes *Mark Antony*.

from New York, by his first wife. The surviving parents married, making these two step-brother and sister. The awful tragedy which he and Miss Harris witnessed perhaps brought them into a singular sympathy, and in a year or two they were married. They had fortune and high character, children were born to them, and they passed a few years in Washington, respected by all; but those who were in their especial intimacy knew that there was a cloud always hanging over the spirit of Rathbone. The scene of that fearful night left an impression on his nerves from which they never recovered. Finally the family went abroad, and shortly afterward the world was shocked to learn that Major Rathbone had shot and killed the wife whom he had tenderly loved.

Sergeant Boston Corbett was a hat finisher by occupation. The regiment to which he belonged (16th New York Cavalry) was stationed at Vienna, Va., about twelve miles from Washington. They first heard of the assassination on Saturday, the 15th, and the regiment was immediately ordered out on a scout, but without success. The next day a detachment was sent to Washington to be in readiness to scour the country for the assassins, and another detachment took part in the funeral procession on the 19th, escorting the President's body from the White House to the Capitol. On their return from the procession, and before they had reached camp, Lieutenant E. P. Doherty was called upon to go on another scout after Booth, and, calling for twenty-five men, started into Maryland, crossing the Eastern Branch over the Anacostia bridge, and followed the route Booth took, until they learned that he had crossed the river into Virginia. They returned to Washington, and immediately started for the Sixth Street wharf, where they took the steamer, landing at Belle Plain. It was this party that surrounded the barn, one of which was Corbett, who shot Booth.

After the war Corbett led a wandering life over the country, canvassing, peddling, and doing odd jobs. He was appointed doorkeeper in the House of Representatives of the State of Kansas. In the session of 1887, when in a crazy fit, he drew a couple of revolvers and prorogued the House of Representatives—that is, they scampered

BOSTON CORBETT.
Who shot Booth in Garrett's barn, April 26, 1865.

and climbed over each other to get out. They managed to quiet him down and got control of him without anyone being hurt. He was examined mentally, placed in an asylum, from which he escaped, and is marked on record as dead. Mr. George A. Huron of Topeka was appointed his guardian by the Probate Court of Shawnee County, Kansas, in 1887.

Corbett has a piece of land in Cloud County, Kansas, and some pension money due, and the guardian wants

THOMAS A. JONES.

The man who carried provisions to Booth and Herold for six days, from the 16th to 21st of April, piloted them to the river, and pushed them off in his own fish boat, for which Booth paid him seventeen dollars.

the charge of insanity removed, so that he may come in control of his property. He has for the four years past been a traveling salesman for a Topeka patent medicine concern. His territory is Oklahoma and Texas, and his headquarters and home are at Enid in Oklahoma. He is now sixty-two years old.

In the month of April, 1894, an old man, seventy-six years of age, called at the house where the martyred President died. After viewing the room he said: " My name is Thomas A. Jones, and I am the man who cared for and fed Booth and Herold while they were in hiding, after committing the awful deed." He was asked to tell the story, and the following is what he said:

" On Easter Sunday morning, 1865, a boy came to my house and told me Samuel Cox, my foster-brother, wanted me to come over to his place, as he wished to see me about some seed corn. I knew that was not the real cause of his sending for me, but

RESIDENCE OF COLONEL SAMUEL COX.

Booth and Herold were directed to this place by Dr. Mudd, and upon their arrival Sunday morning, April 16, Colonel Cox directed his man, Franklin Robey, to pilot them to a thicket.

I saddled my horse at once, and went with the boy. The distance to Rich Hill was about four miles northeast of my house. Cox met me at the gate, and we walked quite a distance out from the house, so that our conversation could not be heard. Cox said: 'There were two men called at my house this morning before daybreak, and I think one was Booth. Now, we want you to take charge of them, feed and care for them, and get them across the river as soon as you can. We must help them, as they are on our side' (meaning the Confederate side). In the cause of the Confederacy I was willing to risk my life, as I had often done, but the war was at an end; the cause I loved was lost. I knew to assist in any way the assassin of Lincoln would jeopardize my life. I knew that southern Maryland was full of detectives then, eager to avenge the murder of their loved Lincoln. After weighing the matter a few moments, I said: 'I will see what I can do, but must see these men first; where are they?' Cox then told me that his overseer, Franklin Robey, had piloted them to a thick piece of pine and advised them to keep perfectly quiet, and promised to send someone to them. They agreed upon a certain signal by which they would know the man who came to them was from Robey (the signal was a certain whistle). Cox warned me to be cautious how I approached them, as they were fully armed and might shoot me by mistake. I left Cox and rode toward the spot, fully realizing the risk I was undertaking; but I did not hesitate. My word was passed, and that settled my determination. The place where Booth and Herold were in hiding was about one mile south of the present village of Cox's Station, which is five miles from Pope's Creek. As I drew near the hiding place of the fugitives, I stopped and gave the signal. Presently a young man

came cautiously out of the thicket and stood before me;
he was armed and ready to shoot, if need be. ' Who are
you, and what do you want?' he asked. ' I came from

THE FUGITIVES' RETREAT.

The clear spot between the two trees is the spot where Booth and Herold
were secreted for six days. It was on the land of Captain Michael Stone
Robertson. The public road and railroad pass close to the spot.

Cox; I am a friend; you have nothing to fear.' He
looked searchingly at me a moment, then said: ' Follow
me,' and led the way for about thirty yards into the thick
undergrowth, to where Booth was lying. ' This is a
friend sent by Captain Cox,' he said; and that was my
introduction to John Wilkes Booth. He was lying on
the wet, cold ground, his head supported by his hand.
His weapons of defense were close beside him; an old
blanket was partly drawn over him. His slouch hat and
crutch were lying by him, he was exceedingly pale, and
his features bore traces of intense suffering. I have

seldom seen a more handsome man. His voice was pleasant and his manner polite."

As the speaker paused and remained silent a few moments, I could not help but draw a comparison—Booth the assassin and Booth the actor. It must be understood that he was not or had not been acting at this time, and in fact for some weeks prior to this he had not been upon the stage; yet there flashed before my mind the brilliant scene of the theater, where in the past he had so often appeared, with its lights, its music, its throngs of patrons, its gayety, all gathered to do honor to the star behind the footlights—John Wilkes Booth. His friends were many, his admirers legion, his future in his own hands, to make or mar; and yet he chose to perform, as the closing act of his life, that awful tragedy that should sink him into the abyss of disgraceful oblivion—pitied, yet despised.

In resuming, Mr. Jones said: "Murderer though I knew him to be, my sympathies were so enlisted in his behalf that I determined to do all I could to get him into Virginia, and so assured him, but told him he would have to remain quiet for the present; I would bring their food every day, and at the earliest possible moment would get them across the river. He held out his hand and thanked me; also said: 'I killed President Lincoln, and knew the United States Government would use every means in its power to capture me; but John Wilkes Booth will never be taken alive!' I visited them daily, giving them food and newspapers and any information that I could, for six days. Each day I made it my business to gain any information I might, and the following day to report to Booth. The third day, or Tuesday following the time I had promised to care for Booth, court was held in Port Tobacco. I knew I would see and hear

a great deal concerning the assassination and the probable whereabouts of the assassin. It was at this time I met
Captain Williams, a detective. He was standing in the
barroom of Brawner's Hotel (now St. Charles Hotel) in
the act of drinking with several gentlemen. Someone introduced me to him, and he politely asked me to drink.
Just as we were about to take the drink, he said to me:
' I am authorized by the United States Government to

ST. CHARLES HOTEL, PORT TOBACCO.

It was in this hotel that Detective William Williams offered Jones one
hundred thousand dollars to tell him where Booth was secreted, but
Jones refused.

pay one hundred thousand dollars for Booth, dead or
alive.' I looked him in the eye and said: ' That's a good
deal of money to give for one man.' "

I here asked Jones if it was any temptation, being in the reduced circumstances he was at the time. He proudly answered: " No, indeed; my word could not be bought for a hundred times that amount. I considered it a sacred trust. The little I had accumulated was irrevocably lost, but, thank God, I still possessed something I could call my own, and its name was Honor!

" Wednesday and Thursday passed uneventfully. As the days rolled away Booth's impatience to cross the river became almost unbearable; but the time to move had not yet arrived. So through six long, wearisome days and five dark, restless nights Booth lay there in hiding. The only breaks in the monotony of that week were my daily visits, and the food and newspapers I carried him. He never tired of the newspapers, and there, surrounded by the sighing pines, he read the world's just condemnation of his deed and the price that was offered for his life. On Friday evening, April 21, the opportune time seemed to have presented itself. I rode to Allen's Fresh, about three miles east of my house, a small village situated where Zekiah Swamp ends and Wicomico River begins. Now or never, I thought, is my chance." Mr. Jones passed his hand over his brow and said: " That was many years ago, but so indelibly were the events of that evening impressed upon my mind that I can in imagination see and hear all that transpired. It was dark when I reached the place. I had never visited the fugitives at night, so approached with more than usual caution and gave the signal. Herold answered me, and led the way to Booth. I told them the coast seemed clear, and the darkness favored us, and we decided to make the attempt to cross the Potomac.

" Booth was obliged to ride my horse, and I advised Herold to walk beside him, while I would precede them about fifty yards. When I came to a certain place I would whistle, and they were to come forward until they reached me. I would then go forward fifty yards more, and when they heard the signal, but not before, they should advance until they reached me; and thus we would proceed until we reached the river. The route we

ALLEN'S FRESH.

Three miles from Huckleberry, the home of Thomas A. Jones. Mr. Jones visited this place on Friday the 21st, and while here first learned that the soldiers had all gone farther south. This was his opportunity, and he grasped it by starting Booth and Herold from the thicket to the river.

had to take led us through the pines about one mile and a half, then down the public road another mile, to the corner of my farm. The part of our journey that lay over the public road I most dreaded—first, because we were very liable to meet someone on the road, and second, because we had to pass two dwelling houses close to the road. One was occupied by a negro named Sam Thomas, where there were children always around; the other was the home of John Ware, where there were several dogs. The night was intensely dark. You could not see your hand before you. As we journeyed slowly and cautiously along my feelings were wrought up to an intense degree. Every slight noise would startle me. At last, after what seemed an interminable age, we reached the place. We stopped near the stable, about

HUCKLEBERRY, THE HOME OF THOMAS A. JONES.

Booth and Herold were taken past this house, and Booth begged piteously to be taken in, but Jones refused, and went himself to get them something to eat.

fifty yards from my house. It was then between nine and ten o'clock. 'Wait here,' I said, ' while I go in and get you some supper, which you can eat while I get something for myself.' With a look I shall never forget, Booth said: ' Please let me go to the house and get some of your hot coffee.' It made my heart ache to hear this piteous request almost at my very threshold, and yet

THE POINT FROM WHICH THE FUGITIVES STARTED TO CROSS THE POTOMAC.

The crossing was made on the night of the 21st of April. The figure seen is that of Henry Woodland, the former slave of Thomas A. Jones, and the assistant of Jones in getting Booth and Herold off.

I had to deny him. My sympathies were never so touched, and with difficulty I said: ' My friend, it would be certain capture, and we would all be lost. Remember, this is your last chance.' He replied: ' So be it.' I went to the house and took what I thought would be enough for two men and carried it out to them, with some hot coffee. After supper we resumed our journey across the open field toward the longed-for river. When about three hundred yards from the river, Herold and myself assisted Booth to dismount. The path was steep and narrow, and for three men to walk down it abreast was not the least difficult part of that night's work. At length we reached the shore and found the boat. It was a flat-bottomed one, about twelve feet long, of a dark lead color. We placed Booth in the stern with an oar to steer, Herold taking the bow seat to row. The night was ink-black. I could not see either of the men, and had to feel for them, and as I was in the act of pushing the boat off Booth said: 'Wait a minute, old fellow.' He then offered me some money. I took seventeen dollars, the price of the boat. In a voice choked with emotion he said: 'God bless you, my dear friend, for all you have done for me. Good-by, good-by!' I pushed the boat off, and it glided out in the darkness. I could see nothing, and the only sound was the swish of the waves made by the little boat. Never in all my life did my heart go out in more pity and sympathy for my fellow-man than that night. I stood on the shore and listened till the sound of the oars died away in the distance, then climbed the hill and took my way home, and my sleep was more quiet and peaceful than it had been for some time."

CHAPTER VI.

FUNERAL CEREMONIES AND REMOVAL OF REMAINS TO SPRINGFIELD, ILL.

THE funeral service was held in the East Room of the White House, at twelve o'clock, noon, on the 19th, after which the body was removed to the funeral car, and at two o'clock the procession formed and started down Pennsylvania Avenue amid the tolling of bells and firing of minute guns. On the arrival at the eastern entrance of the Capitol the coffin was carried into the rotunda and placed on a catafalque, where the body was exposed to view until the 21st. At seven o'clock on the morning of that day the body was escorted to the Baltimore & Ohio railroad station, and at eight o'clock the funeral train started on its mournful journey of fifteen hundred miles to the final resting place, stopping at Baltimore, Harrisburg, Philadelphia, New York City, Albany, Buffalo, Cleveland, and Columbus, O., Indianapolis, Ind., and Chicago, Ill., arriving at Springfield on the 3d day of May. At all of these places the people were permitted to look upon the face of their dead President. At Philadelphia his remains lay in state in the room in which the history of our nation began, eighty-five years before, and where President Lincoln stood on the 22d of February, 1861, while on his journey from Springfield to Washington, and said, in referring to that sentiment in the Declaration of Independence which gave liberty to the people of this country: ' But if this country cannot be saved without giving up that principle, I was about to

THE CAPITOL AT WASHINGTON.

say I would rather be assassinated on this spot than to surrender it." The old bell that rang liberty throughout the land hung silent and dumb, but its echoes will never die out, and the gaunt and rugged form of the martyred President lay amid the memories of that hall close to the bell, April 22, 1865, four years and two months after he made those prophetic remarks. The world will never forget that he sounded the note of liberty, and rung out the joy of a nation redeemed. It seems strange that a wilderness unknown to the men who made the Declaration of Independence should give birth to a man so inspired as to fulfill all its promises.

During the journey through the nights the train was brilliantly illumined by bonfires that lighted up the country for miles around, turning darkness into day. People came in buggies and wagons for a great distance to greet the train, men stood with uncovered heads, bands played their funeral dirges, while a requiem was sung for the dead. At many stations whole companies of soldiers were drawn up in line with reversed arms; young ladies dressed in white, with flags draped, chanted their slow, mournful airs. Large arches of evergreen and flowers were formed above the track. At Richmond, Ind., the train slowly passed under a beautiful arch decorated with the national colors and colored lamps, and a tableau of Genius of Liberty weeping over the coffin of Lincoln was also passed, guarded on either side by soldiers and sailors, while a band played a mournful dirge.

The funeral train left Chicago at half-past nine o'clock on the night of May 2, the distance to Springfield being 185 miles. The track seemed to be illuminated the whole way, showing many appropriate mottoes. The most suggestive were, " Come Home," " Go to Thy Rest," " Ours the Cross, Thine the Crown," " He has Fulfilled his Mission."

His remains were received at Springfield by the plain people on the bright May morning, when spring showers of the previous night had freshened the prairie flowers and the blossoms of the orchard, and the birds were jubilant with their sweet songs.

The " pilot engine," draped in mourning, made its appearance in advance of the funeral train, which consisted of nine cars. It was announced to arrive at eight o'clock, but did not reach the depot until a few minutes before nine.

The remains were transferred from the funeral car to the beautiful hearse tendered by the mayor of St. Louis. After the procession had been formed, it proceeded from the Chicago, Alton & St. Louis Railroad to the State House, entering through the east gate and passing to the Hall of Representatives by the north entrance. The coffin was placed on the catafalque, and a few minutes' past 10 o'clock A. M. the vast crowd was admitted to view the remains.

At half-past eleven on the 4th the cortege moved to Oak Ridge Cemetery, where the body was placed in a temporary vault, when Bishop Matthew Simpson delivered the funeral address, and Abraham Lincoln was left alone in the grass-green valley, where the little brook sweeping by his tomb sung each day a requiem.

THE TEMPORARY VAULT,

Oak Ridge Cemetery, Springfield, Ill., in which the body of Abraham
Lincoln was placed May 4, 1865.

CHAPTER VII.

TRIAL AND PUNISHMENT OF THE CONSPIRATORS.

THE assassination of President Lincoln was a military crime. He was killed while actually in command of the army, as Commander-in-Chief; consequently the conspirators were excluded from any right to a trial in the civil courts. President Andrew Johnson asked Attorney-General James Speed whether the persons charged with the offense of having assassinated the President should be tried before a military tribunal or a civil court. The Attorney-General rendered the following decision:

" That if the persons who are charged with assassination of the President committed the deed as public enemies, as I believe they did, and whether they did or not is a question to be decided by the tribunal before which they are tried, they not only can, but ought to be, tried before a military tribunal. If the persons charged have offended against the laws of war, it would be palpably wrong for the military to hand them over to the civil courts, as it would be wrong in a civil court to convict a man of murder who had in time of war killed another in battle."

The Secretary of War announced in an official bulletin that all persons who had harbored or secreted the conspirators, or who had aided or assisted their escape, should be " subject to trial before a military commission, and the punishment is death. Let the stain of innocent blood be removed from the land by the arrest and punishment of the murderers! All good citizens are exhorted to aid public justice on this occasion. Every man should consider his own innocence charged with this solemn duty, and rest neither night nor day till it is accomplished."

President Johnson, after having considered the reports of the officials charged with the preliminary examination of testimony and having obtained the opinion of Attorney-General Speed on the manner in which those of the suspected conspirators who had been arrested should be tried, issued a special order, dated May 1, 1865, calling upon the Assistant Adjutant-General to detail nine competent military officers to serve as a commission for the trial of said parties. The following were appointed:

Major-General David Hunter, U. S. V.

Major-General Lew Wallace, U. S. V.

Brevet Major-General August V. Kautz, U. S. V.

Brigadier-General Alvin P. Howe, U. S. V.

Brigadier-General Robert S. Foster, U. S. V.

Brevet Brigadier-General James A. Ekin, U. S. V.

Brigadier-General T. M. Harris, U. S. V.

Brevet Colonel C. H. Tompkins, U. S. V.

Lieutenant-Colonel David R. Clendenin, 8th Illinois Cavalry.

Brigadier-General Joseph Holt, Judge-Advocate and Recorder, assisted by Judge-Advocate Henry L. Burnett and Hon. John A. Bingham.

Brevet Major-General John F. Hartranft was assigned to duty as special provost-marshal.

A large room in the northeast corner of the third story of the penitentiary, near the cells in which the prisoners were confined, was fitted up for the trial. It was about thirty by forty-five feet square, with a ceiling about

Gen. T. M. Harris.   Gen. Lew Wallace.   Gen. A. V. Kautz.   Brev. Brig.-Gen. Henry L. Burnett.

Col. D. R. Clendenin.   Gen. A. P. Howe.   Gen. David Hunter.   Hon. John A. Bingham.
Col. C. H. Tompkins.   Gen. James A. Ekin.   Gen. Robert S. Foster.   Judge Joseph Holt.

MEMBERS OF THE MILITARY COMMISSION.

eleven feet high, supported by three wooden pillars. Four windows, with heavy iron gratings, afforded tolerable ventilation, and there were two ante-rooms for the accommodation of the court and witnesses. The room was whitewashed and painted for the occasion, a prisoners' dock was constructed along the western side, the floor was covered with cocoa matting, and the tables and chairs were new. Gas was introduced, in case the court should protract its sittings until after dark.

During the trial the members of the court were all in full uniform, and were seated around a large table parallel with the north side of the room. General Hunter, the president, sat at the eastern end. At the foot of this table was another occupied by Judge-Advocate-General Holt, with his assistants, Hon. John A. Bingham and Colonel H. L. Burnett. In the center of the room was a stand for witnesses, who were required to face the court while being examined. Behind the witness stand, and parallel with the southern side of the room, was a long table, which was occupied by reporters and correspondents during the public sessions of the court. At the foot of this table sat the counsel for the prisoners after they had been introduced.

The prisoners' dock was a platform raised about one foot from the floor, and about four feet broad, with a strong railing in front of it. Along this dock sat the accused. Mrs. Surratt had the left-hand corner to herself, a passageway to the door leading to the cells intervening between her and the seven male prisoners, who sat sandwiched with six soldiers, who wore the light blue uniform of the Veteran Reserve Corps. Dr. Mudd wore handcuffs connected with chains, but the bracelets of the other male prisoners were joined by wide bars of iron ten inches long, which kept their arms apart. All the prisoners except Mrs. Surratt wore anklets connected by short chains, which hampered their walk, and heavy iron balls were also attached by chains to the limbs of Payne and Atzerodt.

During the confinement in the penitentiary the prisoners, with the exception of Mrs. Surratt, wore caps drawn over their heads. The cap was of gray flannel, made roughly, with a string drawn through the end. The cap or mask was tied loosely under the chin. A slit in it served as a hole for the mouth. The cap was left off when the prisoners appeared in the court room. The arms of the male prisoners were fastened at the wrists by handcuffs. They were the kind commonly known as "stiff shackles," so named because the cuffs were fastened to each other by a bar of iron about fourteen inches long, which prevented the moving of one arm without a corresponding movement of the other. The left ankle was fastened by a shackle attached to an iron cone by a chain two feet long. This cone was a foot high and eight inches in diameter at the base. It would weigh about seventy-five pounds. When the prisoners were marched into the court room, two guards put an iron rod through the staple in the apex of the cone and carried it. Each prisoner was confined in a separate cell, attended by four guards. As the prisoners entered and left the room, their fetters clanking at every step, they formed an impressive procession. As seen by the court, the prisoners sat in the following order from the right: Arnold, Dr. Mudd, Spangler, O'Laughlin, Atzerodt, Payne, Herold, and Mrs. Surratt. The prisoners when arrested were first confined in the Old Capitol Prison and on board of the monitors *Montauk* and *Saugus*, anchored off the Navy Yard, whence they were removed to the building originally used as the penitentiary of the

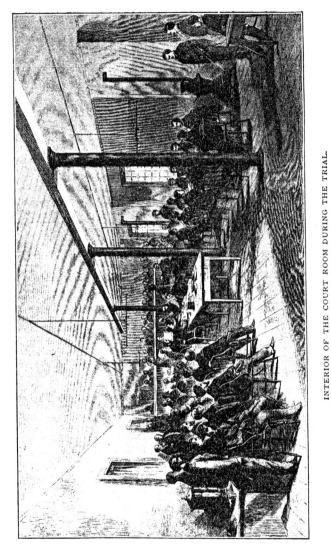

INTERIOR OF THE COURT ROOM DURING THE TRIAL.

District of Columbia, which was within the limits of the
United States Arsenal on Greenleaf's Point.　This is at

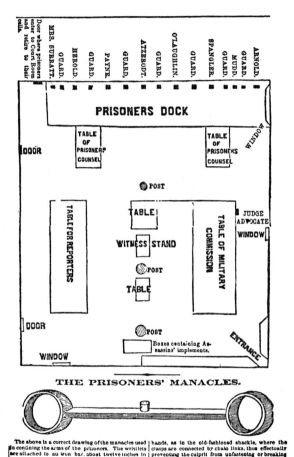

PLAN OF THE COURT ROOM OCCUPIED BY THE MILITARY
COMMISSION.

the junction of the Potomac and the Eastern Branch,
and at the foot of Four-and-a-half Street S. W.　The

following description of the grounds is given by Ben: Perley Poore:

"The tract of land was purchased by a Mr. Greenleaf when Washington was first laid out as a metropolis. He hoped that it would become the business portion of the future city, which George Washington expected would be the tide-water of the great West, by the construction of a canal along the Potomac River as a channel of transmontane transportation. Mr. Greenleaf's 'great expectations' were not realized; and he became so involved that several houses which he erected and nearly completed actually fell gradually to pieces, and were carried away for firewood. The extremity of the point has been used for a United States Arsenal since the last war with Great Britain."

The old penitentiary was erected in 1836, but was afterward enlarged and improved. It was situated on the northern side of the Arsenal grounds. Four-and-a-half Street runs directly from the City Hall and Court-House across the avenue down to the old penitentiary gate. At the breaking out of the War of the Rebellion it was found imperatively necessary to enlarge the Arsenal grounds, and their limits were extended quite a distance north of the penitentiary. The convicts formerly confined there were sent to Albany, N. Y.

Major-General Hartranft, the special provost-marshal detailed for the trial, had placed under his orders a brigade of volunteers and a detachment of the Veteran Reserve Corps. Strong guards were so posted as to render the rescue or escape of the prisoners impossible; and there was in addition a detective force, which exercised a watchful surveillance.

The Commission met at 10 o'clock A. M., Wednesday, May 10, 1865, and the special order of President John-

THE OLD CAPITOL PRISON.

This building was situated on a hill in rear of present Capitol, adjoining "Carroll Prison." It occupied the whole length of a square. Mrs. Surratt was confined as a prisoner in the "Old Capitol Prison," until she was transferred to the monitor.

son convening the Commission was read in the hearing of the prisoners. They were asked if they had any objections to any member of the Commission; to which they all severally replied they had not. The Commission, the Judge-Advocate-General and his associates, and the reporters, having been duly sworn in, the prisoners, Samuel Arnold, Samuel A. Mudd, Edward Spangler, Michael O'Laughlin, George A. Atzerodt, Lewis Payne, David E. Herold, and Mary E. Surratt were arraigned on the charge of conspiracy to assassinate President Lincoln and other officers of the Federal Government. Each prisoner pleaded not guilty to the charge. They were permitted to engage such counsel as they desired to employ. Hon. Reverdy Johnson, who had been solicited to appear in behalf of Mrs. Surratt, was not present, but she conferred with Mr. Frederick Aikin of Washington. Mr. Thomas Ewing, Jr., appeared as counsel for Arnold and Dr. Mudd, Mr. W. E. Doster for Payne and Atzerodt, Mr. Frederick Stone for Dr. Mudd, and Mr. Walter Cox for O'Laughlin. The session of the Commission was not public until the second day, when spectators were admitted to the court room.

Hon. Reverdy Johnson appeared on the 13th as counsel for Mrs. Surratt, but General Harris objected to him as a counsel before the court, on the ground that he did not recognize the moral obligation of an oath that was designed as a test of loyalty. Some debate took place between the two gentlemen, when General Harris withdrew his objections, and, upon the suggestion of General Lew Wallace, the requirement of Mr. Johnson taking the oath was dispensed with, as he had brought with him the certificate of having taken the oath as United States Senator. He then appeared as counsel for Mrs. Surratt.

Mr. Johnson said: " I am here at the instance of that

lady [pointing to Mrs. Surratt], whom I never saw until yesterday, and never heard of, she being a Maryland lady, and thinking that I could be of service to her, protesting, as she has done, her innocence to me. Of the facts I know nothing, because I deemed it right, I deemed it due to the character of the profession to which I belong, and which is not inferior to the noble profession of which you are a member, that she should not go undefended. I knew I was to do it voluntarily, without compensation; the law prohibits me from receiving compensation; but if it did not, understanding her condition, I should never have dreamed of refusing upon the ground of her inability to make compensation.

"I am here to do whatever the evidence will justify me in doing in protecting this lady from the charge upon which she is now being tried for her life. I am here detesting from the very bottom of my heart everyone concerned in this nefarious plot, carried out with such fiendish malice, as much as any member of this court, and I am not here to protect anyone whom, when the evidence is offered, I shall deem to have been guilty —even her."

CHAPTER VIII.

MRS. MARY E. SURRATT was forty-five years of age at the time of the trial. She was raised in Prince George County, Maryland. Her father died when she was quite young. She was considered the belle of Prince George County. In the year 1835 she was married to John H. Surratt, the young couple settling on a farm near Washington, which he had inherited from an uncle. After they had lived there a few years, this house was set on fire by one of their slaves, who seemed to have been infuriated by the cruel treatment to which he had been subjected. Surratt afterward made money as a contractor on the Orange & Alexandria Railroad, and, on his return to Maryland, purchased the place afterward known as Surratt's, where he established a tavern, and later was appointed postmaster. They had three children—a daughter and two sons. One of the latter (Isaac) entered the Confederate army, and the other (John) was the companion of Booth. Mrs. Surratt, now a widow, rented her farm to John M. Lloyd, and removed to Washington in the fall of 1864, where she opened a boarding house at 604 H Street N. W. The daughter (Annie) was an intelligent young lady, having received her education at a Catholic seminary, near Bryantown, Md. Mother and daughter were very devoted to each other. Mrs. Surratt was deeply attached to her church, family, and the Southern Confederacy. No more pronounced secession head-

quarters were established than in her home at Surrattsville, but the family circle in the city was no doubt free
from any designs upon the life of President Lincoln until
J. Wilkes Booth was introduced to her son on the 23d day

MRS. MARY E. SURRATT.

Executed July 7, 1865.

of December, 1864, by Dr. Mudd. After that date
Booth, Payne, and Atzerodt were frequent visitors at her
home. During the trial of the conspirators there was a
strong sentiment manifested in her favor, and there was
much comment as to the degree of her guilt. While she
may not have been privy to the murder of the President,

there was but little doubt as to her approval of the proposed abduction.

The men who composed the Military Commission that tried the conspirators were carefully selected, and for their coolness and good judgment they were especially fitted for the great work that they had been called upon to perform.

It was impossible, at the height of such excitement as prevailed at that time, to have secured for the conspirators a fairer trial than they obtained. Especially is this true regarding Mrs. Surratt. If there had been any reasonable doubt in the minds of the members of the Commission as to her guilt, she would have been acquitted. As fair as Mrs. Surratt's trial was believed to be by all reasonable men, a feeling has existed since that an injustice was done the woman, and the same sentiment has sought to cast blame on the officers who dealt out justice in proportion to the crimes committed.

In the argument of the case, District Attorney Pierpont said: " I know the character of the American people. I know the imagination revolts at the execution of one of the tender sex. But when a woman opens her house to murderers and conspirators, infuses the poison of her own malice into their hearts, and urges them to the crime of murder and treason, I say boldly, as an American officer, that public safety, public duty, requires that an example be made of her conduct."

Annie, the heart-broken daughter, visited her mother constantly, kneeling in the cell at her feet, sobbing, uttering now and then a pitiful scream, till the gloomy corridors rang with her cries. As a last resort she flung herself on the steps of the White House, and made that portal memorable by her grief and tears. But the doors of the Executive Mansion were closed to her, and she was never able to obtain an interview with President Johnson.

Judge Holt was charged with withholding from President Johnson the recommendation of the five members of the court that the sentence of Mrs. Surratt be commuted to imprisonment. For reasons best known to himself, President Johnson did not refute this charge, but after the execution several members of the Cabinet positively declared that the petition had been presented to the President.

General Hartranft was severely censured for placing manacles upon Mrs. Surratt, and he answers this charge by saying that he was marshal of the court before whom the conspirators were tried, had charge of her before, during, and after the trial, and declared that during this period of over two months she never had a manacle or manacles on either hands or feet, and the thought of it was never entertained by anyone in authority. She was shown some favors while in prison. Being a woman, she was allowed to choose what she wished to eat, while the other conspirators were fed on army rations. It was suggested by some of the members of the Commission that, in consequence of the age and sex of Mrs. Surratt, it might possibly be well to change her sentence to imprisonment for life.

President Johnson laid the record of the Military Commission before his Cabinet, and every single member voted to confirm the sentence, and then the President wrote his confirmation of it, signing the warrant for their execution, and the last hope of Mrs. Surratt's friends for her reprieve was blasted. President Johnson firmly believed that Mrs. Surratt participated in the assassination of President Lincoln.

GEORGE A. ATZERODT was about thirty-three years of age, born in Germany, but was raised and lived in Charles County, Maryland, and was by occupation a coach painter at Port Tobacco during the war; also engaged as a blockade runner. He was a short, thick-set, round-shouldered, brawny-armed man, with a stupid expression, high cheek bones, a sallow complexion, small

GEORGE A. ATZERODT.

Was to have killed Vice-President Johnson, but did not make the attempt. Executed July 7, 1865.

grayish-blue eyes, tangled light brown hair, and straggling sandy whiskers and mustache. At the trial he apparently manifested a stoical indifference to what was going on in the court, although an occasional cat-like glance would reveal his anxiety concerning himself. Evidently crafty, cowardly, and mercenary, his own safety was doubtless the all-absorbing subject of his thoughts. Atzerodt made a statement to several parties that Booth and Surratt wanted a man to secure a boat and hold himself in readiness to ferry a party over the Potomac, and he consented to do the work. This was to have taken place near Port Tobacco, but the first plot, to capture the President, failed, and when the second, to kill, was proposed, he declined to have anything to do with it. His statement stands as worthless, for there is no doubt that he fully intended to carry out the instruction of Booth to kill Vice-President Johnson, but he lacked the nerve when the hour of execution came. He was considered by men who knew him to have but little courage, and to be remarkable for his cowardice. He was a good-natured kind of a fellow, and just such a one as the fascinating Booth could win over to do such deeds as were assigned to him. Atzerodt says, in a confession made in his cell on the night before his execution:

" Previous to the arrangement for the murder Booth heard that President Lincoln was to visit a camp.* The coach was to be taken out Seventh Street and Surratt was to jump on the box, as he was the best driver, and drive to the Long Bridge.† This was about the middle of March. Booth, O'Laughlin, Samuel Arnold, Payne, myself, and Herold went to the bridge with two carbines, where we were to wait for Booth and Surratt. We did so until midnight, and returned to Washington. This plan having failed, all was quiet for some time. Booth and Payne went to New York, Arnold and O'Laughlin to

---

* The Soldiers' Home, March 16.
† He probably meant the Navy Yard Bridge.

Baltimore. Booth told me that Surratt was in the Herndon House on the night of the murder, the 14th of April. We were not all together at the Herndon House. The words of Booth were: 'I saw Surratt a few moments ago.' All the parties appeared to be engaged at something that night and were not together. Booth appointed me and Herold to kill Johnson. In going down the street I told Booth we could not do it. Booth said Herold had more courage, and he would do it. The coil of rope at Lloyd's was to stretch across the road to trip the cavalry. When applied to for money, Booth said he would go to New York and get some, as he had some there. Booth told me an actor was to be the assistant in the theater to turn off the gas. Mrs. Surratt, Mrs. Slater, Major Banon, and John Surratt left Washington together, and got horses at Howard's. Mrs. Surratt stopped at Surrattsville, John Surratt and Mrs. Slater crossed, and Banon and Mrs. Surratt came back. Banon was in the Rebel army. Harborn was into it first; he came to Port Tobacco for me with John Surratt during the winter. The boat was at the head of Goose Creek and moved to Nanjemoy Creek. It was a lead-colored, flat-bottom boat, and would carry fifteen men. This boat was bought of James Brawner—the old man. Mrs. Slater went with Booth a great deal. She stopped at the National Hotel."

This statement is very much disconnected, but represents events that took place at various periods of the plot. It was written under trying circumstances, and we cannot wonder at the bungling manner in which it was written.

DAVID E. HEROLD was born in Maryland, receiving his education at Charlotte Hall, in St. Mary's County. His father resided in Washington, on Eighth Street S. E., near the Navy Yard, and was employed for twenty years as principal clerk of the Navy Yard store, at the Navy

DAVID E. HEROLD.

Joined Booth in his flight from Washington, and surrendered in Garrett's barn a few minutes before Booth was shot. Executed July 7, 1865

Yard. He died in 1864, leaving a wife, seven daughters, and one son. The family, with the exception of David, who seldom attended, were members of Christ Church (Episcopal) at the Navy Yard, and were highly esteemed by those who knew them. David was a stupid, insignificant-looking young man, with slender frame, and irresolute, cowardly appearance. He had a narrow forehead, small, dark hazel eyes, thick black hair, and an incipient mustache. At one time he took up pharmacy for a livelihood, and clerked at three different drug stores, the last one for W. S. Thompson, who kept on the southwest corner of Fifteenth Street and Pennsylvania Avenue. For eleven months he was employed in the drug store of Francis S. Walsh, 608 Eighth Street S. E., and during that time lived at his house. While there Mr. Walsh found nothing objectionable in his character, but in many ways he was unstable, and very little reliability could be placed in him. Although twenty-three years of age, he was more like a boy than a man. His conversation was light and trifling, and he was very easily persuaded and led. It is, then, no surprise that such a boy was only wax in the hands of a man of determined and resolute will, of pleasing and fascinating manners, such as J. Wilkes Booth.

LEWIS PAYNE POWELL was the son of the Rev. George C. Powell, a Baptist minister, who lived at the time of the assassination at Live Oak Station, on the railroad between Jacksonville and Tallahassee, Fla. The family consisted of six daughters and three sons. Lewis and his two brothers enlisted in the Confederate army in 1861. His two brothers were killed in battle, and Lewis, in Pickett's charge at Gettysburg, was wounded and taken prisoner. Upon his recovery he was detailed as nurse in a hospital, where he remained until he was sent to another hospital at Baltimore, in October, 1863. From there he deserted, returning to the Confederate army, remaining at Fauquier, Va., until January 1, 1865, when he again deserted and returned to Baltimore, taking rooms with Miss Margaret Branson, a lady whom he met in the hospital at Gettysburg. After he deserted he assumed the name of Payne. It was at Miss Branson's that he first met Booth, and readily fell in with the work of the conspiracy. During the trial Payne was the observed of all observers, as he sat motionless and imperturbed, defiantly returning each gaze at his remarkable face and person. He was very tall, with an athletic, gladiatorial frame, the light knit shirt which was his only upper garment disclosing the massive robustness of animal manhood in its most stalwart type. Neither intellect nor intelligence was discernible in his unflinching dark gray eyes, low forehead, massive jaws, compressed full lips, small nose with large nostrils, and stolid, remorseless expression. His dark hair hung over his forehead, his face was beardless, and his hands were not those of a man who had been accustomed to labor. Payne held himself responsible to a great degree for the execution of Mrs. Surratt. He claimed that had he not gone to her house, where she declared that she had never seen him before, she might have been pardoned; but this declaration of hers formed the strongest barrier to her release. While in jail, as the chances of her reprieve grew less, he cursed his weakness in returning to her house.

Dr. SAMUEL A. MUDD was the most inoffensive and respectable in appearance of all the prisoners. He was forty-five years of age, rather tall, and quite thin, with sharp features, a high bald forehead, astute blue eyes, compressed pale lips, and sandy hair, whiskers, and mustache. He was known throughout the war as a strong sympathizer with the rebellion. In the community in which he lived he was held in high esteem as an honorable gentleman. A determined effort was made during

LEWIS PAYNE.

Executed July 7, 1865.

the trial to clear him of any complicity with the great conspiracy, but the effort was in vain, as the evidence and his own confessions proved his guilt. Statements were made at the time of the trial that Booth forced himself

DR. SAMUEL A. MUDD.

Sentenced for life to Dry Tortugas, and received a full and unconditional pardon from President Andrew Johnson, February 8, 1869.

upon Dr. Mudd, and this is yet claimed by some. In November, 1864, Booth attended St. Mary's Roman Catholic Church near Bryantown, and a few days after he met Dr. William T. Bowman of Bryantown, and asked him if he knew anyone who had any land to sell, and, after getting prices on Bowman's farm, asked him if he had any horses to sell. Mr. Bowman said he could accommodate him, when Booth said he would be down in a couple of weeks and look at the land. Of Mr. John C. Thompson of Charles County at the same time he asked the price of land, and particularly did he inquire about the roads through that part of the country. On this trip Booth stopped a day or two with Dr. Queen, to whom he had a letter of introduction from a party in Canada. Dr. Queen and his son-in-law, Mr. Thompson, attended church near Bryantown, and Booth sat with them in Dr. Queen's pew. It was here that Booth and Dr. Mudd first met, being introduced by Thompson. Booth again visited this part of the country the following month (December), stopping again with Dr. Queen over night. A few days after this visit Dr. Bowman said to Dr. Mudd: " I am going to sell my land." Dr. Mudd asked to whom he expected to sell, and Bowman said: " To a man by the name of Booth, who said he was coming down soon." Dr. Mudd then said: " That fellow promised to buy mine." Booth had no intention of buying lands; he simply wanted to familiarize himself with the roads, and the people in whom he could trust, and it was upon these two visits that the conspiracy was formed to abduct the President. That was his object, so far as this section of country was concerned. Booth stopped over night at Dr. Mudd's during these two visits, and at the time of his first visit in November went with Booth to Squire George Gardiner's, who lived in sight of Dr. Mudd's, not more than a quarter of a mile distant. The two went on horseback. Booth told Mr. Gardiner that he was desirous of purchasing a horse to run a light buggy in which to travel over the

lower counties of Maryland; and that he might look at
the lands, as he desired to buy some. Mr. Gardiner told
him he had but one horse that he could recommend as a
buggy horse, but could not spare it, as he wanted it for
his own use. Mr. Gardiner showed him an old saddle
horse, that he thought would suit him. Booth examined
the animal and said he thought it would answer, as he
only wanted it for a year. It was a dark bay, one-
eyed, and Booth bought and paid for it. Thomas L.
Gardiner, a nephew of Squire Gardiner, said he delivered
the horse to Booth at Bryantown the next day. Booth

ST. MARY'S ROMAN CATHOLIC CHURCH.

One mile south of Bryantown, Md. Dr. Mudd attended this church, and
here first met Booth. His remains lie in the graveyard a few feet from
the church.

kept it at William E. Cleaver's livery stable on Sixth Street, Washington, from the 1st to the 30th of January, 1865, when he told Cleaver that he sold it to Arnold. Arnold paid eight dollars for its keeping for the eight days that it remained in the stable after the so-called purchase.

Dr. Mudd and his brother, Jeremiah T. Mudd, went to Washington on the 23d of December, 1864, returning home the next day. They left their horses at Robert T. Martin's in Anacostia, a hotel about one hundred yards from the Eastern Branch bridge. Persons going to Washington from the vicinity of Bryantown passed by it, and it was a general stopping place for them. The two then went across the bridge to Washington and stayed at the Pennsylvania House all night. They visited the National Hotel after supper, and in a large crowd became separated, but afterward met at the Pennsylvania House. It was during this temporary separation that Dr. Mudd and Booth met, as described by Weichmann and corroborated by Dr. Mudd in a statement made to George W. Dutton, Captain Company C, 10th Regiment Veteran Reserve Corps, commanding the guard that took Dr. Mudd and the other prisoners to the Dry Tortugas, Fla. Captain Dutton said: " During a conversation with Dr. Mudd on the 22d of July, 1865, Mudd confessed that he knew Booth when he came to his house with Herold on the morning after the assassination of the President; that he had known Booth for some time, but was afraid to tell of Booth's having been at his house on the 15th of April, fearing that his own and the lives of his family would be endangered thereby. He also confessed that he was with Booth at the National Hotel on the evening referred to by Weichmann in his testimony; that he came to Washington on that occasion to meet Booth by appointment, as the latter wished to be introduced to John Surratt; that when he and Booth were going to Mrs. Surratt's house to see her son, they met, on Seventh Street, Surratt, who was introduced to Booth, and they had a conversation of a private nature. I will here add that Dr. Mudd had with him a printed copy of the testimony pertaining to his trial, and I had upon a number of occasions referred to the same. I will also say that this confession was voluntary, and made without solicitation, threat, or promise, and was made after the destination of the prisoners was communicated to them, which communication affected Dr. Mudd more than the rest, and he frequently exclaimed, ' Oh, there is now no hope for me! Oh, I cannot live in such a place!' "

When the officers called at Mudd's house the Tuesday after the assassination, he denied that he knew either of the criminals, and at the time of his arrest, on the Friday following, he prevaricated, but finally admitted that he knew Booth. He said he first heard of the assassination at church on the Sunday after it was committed; but that statement was false, for between four and five o'clock on Saturday afternoon, April 15, he called at the house of Francis R. Farrell, who lived halfway between Dr. Mudd's and Bryantown, a short distance off the road. During this visit of not more than fifteen minutes Dr. Mudd said that the President had been assassinated by a man by the name of Booth. When Dr. Mudd was asked whether it was the Booth that was down there the fall before, he replied that he did not know, for there were three or four men by that name; but if that was the one, he knew him. He made no allusion to the two men that had spent the day at his house. Dr. Mudd said that he thought at that time the killing of the President was the worst thing that could have happened, and that it would make it a great deal worse for the country. He received his information of the assassination from a visit to Bryantown in the afternoon, after the soldiers had arrived. Dr. Mudd's second visit to Washington was on the 15th of January, 1865, and according to the testimony his third visit was on the 3d of March, 1865, the day preceding the inauguration, when Booth was to strike the traitorous blow. His fourth visit was on the 23d of March, 1865, in company with a neighbor, Thomas L. Gardiner. This date will be remembered by some of the old inhabitants of Washington as the occasion of the visit of a tornado that swept over the city, unroofing several houses and killing a negro. The two men stayed all night in the city at the residence of Henry A. Clark, returning home the next day. Proof was presented showing that Dr. Mudd did not converse with Booth during this visit, as quite a party of men spent the evening, until between twelve and one o'clock, at the office of Dr. Charles Clark. By testimony at the trial the first and second visits were proven to have been made, but no mention was made of those of January 15 and March 3. Dr. Mudd's friends attempted to prove an alibi on all dates except the first two.

SAMUEL ARNOLD was a native of Maryland. His parents resided in Baltimore, and a brother lived at Hookstown, about six miles from Baltimore. He was twenty-eight years of age at the time of the assassination. He joined the Confederate army at the breaking out of the rebellion.

EDWARD SPANGLER was a middle-aged man, with a large, unintelligent face, swollen evidently by intem-

perance, a low forehead, gray eyes, and brown hair. He
was born in the interior of Pennsylvania, where he had
respectable connections. He considered Baltimore his

SAMUEL ARNOLD.

Sentenced for life to Dry Tortugas, Fla.   Released from prison March 21,
1869, by pardon from President Andrew Johnson.

home, having buried his wife there a year previous to
the assassination. He usually spent his summer months,
during the vacation of the theater, chiefly at crab-
bing, at which he was considered an expert. He does not
appear to have been in the conspiracy at an earlier period
than a few hours before the commission of the crime. If
he was guilty, his participation would seem to have been

in preparing the means of escape by keeping the passage-way clear on the stage, closing the back door after Booth had passed through, so as to retard the movements of pursuers, loosening the screws to the locks in the doors

EDWARD SPANGLER.

Stage hand at Ford's Theater. Sentenced to Dry Tortugas for six years. Released from prison March 21, 1869, having received an official pardon from President Andrew Johnson.

leading to the President's box, and preparing the bar of wood with which to fasten the door leading into the pas-sageway from the audience. He knew the purposes of Booth, and promised to help him.

The parents of MICHAEL O'LAUGHLIN lived in Baltimore for thirty years preceding the assassination. Michael went there from the South during the war, and on the 16th of June, 1863, took the oath of allegiance in the

MICHAEL O'LAUGHLIN.

Sentenced for life to Dry Tortugas, Fla. Died of yellow fever while in prison, September 23, 1867.

office of Marshal James L. McPhail at Baltimore. He had been in the Confederate army previous to taking the oath. He was a schoolmate of J. Wilkes Booth, and his family lived in property owned by Booth's mother. He was a small, delicate-looking man, with rather pleasing features, uneasy black eyes, bushy black hair, a heavy black mustache and imperial, and a most anxious expression of countenance, shaded by a sad, remorseful look.

The following description of Dry Tortugas is from the *Scientific American:*

" Fort Jefferson, Dry Tortugas, Fla., is called by military men the safest fort in the world, and the most useless. It is one of the largest fortifications of masonry the United States Government has ever built, and one of the most expensive. During the Civil War it was used for a military prison, and at present it is used for a Federal quarantine station. It has been utterly worthless from the beginning, except the use it was put to during the war. It commands nothing but two or three sand keys and an unbroken stretch of blue water over which the navies of the world might pass without coming within range of its guns. It is more than one hundred miles from the nearest point of the mainland. The first appropriation by Congress for its construction was made in 1844.

" It was in this fort that Dr. Mudd, O'Laughlin, Spangler, and Arnold were confined for the part they took in the assassination of President Lincoln. The room in which Dr. Mudd was confined was twelve feet wide by twenty feet long, with stone floor, and lighted dimly by an open port-hole. Someone had painted upon the heavy plank door, in large letters, ' Leave hope behind who enters here.' Dr. Mudd did not leave hope behind when he entered the bastion cell, although he remained a prisoner until 1869. An unusually deadly epidemic of yellow fever broke out in the fort, soldiers and prisoners dying by the score every day, and all the

neighboring sand keys were dotted with graves.   Every
surgeon on the post had been carried away, and the commandant was almost in despair, when Dr. Mudd offered
his professional services.   They were gladly accepted,

FORT JEFFERSON, DRY TORTUGAS, FLA.,

In which four of the conspirators, Dr. Mudd, O'Laughlin, Arnold, and
Spangler, were confined.

and his first act was the enlargement of all the port-
holes in the upper casements, to give his patients more
air.   This treatment gave good results, and he soon had
the epidemic under control.   All the officers of the post
united in signing a petition to President Johnson ask-

ing for his release on account of the valuable services
rendered, and he was pardoned February 8, 1869, and
was released from confinement March 8. Arnold and
Spangler were released from the same prison March 21,
1869. Michael O'Laughlin died of yellow fever while
in the fort, September 23, 1867."

CHAPTER IX.

LOUIS J. WEICHMANN.

ONE of the most interesting persons in the conspiracy trial was Mr. L. J. Weichmann, who was the chief witness for the Government.

Mr. Weichmann was born in 1842, in Baltimore, Md., of honest, hard-working Germans, the mother being a strong Catholic, and the father equally as pronounced a Lutheran. In 1844 his father removed to the city of Washington, where he carried on the business of merchant tailoring until 1853, when he concluded to make his home in Philadelphia. In Washington the physician of his father's family was Dr. Jonathan F. May, who subsequently became the physician of J. Wilkes Booth, and identified his body, and among Mr. Weichmann's acquaintances at that early day was Petersen, the tailor, in whose house President Lincoln died.

In Philadelphia young Mr. Weichmann was sent to the public schools, and in 1859 was graduated from the High School with a two years' course.

Now began the worriment of choosing a business or profession in life for the young man. After mature deliberation on the part of his parents, it was decided that he should become a student for the Catholic priesthood. His father had become a convert to that Church by this time. Accordingly negotiations were opened with a prominent clergyman in Washington, Rev. E. Q. S. Waldron, and finally a bishop was secured for whom

Weichmann was to study and in whose diocese he was to labor—the Rt. Rev. John McGill, D. D., Bishop of Richmond, Va.

Weichmann was now (March 1, 1859) sent to the preparatory college of St. Charles in Howard County, Mary-

LOUIS J. WEICHMANN.

A boarder at Mrs. Surratt's, who, in his testimony before the Commission, gave some convincing proofs of the guilt of Mrs. Surratt, although he was innocent of any knowledge of her designs until after the testimony given by John M. Lloyd.

land, twenty-five miles from Baltimore, an institution under the care of the Sulpician Fathers, a French religious order having for its object the training of young men for the Catholic priesthood.

Everything here went on as pleasantly as possible for the novice, who was much pleased with his new home, and became strongly attached to the vocation marked out for him.

In September, 1859, among the new arrivals at this
place was John Harrison Surratt. The same clergyman,
Rev. Mr. Waldron, who had recommended Weichmann
to St. Charles also recommended Surratt, and the bishop
chosen for him was Rt. Rev. Augustine Verot, D. D., of
St. Augustine, Fla. Surratt at that time was sixteen
years of age. He was tall and slender, dignified in manner, genial in nature, and at once won many friends
among the students. He was a very pronounced
Southern man, but in no instance did he make himself
offensive to anyone by his views.

At this school John H. Surratt was an exemplary
student, and when he left in 1862 it was with genuine
feelings of regret on the part of the president, Rev.
Oliver Jenkins, who had become much attached to him.

Weichmann also left school in July, 1862, going to his
home in Philadelphia, where he spent his vacation. He
endeavored to get permission from his bishop to enter
the larger seminary at Baltimore, but in consequence of
the war was unable to do so. In this dilemma he resolved to devote himself to teaching. He again had re-
course to Dr. Waldron, for whom he went to teach in
September, at Pikesville, Md., but did not remain longer
with him than two months. Then Mr. Weichmann went
to teach for Rev. Wm. Mahony, at Little Texas, Md.,
on the line of the Northern Central Railroad, about
twenty miles from Baltimore. Here he remained until
December, 1863, when his schoolhouse was burned
down, and he was obliged to look elsewhere for employment. A paper, the *Catholic Mirror*, fell into his
hands about that time. In it he saw an advertisement of
Rev. Charles I. White, D. D., of Washington, D. C., who
desired a teacher for St. Matthew's Institute on Nine-
teenth Street, between G and H. Mr. Weichmann an-

swered the advertisement, inclosing a note of recommendation from Father Mahony. The place was won without much difficulty, and in this way it was that Mr. Weichmann came to Washington, then the center of military operations for the preservation and restoration of the Union.

John H. Surratt in the meantime had returned to his home at Surrattsville in Maryland. This place was distant from Washington about thirteen miles, and was situated on the line of the Bryantown road, running direct from Washington to the Potomac River. In September, 1862, John H. Surratt was appointed postmaster of Surrattsville, which position he retained until November 17, 1863, when he was succeeded by Mr. Andrew V. Roby. As postmaster he was compelled to take the oath of allegiance to the United States Government. His father, John H. Surratt, Sr., a good Union man, died in July, 1862.

When Surratt learned that his old friend Weichmann was in Washington, he promptly called on him at his school, was pleasantly received, and the old college acquaintance was feelingly renewed. Henceforth Surratt was one of his constant visitors and friends, and was always received pleasantly and treated generously.

In the early spring of 1863 Surratt invited Weichmann to his home. The invitation was eagerly accepted. When Weichmann reached Surrattsville he was introduced to Mrs. Surratt and her daughter Annie, and was received and treated most courteously. He went down on one Friday and remained until the following Monday morning.

Mrs. Surratt's family at that time consisted of her son, John, and her daughter, Annie. There was an older son by the name of Isaac, but he had left at the beginning

of the war, and had gone south and sought employment
in his chosen profession of engineer, in the Confederate
army. He was the oldest of the family, Annie the second, and John the youngest. Mrs. Surratt was then
about forty-five years of age.

On the morning after his arrival Weichmann was
awakened quite early from his sleep by the sound of
music under his window. He was soon called down by
Surratt. He saw a party of musicians, a portion of the
Marine Band of Washington, who had come down to
serenade some newly elected county officials. With them
was a sprightly black-haired and frowsy-headed young
man, who was " hail fellow, well met " among the party.
Weichmann was soon introduced to him as Mr. David
E. Herold. Two years later this young man became one
of the conspirators against Lincoln. He it was who escaped with Booth from Washington on the night of the
assassination, was taken in the burning Garrett barn,
and subsequently hanged. In this way it was that Mr.
Weichmann made Herold's acquaintance two years before the murder, and thus it was shown that Surratt was
Herold's friend at that early date.

During this visit Weichmann spoke of his intention to
visit St. Charles College during the approaching Easter
holidays, and it was arranged for Surratt to go along.
They reached the college on Thursday, April 2, 1863, and
were gladly welcomed by the students and professors.
They spent a very pleasant time in the old college
grounds, and when the hour came to leave, it was with
sincere regret. Weichmann told Father Denis that he
would visit Little Texas. Father Denis then told him
that he would find there a young man, one Henri B. de
Ste. Marie, who had been one of his pupils in the college
at Montreal, and handing Weichmann an Italian paper,

the *Eco d'Italia*, to give to Mr. Ste. Marie, remarked that Ste. Marie was an excellent student, and spoke both French and Italian well.

When they reached Little Texas, Weichmann was presented to Mr. Ste. Marie, and, in turn, he introduced Mr. Surratt to his newly found friend. This was a remarkable introduction, and subsequently was worth just ten thousand dollars to Ste. Marie, for he it was who, nearly three years later, identified Zouave Surratt while serving in the Papal army at Veroli, Italy. That introduction and subsequent identification in Italy will never be forgotten by John H. Surratt as long as he lives.

On the 7th of January, 1864, Mr. Weichmann was appointed a clerk in the War Department, at a salary of eighty dollars per month. This change in his pecuniary circumstances was in every way a help to the recipient. He soon moved into another boarding-house, kept by a Mr. Purnell, a colored caterer. In this house one of the boarders was General A. P. Howe, subsequently a member of the Commission which tried Surratt's mother.

In August, 1864, Mr. Weichmann became a member of the "War Department Rifles," a regiment from among the clerks of the War Department for the defense of Washington City, and continued with it until the end of the war.

In the fall of 1864 he again visited Surrattsville, and was received as pleasantly as on the occasion of his first visit. It was at that time that Mrs. Surratt and her son announced to him their intention to remove to Washington, and to occupy their home, No. 541 H Street. Weichmann was invited to become a boarder and resident. He agreed to do so, and stipulated to pay thirty-five dollars per month for board and room.

Accordingly on the 1st of November, 1864, Mrs. Surratt took possession of her city home. Her son and daughter were there from the start, but she herself did not go there until December 1, 1864. On that day she leased her Surrattsville home to John M. Lloyd for five hundred dollars per annum, Weichmann being a witness to the lease. Mrs. Surratt's Washington home was soon filled with good and desirable boarders. A Mr. Holohan with his wife and two children occupied the two front second-story rooms. A Miss Honora Fitzpatrick, a good woman and most excellent lady, roomed with the daughter, Annie, and a young girl about nine years of age, named Appollonia Dean, was also one of the inmates. Thus the house was full from the start, and was a paying institution. It was a pleasant and happy home during November and December, 1864, and in all that was developed at the two trials of 1865 and 1867 there was not so much as the scratch of a pin's head alleged against that home during that period. But its peace was short-lived—John Wilkes Booth had not yet crossed its threshold.

On the 23d of December, 1864, Louis J. Weichmann and John H. Surratt were standing in front of this house, and having a very pleasant and social time together. Weichmann expressed a desire to go down toward Pennsylvania Avenue, as he desired to purchase a few Christmas presents for his sisters in Philadelphia, wishing to give them at the approaching holidays. Surratt promptly and willingly consented to accompany him. Neither Weichmann nor Surratt expected to meet anyone.

When about halfway down Seventh Street, directly opposite Odd Fellows' Hall, somebody called out, "Surratt! Surratt!"

"John, someone is calling you," said Weichmann.

Quickly Surratt turned and recognized in the caller an old friend—Dr. Samuel A. Mudd, from Bryantown, Md. Dr. Mudd was accompanied by a stranger.

" Why, doctor, how do you do? Let me present to you my friend, Mr. Weichmann."

The doctor gave Mr. Weichmann his hand, and pleasantly acknowledged the introduction, and then bringing forward his companion said, " And you, gentlemen, let me introduce to you my friend, Mr. Boone."

Mr. Boone thereupon shook hands with Surratt and Weichmann, saying at the same time: " Gentlemen, retrace your steps and come to my rooms at the hotel. We will have some refreshments together."

The invitation was accepted. On reaching his room, No. 82, at the National Hotel, Boone at once pulled the call bell, and of the waiter who responded he requested that he serve milk punches and cigars for four. This was promptly done, the punches were sipped, the cigars puffed, and a pleasant and enjoyable time was had.

When this was over, Dr. Mudd arose, went into the entry that led past the room, and called out Booth after him. (All this time Weichmann was under the impression that the name given him was Boone.) These two men probably remained in the entry ten minutes or more, then returned and called out Surratt. They now stayed out some time longer, and on returning to the room Dr. Mudd approaching Mr. Weichmann said, " Too bad, too bad! to leave you alone so long; very ungentlemanly and impolite. Mr. Boone had some private business with me. The fact is, he wishes to purchase my farm, but don't want to give me enough for it." Boone also said something to the same effect.

Then these three men seated themselves around a table about six feet from Weichmann, and began a conversation audible only as to sound, no portion of which he did or could distinguish.

After this was over the party broke up, and Dr. Mudd asked the gentlemen around to his room at the Pennsylvania House on C Street. On arriving there Boone and Surratt seated themselves together on a sofa near the blazing hearth, and Weichmann and Mudd had an interview to themselves. Mudd was a thoroughly Union man in all his utterances, and not a disloyal word was uttered by him.

The company separated about ten o'clock, the gentlemen bidding each other good-night very pleasantly. That night on the way home Surratt remarked to Weichmann that the brilliant young man he had met was no less a personage than John Wilkes Booth, the famous actor. That was Weichmann's first meeting with Booth, and his first and only meeting with Mudd.

Immediately after this introduction to Booth on December 23, Surratt one day told Weichmann that he was going to invest in a cotton speculation; that an elderly gentleman residing in the neighborhood would advance him three thousand dollars for that purpose; that he was in pursuance going to Europe, from Europe to Nassau, and from Nassau to Matamoras, Mexico, where he expected to find his brother, Isaac.

On another occasion Weichmann asked Mrs. Surratt what John had to do with the purchase of Mudd's farm, and why he had become an agent for Booth. Her answer was, "Oh, Dr. Mudd and the people of Charles County are getting tired of Booth, and they are pushing him off on John."

When the Government came to review this evidence, it charged that it was a conference looking to the execution of the conspiracy, which so impressed the prisoner (Mudd) and his counsel (General Ewing) that they endeavored to destroy the credibility of Mr. Weichmann; but said Judge Bingham: " I may say in reference to the witness, Weichmann, that they have not contradicted a single fact to which he has testified in this issue, nor have they found a breath of suspicion against his character." And Bingham went on to speak about two of these men going into the entry to have a private talk, then the third, and then returning to the room and apologizing for the privacy of the interview, Mudd saying that Booth wanted to purchase his farm. Bingham said if it was necessary to go into that hall and talk about the purchase of Mudd's farm, why should they return to the room and disclose that fact to the very man from whom they had concealed it?

This evidence was, indeed, very important, for on the night of the assassination Booth's second halting place was Dr. Mudd's house, which the assassins reached about two o'clock on the morning of the 15th of April, 1865. Dr. Mudd himself admitted Booth and Herold to his home, and they remained there nearly all day. Dr. Mudd set Booth's broken leg, had a crutch made for him, gave him a razor with which to remove his mustache, and then when the time came for the men to leave, accompanied them some distance along the road.

Three days after the murder Lieutenant Alexander Lovett came to Mudd's place, having traced the assassins to that point. To him Dr. Mudd denied all knowledge of Booth, saying that he had heard of an eminent tragedian by the name of Edwin Booth, but he did not know John Wilkes Booth.

The detectives left, but returned in a few days and arrested Dr. Mudd, who now confessed that he knew

Booth and Herold when they came to him; that he was introduced to Booth in the fall of 1864 by one Mr. Thompson. These prevarications cost Dr. Mudd very dearly.

When the conspiracy trial took place, Weichmann was asked:

" Who introduced you to John Wilkes Booth? "

" Dr. Samuel A. Mudd," was the answer.

" Point him out among the prisoners at the bar."

Weichmann pointed him out, and Dr. Mudd's face grew white as paper, and he would have given his farm and every dollar he owned in the world if he could have destroyed this evidence. But that was impossible. He was convicted and sent to Dry Tortugas for life.

When on his way on board the gunboat, he confessed to Captain George W. Dutton, who had him in charge, that Weichmann had told the truth; that he had come that night to Washington to meet Booth by appointment; that Booth was to introduce him to John H. Surratt, and that he was on his way to Mrs. Surratt's house for that purpose when the accidental meeting took place on Seventh Street. Captain Dutton made affidavit to that effect, and it is now on file in the War Department.

Surratt, in his lecture of December 8, 1870, says: " *In the fall of 1864 I was introduced to John Wilkes Booth.*" But again in a published interview on April 3, 1898, with one Hanson Hiss, he says: " In the first place, Wilkes Booth was never introduced to me by Dr. Mudd on the street or anywhere else. Booth came to me with a letter of introduction from a valued and trusted friend. In the second place, Weichmann was nowhere near when Booth presented his letter."

These admissions on the part of Surratt clearly prove that he was practicing the grossest deception on Mr.

Weichmann from the beginning of his acquaintance with Booth, and that he already knew who Booth was when the latter was introduced to Weichmann on Seventh Street as Mr. Boone, and was already a member of the conspiracy.

On the 28th of December, 1864, Surratt obtained employment in the Adams Express Company. This position he did not retain very long, for on or about the 15th of January, 1865, he went to the agent of the company and desired leave of absence to go into the country with his mother, as her protector. He was refused, and then his mother went and interceded for him, saying she was going into the country and desired him along as her protector. Mr. Dunn, the express agent, also refused her petition. Surratt then left the company, and never returned to draw the pay due him. That John Wilkes Booth was interested in this visit of Surratt is shown by the fact that two years after, when the National Hotel clerk, Dawson, was overhauling Booth's clothing, there dropped from the pocket of a vest once worn by Booth a little card with this inscription:

I tried to secure leave, but failed.—J. HARRISON SURRATT.

Weichmann, under oath, identified the handwriting as that of Surratt, and thus it was clearly shown that Booth was much interested in Surratt's trip to the country.

When Atzerodt was on trial for his life, he stated that Surratt came to him in the middle of January and secured a boat on which the President, when abducted, was to be ferried across the river. The boat was capable of holding fifteen persons. He said that Surratt induced him to join the conspiracy to capture the President under promises of a great fortune.

And it was not long before Atzerodt found his way to the Surratt home. One day in the latter part of January, on returning from his work, Weichmann met in the parlor of the house a man who was introduced to him as Mr. Atzerodt. There were in the room at the time Mrs. Surratt, John Surratt, the daughter Annie, and Miss Fitzpatrick. The young ladies could not pronounce the stranger's name well, and hearing that he came from Port Tobacco they jestingly styled him Mr. Port Tobacco. Little did these young people then realize that they were giving him a name by which he would be known ever afterward, and by which he would pass into history!

Atzerodt was a simple, good-hearted countryman, full of wit and humor. He had a big head, with an abundance of curly hair, but his figure was unprepossessing, and his head and face seemed to be wedged between his shoulders. This man became a frequent visitor at Mrs. Surratt's house, and he was very intimate with the son. He boarded and roomed, when in the city, at the Pennsylvania House on C Street.

In the early part of February, 1865, Surratt went to New York. According to his admissions to Weichmann, he called at the Booth home while there, and was never done talking about the large and handsome house in which the Booths lived.

One evening toward the close of February a carriage was driven to the front of Mrs. Surratt's house. In it were John Surratt and a woman who was closely veiled. She jumped out of the buggy in a very sprightly way and went into the house. Mr. Weichmann was called and asked to bring her trunk, which was a small affair, into the house, but he was never introduced to the woman, and at no time did he see her face. She wore what was known in those days as a " mask," a thin veil reaching down to the chin. She remained in the house on that occasion only one night, and when Mr. Weichmann awoke in the morning she was gone. He subsequently learned that she was a dispatch bearer and blockade runner.

The next arrival about the same time was one "Spencer Howell," as he was called, who remained in the house two days, and who was also engaged in running the blockade. Mr. Weichmann had a good deal of talk with him, but gleaned nothing of a very important nature. He was arrested not long after his departure from the Surratt home, early in March, thrown into prison, and was there at the time of the death of Mr. Lincoln.

Before leaving Mrs. Surratt's house he had taught Weichmann a cipher, which investigation showed was the same as used by Booth and by the Confederates; but Weichmann did not know this, and the only use he ever made of it was to translate into it Longfellow's "Psalm of Life."

But a bigger surprise than any yet was in store for the young and unsuspecting boarder. Along about this time, when the family were assembled in the parlor one evening, the front doorbell was heard to ring. Stepping quickly to the door, only a few feet away, Mr. Weichmann opened it and saw before him a tall six-foot man, who wore a big black, shabby overcoat, with his hands buried deep in his coat pockets.

"Good evening!" said the stranger; "does Mr. Surratt live here?"

"He does," was the reply.

"Is he in?"

"He is not."

"Well, then, I would like to see Mrs. Surratt."

" Your name? "

" Louis Wood."

Mr. Weichmann stepped to the parlor and informed Mrs. Surratt that a gentleman giving the name of Wood was at the front door, and would like to see her.

She bade him be admitted. Then the big man came into the house, spoke a few words to Mrs. Surratt, who said: " Mr. Weichmann, this is a poor man who has had nothing to eat; but my dining room is disarranged. Would you mind taking his meal to him in your room? "

And then Mr. Weichmann, in his goodness of heart, served the man's supper to him in his own bedroom. He had never seen him before, did not know him, and he might just as readily have dropped from the clouds of heaven or from anywhere else for all he knew.

The man ate voraciously, as if very hungry. He had the eye of an eagle, and his hair was black as jet. Once Weichmann asked him where he was from. " Baltimore," was the laconic reply. " What are you doing there? " " I am a clerk in the china store of a Mr. Parr." That was all. When the meal was over Wood went at once to bed, and in the morning when Weichmann arose his mysterious visitor was gone. Little did Weichmann dream that he was entertaining one who subsequently proved to be one of the greatest villains of the age, a man then in the pay of J. Wilkes Booth—the notorious Lewis Payne, the would-be assassin of Secretary Seward.

On the 3d of March Booth was in Mrs. Surratt's parlor a portion of the evening, and from there went with Surratt and Weichmann to witness the expiration of the Congress then in session.

As fate would have it, Weichmann was again spending the evening with the family on the night of March 13. The doorbell again rang, and Mr. Weichmann once more answered the summons. He saw the same man standing before him whom he had let into the house only a few weeks before, but a complete transformation had been effected in his appearance. In place of the shabby clothes he wore on the occasion of his first visit, he was now arrayed in a new and complete suit of gray. He had on a new, jaunty hat and wore a pretty black necktie.

"Good-evening!" he said to Weichmann; "is Mr. Surratt in?" Being told that Surratt was not at home, he then asked for Mrs. Surratt, giving his name as Lewis Payne, and thus he was introduced to all assembled in the parlor.

It, however, ran in Weichmann's mind all the time that Payne was not the name given at the time of the first visit, but so little impression had his first appearance made on Weichmann, that the latter was puzzled for a time to remember the name originally given.

He was very polite in his manners with the ladies, lifted the piano cover for Miss Surratt, who played and sang a few songs for him. Then he sat down to a game of euchre, and one of the ladies (Miss Fitzpatrick) called him Mr. Wood. Then it was that his first name came back to Weichmann, who began to wonder why this man was using an assumed name, and what he was doing there, anyhow. What was at the bottom of it all? On this occasion he was no longer a clerk in a china store, but represented himself as a Baptist preacher.

The following day, March 14, Surratt returned home late in the afternoon. While Weichmann was in his room seated at his table writing, Payne walked in. Surratt at the time was lying on the bed. Payne looked at him and said, "Is this Mr. Surratt?" Weichmann answered, "Yes, sir, it is." Payne then observed, "I would like to talk privately with Mr. Surratt." This was all a pretense, a make-believe to deceive Weichmann, for there is no doubt that Surratt already knew who Payne was.

The next day, March 15, on returning from his work Weichmann found a false mustache on his table. Not thinking much about it, and intending to have a little fun with it, he threw it into a box that stood there.

Then Weichmann, not seeing Surratt or Payne around, went up to the back attic. Just as he opened the door he saw there the two men seated together on a bed surrounded by spurs, bowie knives, and revolvers. The moment the door opened they almost instantly and unconsciously threw their hands over the weapons as if to conceal them. Weichmann did not like this, and went down and told Mrs. Surratt what he had seen. She told him that he must not think anything of that, as he knew her son was in the habit of going into the country, and he had to have these things as a protection.

The same day Surratt showed Weichmann a box ticket for the theater, which had been given him by Booth. Weichmann expressed a desire to go, but Surratt did not wish him along, for private reasons. Finally Surratt selected Miss Dean and Miss Fitzpatrick to accompany him. They all went in a hack.

Toward the end of the play Booth came to the box and called Surratt and Payne out into the entry. He was very much excited. What these men were after that night can only be conjectured. The box they occupied was the President's. When the play was over, Surratt and Payne returned the ladies to the house, but themselves stayed away all night. As will be seen from the confession of Samuel Arnold, a meeting was held at the Lichau House that night, March 15, at which the seven conspirators were present, and the proceedings of which are fully described in Arnold's confession and Surratt's lecture, to which reference has already been made.

The next day, March 16, was a very important one. Weichmann had been at his desk in the War Department all day, and as usual wended his way homeward at the close of the day's work. On reaching his room he saw no one; then, pulling a call bell, he requested Dan, the mulatto boy who did the chores around the place, to bring some water, in the meantime asking him where John Surratt was.

" Massa Surratt done gone from the front of the house about two o'clock this afternoon with six or seven others on horseback," was the reply.

" With six or seven on horseback, Dan; who were they? "

" One was Mr. Booth, then Massa Surratt, Payne who is staying here, Atzerodt, Dave Herold, and the other two I don't know," responded Dan; but subsequent developments proved they were Arnold and O'Laughlin.

It was a great pity the Government could not utilize this poor colored boy as a witness, but he was of weak mind, was easily confused, and so his evidence was inadmissible. His story, however, is confirmed by what happened afterward.

On going down to dinner that day Weichmann met Mrs. Surratt in the hall. She was weeping bitterly, and said: " Mr. Weichmann, go down to your dinner and make the best of it you can. John is gone away! John is gone away! " By this time Weichmann's curiosity was pretty well aroused, but he didn't know what to make of it all.

After his dinner he returned to his room and sat down to read, entirely unsuspicious of what was coming. At about six or half-past six o'clock Surratt burst into the room. He was very much excited; the legs of his pantaloons were inside his boot tops. Seeing Weichmann, he drew a pistol hastily from his vest pocket, leveled it at him, and said: " My prospects are gone; my hopes are blasted. Can you get me a clerkship? I want something to do."

" Oh, you foolish fellow! why don't you settle down and be contented? I don't understand you lately, since your acquaintance with the actor," said Weichmann.

He had hardly ceased speaking before Payne came into the room, very much flushed in countenance, but more self-possessed than Surratt. He did not say a word, but once he raised his vest as if in the act of fastening a suspender, and then Weichmann saw a big revolver resting on his hip.

In a short time Booth also came into the room. He wore a small slouch hat, with rim turned down, and had a riding whip in his hand. He walked around two or three times excitedly in a circle, as it were, snapping his whip. Then Weichmann said, " Hello, Booth! "

" Why, you here! I didn't see you," answered Booth, who now gave a signal to the others, and the three men then left the room and went to the attic upstairs.

In about a half hour they descended, and left the house. That was the last time, prior to the assassination, that Payne was in Mrs. Surratt's house, and Weichmann's eyes did not rest on him again until he confronted him as a witness at the conspiracy trial.

The doings of the day, however, had unnerved Weichmann, and he now for the first time since his advent in the Surratt house became suspicious that something wrong was going on among the men. He had seen them come and go and had treated them respectfully and kindly. Booth and Atzerodt were constant visitors.

Herold came there once or twice while Payne was there. He used to wonder why this sudden and great friendship had sprung up between the actor and Surratt, but he could not understand it.

Accordingly, after supper on the night of March 16 Mr. Weichmann started for the rooms of one Captain D. H. Gleason, a clerk in the same office with him, and to whom he used to tell numbers of little things happening at his boarding-house by way of chat and gossip, but he did not find the captain at home that night. The next day, however, he told him at the office of the occurrences just as detailed here.

"By God, that is strange!" said Gleason; "there is something wrong going on there, Weichmann."

They talked the matter over, and a number of possibilities were suggested, such as running the blockade, releasing prisoners, cotton speculation, oil speculation, etc., but no conclusion was reached.

It was suggested that probably it would be a good thing to go and tell the Secretary of War, but finally Gleason said that "inasmuch as what these men were after had failed, it would be a good thing to keep an eye on them, and if anything again came up, to promptly report it to the authorities, secure horses if need be, and pursue them." But nothing occurred to again excite Weichmann's suspicions. When, however, the assassination took place, Gleason put the War Department in possession of the facts stated, and Weichmann was called on for an explanation, which, it is needless to say, he made in a prompt and satisfactory way.

Now, what were these men after that day? Weichmann did not know what it meant until Samuel Arnold's confession was published in 1869 and Surratt's lecture delivered in December, 1870. Then, for the first time, it became publicly known that these men had started out that day to capture Mr. Lincoln at the Soldiers' Home. A play had been arranged at the above place, called "Still Waters Run Deep," and Mr. Lester Wallack, E. L. Davenport, and John Matthews had been secured as players. At the last moment, however, the President did not come, but sent in his stead Mr. Chase, his Secretary of the Treasury, and then Surratt tells us in his lecture that they were much disappointed because the President had not come. "They did not want Mr. Chase; they wanted a bigger chase."

The President was to have been seized at the end of the play while on his way home. Surratt, because of his familiarity with the roads, was to jump on the box, seize the reins, and do the driving by way of Oldfield and Benning's bridge, and they were to go as rapidly as possible through lower Maryland, and before the evening of the same day they calculated to deliver Mr. Lincoln inside the Confederate lines; but the scheme, as has been seen, resulted in a big fiasco, all because the "bigger chase" had not come.

That was the end of the abduction plot, and there is no evidence in existence to show that after that date it was ever renewed or attempted again. Surratt says this in his lecture, and Samuel Arnold confirms it in his confession. He and O'Laughlin went now to Baltimore. On the 29th of March Arnold secured a position in the store of John W. Wharton, a sutler at Fortress Monroe, and was there when the assassination took place. Booth, about April 1, sold the horses and buggy he had provided for capturing the President at the theater.

Henceforth another plan was in Booth's mind, which, as results proved, was eminently successful—the killing of Lincoln.

On the 18th of March Booth played at Ford's Theater, for the benefit of his friend John McCullough, in the play of the " Apostate," he himself assuming the character of Pescara, the infamous duke of Alba. He had given a number of tickets to Surratt, who invited Mr. Holohan and his friend Weichmann. At the play were also seen Herold and Atzerodt. When the play was over Weichmann left the theater with Surratt and Holohan, but Surratt, looking around and finding that Atzerodt and Herold were not coming, sent Weichmann to tell them to hurry up and come to Mr. Kloman's saloon on Seventh Street to partake of an oyster supper. When Weichmann went into the restaurant next the theater he saw Booth in close conversation with Herold and Atzerodt. Booth left his companions and asked Weichmann to take a drink with him, who did so, and partook of a glass of ale.

After this Herold and Atzerodt left the restaurant and joined the rest of the company at Kloman's.

On the 23d of the month Weichmann was surprised to see Mrs. Holohan come to the office where he was employed. She had for him a telegram, which she handed him. Weichmann opened it. It read as follows:

NEW YORK, March 23, 1865.

—— WICKMAN, Esq., No. 541 H Street, Washington, D. C.

Tell John telegraph number and street at once.

(Signed) J. BOOTH.

Weichmann thought strange of this; he could not understand why Booth should address him a telegram, and laughingly showed it to the other clerks. The same afternoon, however, after his work, on his way home, he met Surratt at the corner of Seventh and F streets. He handed him the message, asking him why it was addressed as it was, and what street and number were meant. Surratt answered, " Don't be so damned inquisitive." Then he stepped to the window of the delivery office, and inquired for a letter for " James Sturdy," and a letter bearing that address was given him. It was from New York, and was written in a very bad hand. It was signed " Wood "—the same man who had been at Mrs. Surratt's house under that name, viz., Payne.

That evening after dinner Weichmann went out with Surratt at his invitation. They first called at a Catholic school at the corner of Tenth and G streets, where a young lady by the name of Anna Ward was employed as a teacher, whom Surratt saw and with whom he had some conversation. What the nature of it was, Weichmann did not know. From here Surratt went to the Herndon House at the corner of Ninth and F streets and called for a Mrs. Murray, with whom he desired to converse alone; but Mrs. Murray was slightly deaf, and did not understand him. Then he spoke out more boldly, and said: " Did not Miss Anna Ward engage a room for a sick man who was to have his meals sent up to him, and who would be here Monday, March 27?" Mrs. Murray acknowledged this to be so. The " sick " man arrived and took possession of the room on the date named. This was Payne, as subsequent developments showed, for Weichmann, happening to meet Atzerodt one day on the street, asked him if it was Payne who was staying at the Herndon House, and Atzerodt said it was.

Mrs. Surratt knew that it was Payne, for Weichmann told her what Atzerodt had said to him, and she was very angry about it. During the week ending April 8, while on her way from St. Patrick's Church, she called on Payne at the Herndon House, and had an interview with him, the testimony to this effect being given by

Miss Fitzpatrick and Weichmann at the trial of Surratt, in 1867.

Weichmann has always felt that Booth's telegram was sent direct to him for the purpose of compromising him. He was always at a loss to know why it should have been sent to him at all. He had no intimacy whatever with Booth, and never wrote to him or visited him at his rooms except at the request of Mrs. Surratt.

On Saturday morning, March 25, just as Weichmann came down for his breakfast, on looking out of his window he was surprised to see Surratt, his mother, and Mrs. Slater, all in a carriage with a pair of white horses attached. Mrs. Slater had probably been in the house the previous night, but not to his knowledge.

They drove away; not a word was said to him, Surratt not having politeness enough to say good-by. When Mrs. Surratt returned home alone that evening, Weichmann asked her what had become of her son, and she said, " He has gone to Richmond to secure a clerkship." She asked Weichmann to go to Brooke Stabler and say to him that the white horses and buggy would not be returned until the following Sunday. Weichmann made some objection to this. Said she, " Oh, Brooke considers John, Herold, and Atzerodt a party of young sports, and I want him to think them so."

On Sunday, March 26, as he was about to leave the house for church, Mrs. Surratt requested Weichmann to go to the National Hotel and ask Mr. Booth to call on her in the afternoon. On his way down Sixth Street Weichmann met Atzerodt, who was also going to see Booth. When they arrived at the hotel they found Booth at the front door. Weichmann communicated his message, stating that Mrs. Surratt desired to see him in the afternoon. Booth went to her house, and she had an interview with him near the head of the kitchen stairs.

On Sunday, April 2, Mrs. Surratt again requested Mr. Weichmann to go to the National Hotel and say that she wanted to see Booth, and if he was not there to call on Atzerodt and tell him to come around to the house.

Booth was not in the city at that time, and Weichmann went around to the Pennsylvania House, where he found Atzerodt standing in front of the hotel and holding two horses by the bridles. Weichmann asked him, " Whose horses are those? " " One," he said, " is mine and the other is Booth's." " I thought they were John Surratt's horses." " No," he responded, " they are mine." Weichmann had once seen a bill for livery in Surratt's name, and Mrs. Surratt said they were John's horses. Atzerodt asked Weichmann to mount one of them, and ride to church. This he did.

The same afternoon Mr. Jenkins, Mrs. Surratt's brother, who was at the house, desired to go home, and she again sent Weichmann around to Atzerodt to see if he could borrow one of John's horses. Atzerodt, however, refused, saying he would have to see Mr. Payne about it. " What has Payne to do with it? " asked Weichmann. " A heap," answered Atzerodt. Then Jenkins, Atzerodt, and Weichmann went around to Payne's boarding place. Atzerodt went in, but soon returned with a refusal on the part of Payne. This nettled Mrs. Surratt, who said she thought very mean of Atzerodt for this, for she had loaned him the last five dollars out of her pocket.

On the 3d of April the fall of Richmond was celebrated in Washington. Weichmann was sitting in the parlor in the afternoon, about five o'clock, worn out with the rejoicing and excitement of the occasion. Suddenly the door opened, and in walked John Surratt. " Why, Surratt," said Weichmann, " I thought you had gone to Richmond. Don't you know that Richmond has been evacuated? " " No, it has not," said Surratt; " I saw Davis and Benjamin in Richmond, and they told me it would not be evacuated."

Then Surratt went upstairs, and in a few minutes Weichmann followed him. Surratt changed his under-clothing; his outer clothes were new. He desired Weich-mann to change some money for him, and showed him some twenty-dollar gold pieces and some Treasury notes. Weichmann could not make the change, and then Sur-ratt called on Mr. Holohan, who accommodated him.

The same evening Surratt invited Weichmann down to Pennsylvania Avenue to eat some oysters with him. This was done, and at about eight o'clock Surratt left him, saying he would leave town for Montreal the follow-ing morning. Surratt stayed all that night at the Na-tional Hotel. That was the last time Weichmann ever spoke to him. He did not lay eyes on Surratt again until he appeared as a witness against him at his trial in 1867.

On Monday evening, April 10, Weichmann was again in Mrs. Surratt's parlor. Booth and Miss Anna Ward were also there. Suddenly Booth went across to Miss Ward and said, " Let me see the address of that lady again." Miss Ward then handed him a letter, which he read and returned. After he was gone Annie Surratt read the letter to Weichmann, saying, " It was too bad to practice such deception on him." The letter proved to be from her brother, but Weichmann did not remem-ber its contents.

The same evening Mrs. Surratt told him that it was necessary for her to go into the country the following day to see a Mr. John Nothey in reference to the money due on some land which he had purchased from her husband, and asked him if he would please drive her down. This he consented to do. He then went and asked the permission of his superior officers to be absent for the day. On the following morning, April 11, Mrs. Surratt requested him to go to Mr. Booth at the National Hotel and ask him for the loan of his horse and buggy. When Weichmann saw Booth he was informed by him that he had sold his horse and buggy, but he gave him ten dollars to hire a team for her. This Weichmann did. On the way to Surrattsville, near Uniontown, they happened to meet John M. Lloyd, who was coming to the city. Mrs. Surratt called him to her, and when he came she had a whispered conversation with him which Weichmann did not hear. Lloyd says she told him to get the "shooting-irons" out ready; that they would be wanted soon, and that she spoke in such a way that no one else would understand.

She then went to Surrattsville, where she met Mr. Nothey and had an interview with him of a couple hours' duration in the presence of a Mr. Bennett Gwynn, and some kind of arrangement was made in reference to paying the debt. She then returned home, which she reached at about six o'clock in the evening.

On the morning of the 14th of April (Good Friday) Weichmann, after taking his breakfast, went to St. Patrick's Church and assisted at the early service there. When that was over he went to his desk and was there until ten or half-past ten o'clock. At that time a circular letter was read from the Secretary of War, Mr. Stanton, to the effect that all his employees whose churches had divine service that day were relieved from duty for the remainder of the day. Weichmann took advantage of the order and went to hear mass at St. Matthew's Church, where Dr. White, his old employer, officiated, preaching the sermon. At the end of the service, about half-past twelve, he returned to his boarding-house, meeting several friends on the way. When he reached the place he took lunch with the family, and when that was over went to his room, expecting to remain there the rest of the afternoon, and without any thought at all of going anywhere.

At about two o'clock he heard a rap at his room door, and on opening it saw standing there Mrs. Surratt with a letter in her hand. Said she, " Mr. Weichmann, I have here a letter from Mr. Calvert, and I find it necessary to go into the country again to see Mr. John K. Nothey. Here are ten dollars. Would you mind hiring a buggy for me, and driving me down." Certainly Weichmann did not mind. He was glad of the chance, as it was his second opportunity in life to handle a horse and a pair of reins. He did not mistrust this woman for a single instant. Putting on his hat he went downstairs, and, just as he opened the front door, there stood John Wilkes Booth with his hand on the front doorbell ready to pull it! Booth extended his hand, exchanged pleasant greetings, and then went into the parlor.

Weichmann hired the horse and buggy, paying six dollars for their use, returning the change to Mrs. Surratt. At the stables he saw Atzerodt. Weichmann asked him what he was doing there, and he said that he was going to take a ride into the country, and that he was trying to get a horse for Payne.

Returning to the house, Weichmann left the horse and buggy in front of the door, and went to his room for some articles of clothing. As he descended and walked past the parlor, he saw Booth and Mrs. Surratt in close conversation. Mrs. Surratt was facing the entry, and Booth had his back to it. In a short time Booth came down the front steps, and, seeing Weichmann at the curb, waved his hand to him in token of adieu. That was the last Weichmann saw of him alive or dead.

Very soon Mrs. Surratt also came down the front steps, and was in the act of getting in the buggy when she said: "Stop! let me get those things of Booth's." She went into the house, and in a short time returned with two packages in her hand, one about six inches in diameter, done up in brown paper, and the other evidently some business papers. Weichmann never saw the contents of either paper. He was under the impression that the package in brown paper contained some articles of glass or china which she was taking to an old colored woman in the country, of whom she was very fond. She said it was glass, but not *a* glass. The contents of that package turned out to be John Wilkes Booth's field-glass.

When about halfway on the road some soldiers were seen to the left, their horses nibbling the grass, and the soldiers lying down, taking their ease. Mrs. Surratt stopped the buggy, and calling an old man to her, evidently a farmer, wanted to know what those soldiers were doing there. He said they were pickets to guard the road. She then wanted to know if they remained there all night. The old man replied that they were generally called in at seven o'clock in the evening. "I am glad to know that," said she, and drove on.

When they arrived at Surrattsville, about four o'clock, Mrs. Surratt got out of the buggy, and Weichmann remained in it, driving around the neighboring roads of the country for a little pleasure. When he returned, Mrs. Surratt rapped at the parlor window and informed him Mr. Nothey was *not* there. This is a most vital point. She had made no arrangements to meet Nothey at all; and he did not know she was there. It was all a blind to deceive Weichmann as to the real nature of her business. She thereupon dictated the following letter to Nothey, which Weichmann wrote at her request:

SURRATTSVILLE, MD., April 14, 1865.
MR. JOHN NOTHEY.

Dear Sir: I have this day received a letter from Mr. Calvert intimating that either you or your friends have reported to him that I am not willing to settle with you for the land.

You know that I am ready, and have been waiting for these last two years; and now, if you do not come within the next ten days, I will settle with Mr. Calvert and bring suit against you immediately.

Mr. Calvert will give you a deed on receiving payment.

M. E. SURRATT,
Administratrix of John H. Surratt.

That letter was one of the chief grounds of defense in Mrs. Surratt's case. On it she relied mainly to prove that her visit to the country on that day was one of strict business; but the scheme and pretense failed. The letter could have been written in her own home, and mailed from there for a three-cent stamp. It was not necessary to go to the country at all at that time for the alleged purpose.

She was anxious to be home at nine o'clock, saying she had made an engagement with a gentleman to meet her at that hour. Weichmann asked her if it was Booth. She made no reply, yes or no. On the return that evening, Weichmann asked her some questions about Booth, saying he appeared to be without employment, and asking her when he was going to act again. " Booth is done acting," she replied, " and is going to New York very soon, never to return." Then turning around and

looking Mr. Weichmann in the face, she continued:
" Yes, and Booth is crazy on one subject, and the next
time I see him I am going to give him a good scolding."

When about a mile from the city, and having from the
top of a hill caught a view of Washington, swimming
in a flood of light, she said, " I am afraid all this rejoicing
will be turned into mourning and all this glory into sad-
ness." Weichmann asked her what she meant, and she
replied that " after sunshine there was always a storm,
and that the people were too proud and licentious, and
that God would punish them."

Just as the carriage drove from New Jersey Avenue
past the Capitol into Pennsylvania Avenue, sounds of
music were heard in the distance, and then a procession
of Arsenal employees was seen passing up Pennsylvania
Avenue in the direction of the White House.

Mrs. Surratt reached home at about half-past eight,
and then the horse and buggy were returned to Howard's
stable.

At tea that evening Mrs. Surratt showed Weichmann
a letter she said she had received from her son John. It
had been brought to the house by Miss Anna Ward, and
not by the letter carrier. It was dated St. Lawrence Hall,
Canada, April 12, 1865. In it he said he was much
pleased with the city of Montreal and with the French
Cathedral; that he had bought a French pea-jacket, for
which he had paid ten dollars in silver; that board was
too high at the hotel, $2.50 per day in gold, and that he
would probably go to some private boarding-house, or
soon go to Toronto.

That letter was also probably a deception. It was
never seen after that.

While yet at supper footsteps were heard coming up
the front steps on the outside, and then the front door-

bell was heard to ring. There was no servant in the house at the time, and Weichmann said to Mrs. Surratt that he would answer the bell, as she must be very tired after her long drive. She, however, said " No," and went to answer it herself. The door was opened, and the footsteps were heard to enter the front parlor. The gentleman whom she had expected at nine o'clock had arrived. He remained several minutes, and then departed.

As soon as Weichmann had finished his supper he went to the parlor. In a short time he noticed that Mrs. Surratt's cheerfulness had left her. Once she asked him which way the torchlight procession was going that they had seen on Pennsylvania Avenue. Weichmann remarked that it was a procession of Arsenal employees who were going to serenade the President. She said she would like to know, as she was very much interested in it. She had a pair of prayer beads in her hands, and once she asked him to pray for her intentions. He answered her by saying he did not know what her intentions were. She then asked him to pray for them, anyhow.

Her nervousness finally increased so much that she in a manner hurried the young ladies, Annie Surratt, Miss Olivia Jenkins, a sister of Mrs. Surratt then on a visit, Miss Fitzpatrick, and himself to their respective rooms.

All dreamless of the terrible tragedy which was about to be enacted at Ford's Theater, Weichmann retired for the night at about a quarter of ten o'clock, without the slightest suspicion of any wrong. He did not even know of the President's visit to the theater, and was sound asleep when the latter was shot.

The next morning, April 15, he, being slightly indisposed, had gone to the yard, returned to his room, and was hardly in bed again when the front doorbell was pulled very violently. Hastily drawing on a pair of trousers, for he was the only man in the house, he ran downstairs and rapped on the inside of the front door. "Who's there?" he asked. "Detectives," was the reply, "come to search the house for John Wilkes Booth and John H. Surratt." "Neither of them are here," said Weichmann. "Let us in, anyhow; we wish to search the house," cried the detectives. "Before doing so, gentlemen, I will have to get the permission of the mistress of the house." Then Weichmann stepped to Mrs. Surratt's door, which was on the same floor and in the rear of the parlor, rapped at it, and said, "Here, Mrs. Surratt, are some detectives who have come to search the house for John Wilkes Booth and your son." "For God's sake!" said she, "let them come in; I expected the house to be searched."

The detectives now entered the house and searched every nook and corner of it, going into the third story where the young ladies were sleeping, looking into the beds, under them, into the closets—everywhere.

Finally they came into Weichmann's room. "Gentlemen," said he, "what do you mean by searching this house so early in the morning?" Then replied John Clarvoe, one of the men: "Do you mean to tell us that you don't know what happened last night?" Weichmann assured him he did not. "Then," said Clarvoe, at the same time bringing forth a piece of black cravat; "I will tell you. Do you see the blood on that?" "Yes," rejoined the young man. "Well," said Clarvoe, "that is Lincoln's blood. John Wilkes Booth has murdered the President, and your friend, John H. Surratt, the Secretary of State."

Here was a tremendous revelation for this man, and it is a wonder that he did not fall to the floor on the reception of such horrible news. His feelings may be better imagined than described. When he had somewhat recovered his equanimity, he told the detectives that they were probably mistaken as to Surratt. "He is not in the city," said he; "I saw a letter from him last night, dated St. Lawrence Hall, Canada, April 12. Gentlemen, Surratt is in Canada."

Weichmann then went with the detectives downstairs into the parlor. Mrs. Surratt was just coming out of her room. "What do you think," said he to Mrs. Surratt; "John Wilkes Booth has murdered the President!" He kept back the name of her son out of respect to her feelings. "My God, Mr. Weichmann! you don't tell me so," was her answer.

The officers now questioned her as to the whereabouts of her son. She stated she had received a letter from him the last evening, and that he was in Canada. James McDevitt, the leader of the party, pressed her very strongly as to the truth of this, and asked her for the letter, but she made no effort to find it. It never was found and produced in open court, as it should have been. Had that been done, it would have settled the fact as to Surratt's whereabouts on the evening of April 14 beyond controversy.

Weichmann told the detectives that he would report at their headquarters on Tenth Street in the morning at eight o'clock, and would assist them to the full extent of his ability in making an investigation. With this assurance the detectives left the house.

Weichmann returned to the parlor and said to those present that he was sorry that these men had come to the house so soon after the murder, and that, in consequence of the continued visits of Booth to the house, the Government would make a strenuous investigation,

and that everybody living in the house would be held
to accountability.

Annie Surratt on hearing this said, "Oh, ma, Mr.
Weichmann is right. Just think of that man Booth having been here an hour before the murder!" Thus the
fact came to the surface that it was Booth who came up
the front stairs while the supper was being served.

"Annie, come what will," Mrs. Surratt replied, "I am
resigned. I think that John Wilkes Booth was only an
instrument in the hands of the Almighty to punish this
proud and licentious people."

Young Weichmann returned to his room, where only
God witnessed the agony he suffered. About six o'clock
he went out and purchased a paper—the *Chronicle*. He
read a full account, and saw that it was indeed Booth
who murdered the President. But what of the man who
assaulted the Secretary of State? Weichmann read the
description of him, and was convinced that it did not
answer that of Surratt, and thus a big load was lifted
from his heart. He now returned to his boarding-house
for his breakfast.

Breakfast over, Weichmann left the house along with
John T. Holohan, and went to police headquarters on
Tenth Street near E. Here for the first time he met
Major A. C. Richards, the Superintendent of Police in
those days for the city of Washington. He remained all
day with the detectives, who made a visit to Maryland,
going through the counties of Prince George and Charles,
and secured little information of any account. That
night he slept on the floor of the station house. The
next day the party went to Baltimore, met Marshal
McPhail, and secured from him a few items of interest,
and then returned to Washington.

It was now determined to make a visit to Canada as

speedily as possible in pursuit of Surratt, and accordingly
the necessary papers were procured from the War Department, as follows:

HEADQUARTERS DEPARTMENT OF WASHINGTON,
WASHINGTON, D. C., April 16, 1865.

SPECIAL ORDERS No. 68.—Extract.

Special Officers James A. McDevitt, George Holohan, and
Louis J. Weichmann are hereby ordered to New York on important Government business, and, after executing their private
orders, to return to this city and report at these headquarters.
The Quartermaster's Department will furnish the necessary
transportation.

By command of Major-General Augur.

T. INGRAHAM,
Colonel and Provost-Marshal-General, Defenses
North of the Potomac.

Official :

G. B. RUSSEL,
Captain and Asst. Prov.-Mar.-Gen'l.,
Defenses North of the Potomac.

McDevitt and his little party reached Montreal on the
20th of April, and went to St. James Hotel for accommodation. They soon ascertained from the register of
St. Lawrence Hall that Surratt had arrived there on the
6th of April, left on the 12th, and returned on the 18th,
again leaving a few hours later on the same day. They
also ascertained that he was seen one day to leave the
house of one Porterfield, an agent for the Confederacy
then residing in Montreal, in company with another man,
both dressed alike, each one taking a separate carriage
and driving in opposite directions. After this all trace of
Surratt was lost by the Government until his identification by Ste. Marie while serving as a zouave in the Papal
army in Italy, in the early part of 1866.

Weichmann now returned to the United States with
Holohan and McDevitt. They reported at the War De-

partment to General Henry L. Burnett, on the afternoon of April 29, making such statements as they were
in possession of at that time, and were then discharged
by order of the Secretary of War. During the night of
April 29 Weichmann slept in a boarding-house about
half a square from the War Department. In the morning
he ate his breakfast with young Ulysses Grant, who sat
at the same table at his right hand. When the meal was
concluded he left the house with Mr. Gilbert Raynor, an
employee of the office of the Commissary-General of
Prisoners, and took a stroll along Pennsylvania Avenue.
When in front of the War Department General Burnett,
the officer to whom he had made his statements the
previous afternoon, came across the street. Weichmann
introduced his friend Raynor to the General, who politely acknowledged it and shook Mr. Raynor warmly
by the hand. Then Burnett grasped Weichmann by
the arm, for he was very glad to see him, and begged
his companion to excuse him.

Burnett now told Weichmann that the Secretary of
War wanted to see him, and in the course of a few minutes he was ushered into the presence of that great and
stern man. General Burnett was present and made notes
of all that was said. Stanton wanted to know how he
had become acquainted with the Surratt family, and had
made his home with them. Weichmann then told him
that it was due to college acquaintance extending as far
back as 1859, and that he did not suspect either Mrs.
Surratt or her son of disloyalty when he went there to
board, and that he had agreed to pay them thirty-five
dollars for his accommodation. Then the Secretary desired to know how and when he had become acquainted
with Booth. Weichmann then related the story of the
introduction by Dr. Mudd, as related in these pages.

Then Stanton said that was, indeed, very important, and bade Burnett be sure to make a note of it. Then he asked a number of questions, subjecting the young man to an interview of about two hours. At its conclusion Mr. Stanton informed him that he would have to hold him in custody until all the circumstances attending the assassination of Mr. Lincoln had been inquired into. Weichmann looked Stanton squarely in the eye and said: "All right, Mr. Stanton; but by the time this investigation is closed, you will find that I have done my whole duty to the Government." "I hope so," said Stanton. This was the first and only time any restraint was put on Weichmann. Before leaving the Secretary he made a plea in Mrs. Surratt's behalf, but the Secretary replied that the law must take its course.

Weichmann was now committed to the care of General Lafayette Baker, and by him was taken in the street cars to the Carroll prison.

During the week which intervened before the great conspiracy trial began, Mr. Weichmann met bravely every test imposed upon him, and answered truthfully every question asked him. His letters which he had kept for seven years had been seized at the Surratt house, when the arresting party had gone there, and every one of them was read by the War Department officials. Pending this investigation he was discharged from his position which he held for a year and a half in the War Department, and his father, although he had voted for Lincoln in 1864, was also discharged from a position which he held in the United States Arsenal at Philadelphia.

Mr. Weichmann met all this adversity in a firm and manly way, feeling that the Government was not to blame for making the inquiry, but that his trouble was all because he had made his home with Mrs. Surratt and her son out of a pure act of kindness and friendship and from a desire to befriend them, and above all to be with the friend of his schoolboy days.

He was called to the witness stand on May 7, and gave the following testimony, which gave Mrs. Surratt the best character of anyone during the trial.

By Reverdy Johnson:

Q. During the whole of that period you never heard him [Booth] intimate that it was his purpose, or that there was a purpose, to assassinate the President?

A. Never, sir.

Q. You never heard him say anything on the subject, or anybody else, during the whole period from November until the assassination?

A. No, sir.

Q. During the whole of that period what was her [Mrs. Surratt's] character?

A. It was excellent; I have known her since 1863.

Q. During the whole of that time, as far as you could judge, was her character good and amiable?

A. Her character was exemplary and ladylike in every particular.

Q. Then, if I understand you, from November up to the 14th of April, whenever she was here, she was regular in her attendance at her own church, and apparently, as far as you could judge, doing all her duties to God and to man?

A. Yes, sir.

By Ekin:

Q. You were not suspicious of anything of the sort?

A. I would have been the last man in the world to suspect John Surratt, my schoolmate, of the murder of the President of the United States.

He was cross-examined by the seven very able lawyers for the defense, but was in no wise shaken in what he said. On cross-examination he gave Mrs. Surratt the best character of any witness on the stand, and in his testimony he did not say one word of a compromising character or nature against her.

But his testimony more than that of anyone in the case was mainly relied on to establish what is known as a *prima facie* conspiracy.

Judge Bingham said of Weichmann, in his great and closing argument, that the defense had not contradicted a single fact to which he testified, nor had they found a breath of suspicion against his character.

Mr. Weichmann was subsequently reinstated in the Government service, in the Custom House at Philadelphia, which he retained for many years, and resigned on October 1, 1886.

He won by his conduct the personal respect of Stanton, Holt, Bingham, and Burnett, and enjoyed the confidence and best wishes of every member of the Commission.

Perhaps a better conclusion cannot be made of this sketch than by giving extracts from several letters which Mr. Weichmann has already been compelled to make public:

Of him Major Richards says:

EUSTIS, FLA., December 20, 1898.

Mr. L. J. WEICHMANN.

My Dear Sir: I have your letter of December 15, 1898, and in reply I take much pleasure in giving you the information you desire.

You did report to me about eight o'clock on the morning of April 15, 1865, and communicated to me such facts as had come to your knowledge at that time. You acted as special officer with my men, going with them to lower Maryland, Baltimore, and finally to Canada, in pursuit of some of the alleged guilty parties.

In no instance was any statement made by you in relation to the conspiracy found to be false or incorrect, and very many of your assertions were subsequently corroborated by undoubted testimony of which you did not know the existence. No threats or undue influence of any kind were resorted to by any of us to control your actions.

You performed a manly part all the way through, and did your duty in such a manner as to win the admiration of all lovers of the truth.

Let me add that the fact that you were a boarder at Mrs. Surratt's house may have been to you the cause of much personal sacrifice in your worldly prospects, and of much suffering, but for the sake of justice and in behalf of the murdered Lincoln, I deem it a most fortunate event that you were there.

Respectfully yours,

A. C. RICHARDS.

And General Burnett has this to offer:

CINCINNATI, OHIO, January 27, 1867.

There is but one criterion, Weichmann, for any witness, or indeed for any man in any circumstance in life, and that is when stating or relating anything, let that statement be purely the truth; let it then be given fearlessly and faithfully. Truth is ever consistent. It conflicts only with that which is untrue and false in the world. The man who worships at the shrine of truth will triumph in the world; in the end he will put his enemies under his feet.

I reciprocate your expressions of kind feelings. I have always believed that in that trial of Mr. Lincoln's assassins you enacted an honorable and truthful part, and did our struggling country great service.

Yours truly,

H. L. BURNETT.

Mr. Weichmann was also a witness at the trial of John H. Surratt in 1867, and virtually repeated his testimony of 1865.

Probably no one has suffered more persecution and misrepresentation because of his testimony and his duty to the Government at the trial of the conspirators than has Mr. Weichmann. It has been almost continuous, and has been done for the purpose of striking him down and disparaging him before the country, so that the people who were in sympathy with the conspirators could claim that the Commission was wrong in its verdict of 1865 in regard to, at least, one of the parties accused.

It was Mr. Weichmann's intention to have resigned his position under the Government on the 1st of July, 1865, and after a few months' vacation to enter St. Mary's Seminary at Baltimore, Md., for the purpose of continuing his studies for the Catholic priesthood. He had visited Baltimore in consequence of a letter received from the Catholic bishop of Richmond, Va., in the latter part of January, 1865, and had made arrangements with the president of the seminary to that end.

In the meantime the terrible tragedy of the 14th of April occurred, and because of the stand taken by him for the Government, Mr. Weichmann was not able to complete his studies, but was compelled to work out his destiny in another field in life. In this he was most nobly helped by Secretary Stanton and Judge Holt.

CHAPTER X.

Mr. John M. Lloyd, who kept Mrs. Surratt's tavern at Surrattsville, testified during the trial that some five or six weeks before the assassination John H. Surratt, David E. Herold, and George A. Atzerodt came to his house. He said: " Atzerodt and Surratt first drove up to my house in the morning, and went toward T. B., a post-office about five miles below here. They had not been gone more than half an hour when they returned with Herold. All three, when they came into the bar-room, drank, I think. John Surratt then called me into the front parlor, where on the sofa were two carbines with ammunition, also a rope from sixteen to twenty feet in length, and a monkey-wrench. Surratt asked me to take care of these things, and to conceal the carbines. I told him there was no place to conceal them, and I did not wish to keep such things. He then took me into a room I had never been in, immediately above the store room, in the back part of the building. He showed me where I could put the articles underneath the joists of the second floor of the main building. I put them there according to his directions. Surratt said he just wanted them to stay for a few days, and he would call for them. On the Tuesday before the assassination of the President I was coming to Washington, and met Mrs. Surratt on the road at Uniontown [Anacostia]. When she first broached the subject to me about the articles at my place,

I did not know what she had reference to. Then she came out plainer, and asked me about the 'shooting-irons.' I had myself forgotten about their being there. I told her they were hid away far back, and that I was afraid the house might be searched. She told me to get them out ready; that they would be wanted soon. I do not recollect distinctly the first question she put to me. Her language was indistinct, as if she wanted to draw my attention to something, so that no one else would understand. Finally she expressed herself more plainly, and said they would be wanted soon. I told her that I had an idea of having them buried; that I was very uneasy about having them there. On the 14th of April I went to Marlboro to attend a trial, and in the evening when I got home, which I should judge was about five o'clock, I found Mrs. Surratt there. She met me out by the wood-pile as I drove in with some fish and oysters in my buggy. She told me to have those shooting-irons ready that night, there would be some parties who would call for them. She gave me something wrapped in a piece of paper, which I took upstairs and found to be a field-glass. She told me to get two bottles of whisky ready, and that these things were to be called for that night. Just about midnight on Friday Herold came into the house and said, 'Lloyd, for God's sake, make haste and get those things!' I did not make any reply, but went straight and got the carbines, supposing they were the parties Mrs. Surratt had referred to, though she didn't mention any names. From the way he spoke he must have been apprised that I already knew what I was to give him. Mrs. Surratt told me to give the carbines, whisky, and field-glass. I did not give them the rope and monkey-wrench. Booth didn't come in. I did not know him; he was a stranger to me. He remained on his horse. Herold took a bottle of whisky out to Booth, and he drank while mounted. Herold, I think, drank some out of the glass before he went out. I do not think he remained over five minutes. They only took one of the carbines. Booth said he could not take his, because his leg was broken. Just as they were about leaving, the man who was with Herold said: 'I will tell you some news, if you want to hear it,' or something to that effect. I said, 'I am not particular; use your own pleasure about telling it.' 'Well,' he said, 'I am pretty certain that we have assassinated the President and Secretary Seward.' I think that was his language, as well as I can recollect. Whether Herold was present at the time he said that, or whether he was across the street, I am not positive; I was much excited and unnerved at the time. When Herold brought back the bottle from which Booth had drunk the whisky, he remarked to me: 'I owe you a couple of dollars,' and said he: 'Here.' With that he offered me a note, which next morning I found to be one dollar, which about paid for the bottle of liquor they had just pretty nearly drunk. When Booth and Herold left my house they took the road toward T. B., and rode off at a pretty rapid gait."

Mr. Holohan boarded with Mrs. Surratt during the winter and spring and up to the night of the assassination. While there he said that he saw Atzerodt several times, and Payne once at breakfast. Atzerodt seemed to be with John Surratt most of the time. John Wilkes Booth he saw quite frequently with Mrs. Surratt and the ladies in the parlor.

Mr. E. L. Smoot, residing a mile from Surrattsville, testified that on the day after the assassination he met two young men at Surrattsville, and one of them said that John H. Surratt was supposed to be the man who attempted to kill Mr. Seward. The question was asked Mr. Joseph T. Nott, the bartender at the Surratt tavern, if he could tell where John Surratt was. He smiled and said: " I reckon John is in New York by this time." He was asked why he thought so, when he replied: " My God! John knows all about the murder; do you suppose he is going to stay in Washington and let them catch him? I could have told you six months ago this was coming to pass." He put his hand on the shoulder of Mr. Smoot and said: " Keep that in your own skin, my boy. Don't mention that; if you do, it will ruin me forever."

On the morning of the 6th of July the findings of the court, approved by the President, were made public. That morning about nine o'clock General Hartranft, accompanied by the judges of the court and the officers of the prison, went to the cell of each prisoner and read the verdict to him. The four who were condemned—Herold, Payne, Atzerodt, and Mrs. Surratt— were very much affected. The condemned prisoners were taken from their cells and placed in a large room on the ground floor, and their friends and spiritual advisers were allowed to see them. The sight of the seven sisters of Herold weeping around him was affecting to the officers and guards to the last degree.

George Alfred Townsend, a special correspondent, representing the New York *World* at the execution, gave a conscientiously written statement of the penalty paid by the four for the part they took in the great conspiracy, which is as follows:

" I entered a large, grassy yard, surrounded by an exceedingly high wall. On the top of this wall soldiers, with muskets in their hands, were thickly planted. The yard below was broken by irregular buildings of brick. I climbed by a flight of outside stairs to the central building, where many officers were seated at the windows, and looked a while at the strange scene on the grassy plaza. On the left the long, barred, impregnable penitentiary rose. The shady spots beneath it were occupied by huddling spectators. Soldiers were filling their canteens at the pumps. A face or two looked out from the barred jail. The north side of the yard was enclosed on three sides by columns of soldiers drawn up in regular order, the side next to the penitentiary being short to admit of ingress to the prisoners' door; but the opposite column reached entirely up to the north wall. The gallows consisted of a beam resting horizontally in the air, twenty feet from the ground. Four ropes at irregular intervals dangled from it, each noosed at the end. It was upheld by three props, one in the center and one at each end. These props came all the way to the ground, where they were mortised in heavy bars. Midway of them a floor was laid, twenty by twelve feet, held in its position on the farther side by shorter props, of which there were many, and reached by fifteen steps, railed on either side. This floor had no supports on the side nearest the eye, except two temporary rods, at the foot of which two inclined beams pointed menacingly, held in poise by ropes from the gallows floor. Two hinges only held the floor to its firmer half. These were to give way at the fatal moment.

" The traps were two, sustained by two different props. The nooses were on each side of the central support. Close by the foot of the gallows four wooden boxes were at the edge of four newly excavated graves, the fresh earth of which was already dried and brittle in the burning sun.   In these boxes and pits were to be placed the victims when the gallows had let them down.   Not far from these, in silence and darkness beneath the prison

Lt.-Col. G. W. Frederick.   Lt. G. W. Geissinger.   Surg. G. L. Porter.

General John F. Hartranft.
Capt. A. R. Watts.   Lt.-Col. W. H. McCall.   Col. L. A. Dodd.   Capt. C. Roth.

GENERAL JOHN F. HARTRANFT AND STAFF, IN CHARGE OF THE EXECUTION OF THE CONSPIRATORS.

where they had lain so long and so forebodingly, the body of John Wilkes Booth, sealed up in the brick floor, had been moldering.   If the dead can hear, he had listened many a time to the rattle of their manacles upon the stairs; to the drowsy hum of the trial and the buzz of the garrulous spectators; to the moaning or the gibing or the praying in the bolted cells where those whom

kindred fate had given a little lease upon life lay waiting for the terrible pronouncement. The sentence gave
them only till two o'clock, and it was near that time,
when suddenly the wicket opens, the troops spring to
their feet and stand at order arms, the flags go up, the
low order passes from company to company; the spectators huddle a little nearer to the scaffold; all the writers
for the press produce their pencils and notebooks.

" First came a middle-aged woman dressed in black,
bonneted and veiled, walking between two bareheaded
priests. One of these held against his breast a crucifix
of jet, and in the folds of his blue-fringed sash he carried an open breviary, while both of them muttered the
service of the dead. Four soldiers, with muskets at
shoulder, followed, and a captain led the way to the
gallows.

" The second party escorted a small and shambling
German, whose head had a long white cap upon it, rendering more filthy his dull complexion, and upon whose
feet the chains clanked as he slowly advanced, preceded
by two officers, flanked by a Lutheran clergyman, and
followed, as his predecessor, by an armed squad.

" The third preacher and party clustered about a
shabby boy, whose limbs tottered as he progressed.

" The fourth walked in, the shadow of a straight high
statue, whose tawny hair and large blue eyes were suggestive rather of the barbarian striding in in his con-
queror's triumph than the assassin going to the gallows.
All these, captives, priests, guards, and officers, nearly
twenty in all, climbed slowly and solemnly the narrow
steps; and upon four armchairs, stretching across the
stage in the rear of the traps, the condemned were seated
with their spiritual attendants behind them.

" The findings and warrants were immediately read

to the prisoners by General Hartranft in a quiet and respectful tone, an aid holding an umbrella over him. Mrs. Surratt was placed on the right, and the nearest to her was Payne, followed by Herold and Atzerodt. At first Mrs. Surratt was very feeble, and leaned her head upon alternate sides of her armchair in nervous spasms; but now and then, when a sort of wail just issued from her lips, the priest placed before her the crucifix to lull her fearful spirit. All the while the good Fathers Wigett and Walter murmured their low, tender cadences, and now and then the woman's face lost its deadly fear, and took a bold, cognizable survey of the spectators. She wore a robe of dark woolen, no collar, and common shoes of black listing. Her general expression was that of acute suffering, vanishing at times as if by the conjuration of her pride, and again returning in a paroxysm, as she looked at the dreadful rope dangling before her.

"Payne, the strongest criminal in our history, was alone dignified and self-possessed. He wore a closely fitting knit shirt, a sailor's straw hat tied with a ribbon, and dark pantaloons, but no shoes. His collar, cut very low, showed the tremendous muscularity of his neck, and the breadth of his breast was more conspicuous by the manner in which the pinioned arms thrust it forward. His height, his vigor, his glare, made him the strong central figure of the tableau. He looked at death as for one long expected, and not a tremor nor a shock stirred his long, stately limbs; and he died without taking the hand of any living friend.

"Herold, the third condemned, although whimper· ing, had far more grit than I anticipated; he was inquisitive and flippant-faced, and looked at the noose flaunting before him and at the people gathered below. Atzerodt wore a grayish coat, black vest, light pantaloons and slippers, and a white affair on his head, perhaps a handkerchief. He was visited by his mother and a poor ignorant woman with whom he cohabited. He was the picture of despair, and died ridiculously, whistling up his courage.

" When General Hartranft ceased reading, there was

VIEW OF THE SCAFFOLD WHILE THE OFFICERS ARE ADJUSTING THE
NOOSES AROUND THE NECKS OF THE CONDEMNED.

a momentary lull, broken only by the cadences of the priests.

" The Rev. Mr. Gillette addressed the spectators in a deep, impressive tone. The prisoner Payne requested him to thus publicly and sincerely return his thanks to General Hartranft, the other officers, the soldiers, and all persons who had charge of him and had attended him. Dr. Gillette then followed in a fervent prayer in behalf of the prisoners, during which Payne's eyes momentarily filled with tears, and he followed in the prayer with visible feeling.

" Rev. Dr. Olds followed, saying in behalf of the prisoner, David E. Herold, that he tendered his forgiveness to all who had wronged him, and asked the forgiveness of all whom he had wronged. He gave his thanks to the officers and guards for kindnesses rendered him. He hoped that he died in charity with all men and at peace with God. Dr. Olds concluded with a feeling prayer for the prisoner.

" Rev. Dr. Butler then made a similar return of thanks on behalf of George A. Atzerodt for kindness received from his guards and attendants, and concluded with an earnest invocation in behalf of the criminal, saying that the blood of Jesus Christ cleanses from all sin, and asking that God Almighty have mercy upon this man. The two holy fathers having received Mrs. Surratt's confession, after the custom of their creed, observed silence. In this, as in other respects, Mrs. Surratt's last hours were entirely modest and womanly. The stage was still filled with people; the crisis of the occasion had come; the chairs were all withdrawn, and the condemned stood upon their feet, and the process of tying the limbs began.

" It was with a shudder, almost a blush, that I saw an officer gather the ropes tightly three times about the robes of Mrs. Surratt, and bind her ankles with cords. She half fainted, and sank backward upon the attendants, her limbs yielding to the extremity of her terror, but uttering no cry. Payne, with his feet firmly laced together, stood straight as one of the scaffold beams, and braced himself up so stoutly that this in part prevented

the breaking of his neck. Herold stood well beneath
the drop, still whimpering at the lips. Atzerodt, in his

VIEW OF THE SCAFFOLD AFTER THE TRAP WAS SPRUNG.

Captain C. Roth, the executioner, is still living, and says: "I received
orders from General John F. Hartranft to execute Mrs. Surratt, Payne,
Herold, and Atzerodt. The orders were that the execution should take
place at one o'clock, July 7, or as soon thereafter as circumstances would
permit. It did not come off as early as was expected, from the fact that
General Hancock, whose presence was necessary, failed to appear. It was
stated that Mrs. Surratt's counsel undertook to stop the execution by having
Hancock arrested. I saw the gallows built and secured the rope, which was
a three-ply Boston hemp, from the Navy Yard. I made the nooses and
placed them on the beam, saw them adjusted on the victims, then stepped
aside and gave the signal to the men underneath the gallows to spring the
traps. A short time afterward the bodies were taken down and buried."

groveling attitude, while they tied him, began to indulge
in his old vice of gabbing. Again, when the white death-
cap was drawn over his face, he continued to cry out

under it, saying: ' Good-by, shentlemens who is before me now,' and again, ' May we meet in the other world; God help me.' Herold protested against the knot, it being as huge as one's double fist. Mrs. Surratt asked to be supported, that she might not fall. When the death-caps were all drawn over the faces of the prisoners, and they stood in line in the awful suspense between absolute life and immediate death, an officer signaled the executioners, and the great beams were darted against the props simultaneously. The two traps fell with a slam, the four bodies dropped like a single thing. The bodies were allowed to hang about twenty minutes, when Surgeon Otis, U. S. V., and Assistant Surgeons Woodward and Porter, U. S. A., examined them and pronounced all dead.

" In about ten minutes more a ladder was placed against the scaffold and the bodies were cut down and given over to a squad of soldiers, who placed them in plain pine boxes, and lowered them in the graves prepared for them." *

In the minds of many the burial of John Wilkes Booth is yet an unsolved mystery. An illustrated paper, in its first issue after his death, gave a picture of two men throwing his body from a rowboat into the Potomac River. The truth of the matter is, that the body was first buried in a pine gunbox in one of the cells of the

* It has been said, and very generally believed, that the conspirators were all, or nearly so, Catholics; but such was not the case. Of the ten, four were of that faith—Mrs. Surratt, her son, John H. Surratt, Dr. Mudd, and Michael O'Laughlin. Mrs. Surratt was a convert from the Protestant faith. Her husband at one time was a member of the Episcopal Church at Surrattsville. Booth and Herold were Episcopalians, Payne a Baptist and a son of a Baptist minister; Atzerodt claimed to be a Lutheran, and Arnold was a Protestant.

BOOTH LOT IN GREEN MOUNT CEMETERY, BALTIMORE, MD.

The body of J. Wilkes Booth was transferred from the Arsenal grounds, Washington, March, 1869. The monument faces west, and on the east side, close to the monument, beneath the clump of ivy, the remains of J. Wilkes Booth are buried.

old penitentiary in the Arsenal grounds, where it remained until 1867, when the main part of the building was torn down. The body was then removed, with the four that had been executed, to one of the large storehouses situated on the eastern side of the grounds, and there it remained until February, 1869, when President Johnson gave Edwin Booth permission to remove it to Baltimore, Md., where it now reposes in the Booth lot in Greenmount Cemetery. Edwin Booth, after securing the approval of President Johnson for its removal, gave instructions to Mr. J. H. Weaver, an undertaker of Baltimore, to perform that work. Mr. Weaver called to his assistance Harvey & Marr, undertakers, of Washington, who went to the Arsenal grounds and exhumed the remains. Edwin Booth accompanied Mr. Weaver from Baltimore, and with Mr. Harvey went to the Arsenal grounds. Mr. W. R. Speare, the present undertaker, at No. 940 F Street, who was then a boy in the employ of Harvey & Marr, drove the furniture wagon that brought the remains of Booth to the alley in the rear of Ford's Theater, almost to the very door from which he started on the night of April 14, 1865. The wagon backed up to the door of the stable that Booth had formerly used. The box was somewhat decayed, but the lettering on it was legible. When the box was opened and the body taken from the blanket which was wrapped around it, it was found that four years' burial had brought it to decay. The skull was detached, and, when lifted out, a dentist, who had filled Booth's teeth, identified his work, thus proving the identity of the body beyond a doubt. The hair was in its natural state, and hung in long ringlets. A report was made to Edwin Booth, who was in the front office, and who, when informed of the examination, expressed his satisfaction, and

then directed Mr. Weaver to take the body to Baltimore.
A plain coffin was taken out to the stable, the contents
of the box placed in it, and the remains driven to the

— OFFICE OF —

SUP'T GREEN MOUNT CEMETERY,

Baltimore, May 25 1892

The remains of J. Wilkes
Booth were interred in this
Cemetery in February or
March 1869. Being brought
form Washinton. D. C. —
By Jno. H Weaver Undertaker
Since Deceased.
Alex Russell
Foreman

LETTER FROM SUPERINTENDENT OF GREEN MOUNT
CEMETERY.

Baltimore & Ohio train for Baltimore. The bodies of
the conspirators that were executed in the Arsenal
grounds were delivered to their friends and given Chris-
tian burial. The remains of Mrs. Surratt were taken
from the Arsenal grounds to Mount Olivet (Catholic)
Cemetery, northeast of the city, where the pine gunbox
in which she was buried was exchanged for an appropriate casket. A modest headstone bearing only the
name, "Mrs. Surratt," was placed at the grave. Herold
was buried at the Congressional Cemetery, on the banks
of the eastern branch of the Potomac, east of the city;
and Atzerodt sleeps at Glenwood Cemetery, a mile north

of the Capitol. The remains of Payne were buried in Holmead Cemetery, in the northwest part of the city, but in after years were exhumed, as the cemetery was discontinued. The body of Captain Wirz, who was hanged in the Old Capitol Prison, Washington, D. C., for his inhuman treatment of soldiers at Andersonville, lay fifth in a fearful row of graves,—Mrs. Surratt, Payne, Herold, Atzerodt, and Wirz,—but was removed to Mount Olivet at the same time that the others were. Dr. Mudd sleeps in the Catholic Cemetery of St. Mary's Church, near Bryantown, and Spangler died at Dr. Mudd's, February 27, 1875, and was buried in the graveyard connected with St. Peter's Church, within two miles of Dr. Mudd's house. Michael O'Laughlin died of yellow fever while serving his life sentence at Dry Tortugas, Fla., September 23, 1867. President Johnson issued an order February 13, 1869, that the remains of O'Laughlin be delivered to his mother, and they were brought north from Dry Tortugas. Samuel A. Arnold is buried near Baltimore, Md. John H. Surratt, the only one left out of the ten conspirators, is living in Baltimore, Md., engaged as auditor for the Old Bay Line Steamship Company.

CHAPTER XI.

THERE were numerous attempts upon the life of President Lincoln during his Presidential term. It was the purpose of the conspirators to kidnap and hold him in captivity, without injury to his person, until such concessions were made to the Southern leaders as their plan of compromise rendered necessary. The various schemes of abduction having proved futile, some of the more desperate among the conspirators, exasperated by these repeated failures, resolved to dispose of Mr. Lincoln by the dagger or the bullet.

On the occasion of his elevation to the Presidency of the United States, a conspiracy against his life was formed, and followed him from the quiet of his home at Springfield, Ill., to the capital of the nation, and sought in various ways to encompass his assassination; and though various attempts upon his life were made, his spirit never appears to have been embittered in the least against his enemies. Not the least shade of vindictiveness is discernible. Malice seems to have had no place in his nature. As early as the month of January, 1861, knowledge was had that threats were made to assassinate Mr. Lincoln when on his way from his home to Washington. As the time grew near for his departure, the plot thickened, and news reached Washington that another was being formed in Baltimore, and that threats had been made that he should not be inaugurated. Detectives were sent to that city, and it was soon found that such a plot was in existence. The plan was to break or burn one of the bridges north of Baltimore, at the time of Mr. Lincoln's anticipated approach, and, in the confusion of the accidental stoppage of the train, to assassinate him in the cars. The intended route of the President from Illinois to Washington being published, they knew at just what time the train would pass through Baltimore.

Mr. Lincoln's own statement as to his fear of assassination in passing through Baltimore is given, and fully proves the fact that there was a conspiracy to do him harm. He says: " Mr. Norman B. Judd, a warm personal friend from Chicago, sent for me to come to his room (at the Continental Hotel, Philadelphia, February 21). I went, and found there Mr. Allan Pinkerton, a skillful police detective, also from Chicago, who had been employed for some days in Baltimore, watching or searching for suspicious persons there. Pinkerton informed me that a plan had been laid for my assassination, the exact time when I expected to go through Baltimore being publicly known. He was well informed as to the plan, but did not know the conspirators would have pluck enough to execute it. He urged me to go right through with him to Washington that night. I didn't like that. I had made engagements to visit Harrisburg, and to go from there to Baltimore, and I resolved to do so. I could not believe that there was a plot to murder me. I made arrangements, however, with Mr. Judd for my return to Philadelphia the next night, if I should be convinced that there was danger in going through Baltimore. I told him that if I should meet at Harrisburg, as I had at other places, a delegation to go with me to the next place [Baltimore], I should feel safe, and go on.

"When I was making my way back to my room through crowds of people, I met Frederick Seward. We went together to my room, when he told me that he had been sent, at the instance of his father and General Scott, to inform me that their detectives in Baltimore had discovered a plot there to assassinate me. *They knew nothing of Mr. Pinkerton's movements.* I now believe such a plot to be in existence."

Mr. Pinkerton was engaged in the service of the Philadelphia, Wilmington & Baltimore Railroad in February, 1861, to discover the plot and plans of those persons contemplating the destruction of any portion of this great link between New York and the capital at Washington. While in Baltimore with his corps of detectives he acquired the knowledge that a plot was in existence for the assassination of Mr. Lincoln on his passage through Baltimore to Washington to be inaugurated as President.

It was the advice of Mr. Lincoln's friends that he should go to Washington from Philadelphia on the night of the 21st, and, when it was suggested to him, he said: "I cannot go to-night. I have promised to raise the flag over Independence Hall to-morrow morning, and to visit the legislature at Harrisburg. Beyond that I have no engagements. Any plan that may be adopted that will enable me to fulfill these two promises I will carry out, and you can tell me what is concluded upon to-morrow."

He did carry out his two promises, and on the morning of February 22 he raised a new flag over Independence Hall, and then proceeded to Harrisburg.

Mr. Lincoln, in company with Mr. Ward H. Lamon and several officials of the railroad, left Harrisburg between 5 and 6 P. M., February 22, on the return trip to Philadelphia. The Pennsylvania Railroad train consisted of a locomotive and one passenger car. The lamps of the car were not lighted, and the train reached West Philadelphia between ten and eleven, where a carriage was in waiting to convey the President to the depot of the Philadelphia, Wilmington & Baltimore Railroad. Mr. Lincoln wore a light felt hat, and had a gentleman's shawl thrown over his shoulders.* He entered the sleeping car, and the train left at 10.55, reaching Washington the following morning.

Mr. John W. Nichols, a member of Company K, 105th Pennsylvania Volunteers, gives an interesting incident that happened in August, 1864. He was stationed about the middle of that month as a sentinel at the large gate to the Soldiers' Home grounds. The President and his family spent the summer months there. About eleven o'clock he heard a rifle-shot, and shortly afterward Mr. Lincoln dashed up to the gate on horseback, bareheaded, and as he dismounted he said, referring to the horse: " He came pretty near getting away with me, didn't he? He got the bit in his teeth before I could draw the rein." Mr. Nichols asked him where his hat was, and he replied that someone had fired a gun off at the foot of the hill, and that his horse had become scared and jerked his hat off. A corporal accompanied Mr. Nichols down the hill and found the President's hat, returning it to him the next morning. Mr. Lincoln remarked rather unconcernedly that it was some foolish gunner, and requested that the matter be kept quiet. Mr. Nichols felt confident that it was an attempt to kill him.

Previous to the second inauguration of Lincoln rumors were in circulation that he would never be inaug-

* Heavy shawls were worn at that time by many men.

urated. Not much attention was paid to these threats, except that more vigilance was exercised by the police authorities of the capital for the better protection of the person of the President. Great throngs had assembled in Washington to witness the imposing ceremonies attending the second inauguration. A tragedy was planned for this occasion, and the man to perform it was John Wilkes Booth, proofs of which are given in a dozen or more affidavits which form a part of the " Oldroyd Lincoln Memorial Collection."

When the Presidential procession was formed in the Senate chamber, the line of march through the rotunda to the portico, where the inaugural ceremonies were to occur, was flanked by the members of the Capitol police to prevent confusion during the ceremonies. A large number of persons had gained access to the rotunda, but were prevented by the police from joining the procession or reaching the outer door. One man (subsequently learned to be John Wilkes Booth), however, persisted in forcing his way through the ranks against the earnest endeavors of John W. Westfall, one of the policemen on guard here, who, grasping the man, called for assistance, at the same time shouting to the doorkeeper, " Shut that door! " This was at once done, and the procession stopped until the officers, after a severe struggle, overcame the intruder, and placed him in custody below stairs in the guardroom, from whence he was released after the ceremonies of the day were over. It is amazing that any human being could have seriously entertained the thought of assassinating the President in the presence of such a vast assembly. Booth was so frenzied over the repeated failures of his abduction schemes that he determined to take the President's life at the almost certain sacrifice of his own, for, had he been successful, the infuriated people would have instantly avenged the death of Lincoln by a summary and instantaneous visitation of angry judgment. By the brave act of Mr. Westfall the President's life was probably saved, and he was permitted to see the close of the war and dawn of peace. The persons who stopped Booth on that day were not aware who the persistent intruder was, and nothing more was thought of the matter until after the assassination, when a photograph of Booth was shown the Capitol police, and it was at once recognized by Mr. Westfall and others of the force who were engaged in the *mêlée* as that of the man who had forced his way through their ranks on the day of the inauguration.

The Hon. B. B. French, then Commissioner of Public Buildings and Grounds, called the attention of Acting Vice-President Foster and Speaker Colfax to Westfall's great public service, and they immediately authorized the creation of the office of Lieutenant of Police, that he might be the honored incumbent of the place and enjoy the comfort which the increased salary would confer. Did this faithful man enjoy the emoluments of his office during his life? No. The captain of the Capitol Police was informed on the 15th of February, 1876— ten years after Mr. Westfall's commission was signed— that, at a meeting of the Sergeant-at-Arms of the Senate and the Sergeant-at-Arms of the House of Representatives and the Architect of the Capitol, it was ordered that the term of service of J. W. Westfall, lieutenant, should expire on the 1st day of March, 1876. This faithful servant was discharged, and, being too modest and self-respecting to complain, spent his declining years as a watchman in the National Museum, at a salary of fifty dollars per month.

On one occasion General Lafayette C. Baker, chief of

the National Detective Police, carried to Mr. Lincoln two anonymous communications, in which he was threatened with assassination. In a laughing, joking manner the President remarked, " Well, Mr. Baker, what do they want to kill me for? If they kill me, they will run the risk of getting a worse man."

ONE MILLION DOLLARS WANTED, TO HAVE PEACE BY THE FIRST OF MARCH.

If the citizens of the Southern Confederacy *will* furnish me with the cash, or good securities for the same, One Million Dollars, I will cause the lives of Abraham Lincoln, Wm. H. Seward, and Andrew Johnson to be taken by the 1st of March next. This will give us peace, and satisfy the world that cruel tyrants cannot live in a land of liberty. If this is not accomplished, nothing will be claimed beyond the sum of fifty thousand dollars, in advance, which is supposed to be necessary to reach and slaughter the villains. I will give, myself, one thousand dollars toward this patriotic purpose. Everyone wishing to contribute will address Box X, Cahawba, Alabama

December 1, 1864.   .

The above advertisement was published in the Selma (Ala.) *Dispatch* four or five times, and, according to the testimony of John Cantlin, who was foreman of the paper at the time, the author of the manuscript was a Mr. G. W. Gayle of Cahawba, Ala.

While at Andersonville some of the Northern prisoners heard the officers of the prison who were in charge say that if Mr. Lincoln was re-elected he would not live to be inaugurated. They said that a party at the North would attend to the matter.

Mr. Richard Montgomery gave some damaging testimony on the trial, implicating a number of Confederates in Canada. He visited Canada during the summer of 1864, remaining there the greater part of the time until the 1st of April, 1865. He personally knew George N. Sanders, Jacob Thompson, Clement C. Clay, Professor Holcomb, Beverly Tucker, and W. C. Cleary, and frequently met them. In a conversation with Jacob Thompson in the summer of 1864, the latter said he had friends (Confederates) all over the Northern States, who were ready and willing to go any length to serve the cause of the South; that he could at any time have the tyrant Lincoln, and any of his advisers that he chose, put out of his way—and not consider it a crime when done for the cause of the Confederacy. Mr. Montgomery repeated this conversation to Mr. Clay, and he said, " That is so; we are all devoted to our cause, and ready to go any length—to do anything under the sun to serve our cause." In January, 1865, he again met Jacob Thompson in Montreal several times, and in one of the conversations Thompson said that a proposition had been made to him to rid the world of the tyrants Lincoln, Stanton, Grant, and some others. The men who had made the proposition he said he knew were bold, daring men, and able to execute anything they would undertake, without regard to the cost. He said he was in favor of the proposition, but had determined to defer his answer until he consulted with his Government at Richmond, and he was then only waiting its approval. He added that he thought it would be a blessing to the people, both North and South, to have these men killed.

Mr. Montgomery met Payne on several occasions at Niagara Falls and in Canada. Once, in conversation with Mr. Clay, Payne hesitated in telling Montgomery who he was, but finally said that he was a Canadian. Montgomery afterward asked Clay who this man Payne was, and Clay asked: " What did he say? " When told that he said he was a Canadian, Clay laughed and said:

" That is so; he is a Canadian." And he added, " We trust him."

Montgomery was in Canada when arrangements were made to fire the city of New York. He immediately left Canada and carried the news to Washington, as he did of the intended raids upon Buffalo and Rochester, and by this means prevented these several disasters. He also knew of the St. Albans raid, but not the precise point aimed at. Every move received the direct indorsement of Clement C. Clay. The raid on St. Albans, Vt., was made by about twenty-five Confederate soldiers, in October, 1864. They were nearly all of them escaped prisoners, led by Lieutenant Bennett H. Young, a Confederate. While their attempt to burn the town was a failure, they succeeded in robbing three banks to the amount, in the aggregate, of two hundred thousand dollars. They were arrested in Canada by United States forces, but the sympathies of nine-tenths of the Canadians were with Young and his men, and the Canadian Government refused extradition.

In a conversation that Montgomery had with W. C. Cleary, who was a sort of confidential secretary to Mr. Thompson, he said that Booth had been there visiting Thompson twice in the winter; he thought the last time was in December. When Thompson spoke to Montgomery in January, 1865, of the assassination, he said he was in favor of the proposition that had been made to him to put the President, Mr. Stanton, General Grant, and others out of the way; but had deferred giving his answer, as stated above, until he had consulted with and obtained the approval of his Government at Richmond. Montgomery did not know, of his own knowledge, that an answer had been returned, but his impression was, from the remarks of Beverly Tucker, that an answer and approval had been received. During Montgomery's stay in Canada he was in the service of the United States Government, seeking to acquire information in regard to the plans and purposes of the rebels who were assembled there. He adopted the name of James Thompson, and, leading the Confederates to suppose this was his correct name, he made use of another name at the hotel at which he might be stopping. He was intrusted with dispatches from the Confederates in Canada to take to Richmond, and carried back the replies to Canada, taking them both ways through Washington, and making them known to the United States Government. These Confederates in Canada represented themselves as being in the service of the Confederate Government, and Montgomery frequently heard the subject of raids upon our frontier and the burning of cities spoken of by Thompson, Clay, Cleary, Tucker, and Sanders. Clay and Thompson represented themselves as acting under the sanction of their Government, and as having full power from it to do anything that they deemed expedient for the benefit of their cause. Mr. Clay, in speaking about the necessary funds for these raids, said he always had plenty of money to pay for anything that was worth paying for.

During the trial strong evidence against Jefferson Davis and the agents of the Southern Confederacy was presented. One of the principal witnesses was Sanford Conover, who represented himself as a native of New York, but resided in South Carolina when the Rebellion broke out. He was conscripted into the Southern army, but was detailed as a clerk in the War Office at Richmond. Here he remained for six months, when he " ran the blockade," by walking out of Richmond and much of the way through Virginia to the North, where he went to Canada. His testimony, and that of Richard Montgomery, clearly shows that all parties named were engaged, not only in plots to murder, but also to burn various cities of the North, destroy the Croton waterworks at New York, and introduce yellow fever into the country by means of infected clothing brought from Nassau. All of the above swore positively that the assassination was a matter of common conversation, and that they knew Booth and Payne to be on intimate terms with the rebel agents. Much incidental testimony bearing upon the subject was introduced during the trial. In the testimony of Conover, Montgomery, and Merritt it was clearly shown that Thompson, Sanders, and Clay made their boasts that they had money in Canada for the purpose of aiding the abducting or assassination of President Lincoln. The officers of the Ontario Bank of Montreal testified that during the year of the assassination Jacob Thompson had on deposit in that bank the sum of $649,000, and that this deposit to his credit was from the negotiation of bills of exchange drawn by the Secretary of the Treasury of the Confederate States on Frazier, Trenholm & Co., of Liverpool, England, who were known to be the financial agents of the Confederate States. When Booth was shot in Garrett's barn, upon his person was found the following bills of exchange:

No. 1492.

THE ONTARIO BANK, MONTREAL BRANCH.

Montreal, 27th October, 1864.

Exchange for £61 12s. 10d.

Sixty days after sight of this first exchange, second and third of the same tenor and date, pay to the order of J. Wilkes Booth £61 12s. 10d. sterling, value received, and charge to the account of this office.

H. Stanus, Manager.

To Messrs. Glynn, Mills & Co., London.

After the surrender of Lee's army Thompson and Sanders in Canada sent a communication to Washington, asking leave to pass through the States. The Secretary of War seriously opposed granting their request, but Mr. Lincoln, in the kindness of his heart, said: " Let us close our eyes, and let them pass unnoticed."

CHAPTER XII.

As has been stated in a previous chapter, John H. Surratt, in obedience to the wishes of his mother, is supposed to have left Washington the latter part of the day of April 14, 1865.

The name John Harrison was entered upon the register at St. Lawrence Hall, Montreal, Canada, 12.30 P. M., the 18th day of April, 1865. That name was written by John H. Surratt. He did not eat or sleep here, but immediately went to the house of a man named Porterfield, where he remained for a few days in concealment. Mr. Porterfield was a Southern gentleman, but became a British subject. He was for some time a banker or broker for the Ontario Bank in Canada, and was, it is said, the agent who took charge of the money plundered during the St. Albans raid.

Rev. Charles Boucher, a Catholic priest of the parish of St. Liboire, about forty miles from Montreal, testified that John H. Surratt came to his house in a cart between nine and ten o'clock on the night of the 22d of April, in company with Joseph T. Du Tilly, and remained in his house about three months.

St. Liboire was at that time a new village and thinly settled, and a very appropriate hiding place for a criminal. Mr. Boucher said that he had been notified that a man by the name of Charles Armstrong was coming to

his house on account of his health, and because of being
compromised in the American war. About twelve days
after Armstrong's arrival, so the reverend gentleman

JOHN H. SURRATT.

Implicated in the attempt to kidnap President Lincoln, escaped from
Washington, went abroad, and joined the Papal Zouaves; was recognized,
arrested, and brought to Washington, and held for trial, but the jury disa-
greeing he went free.

said, he made himself known to his hostess as John H.
Surratt. During his concealment he frequently went
hunting, either alone or in company with others. The
latter part of July Mr. Boucher took him secretly
to Father Lapierre, a Catholic priest, who kept him in
his own father's house for some time, after which La-

pierre and Boucher accompanied Surratt in a carriage to the steamer *Montreal* for Quebec. Father Lapierre kept Surratt under lock and key during the voyage from Montreal to Quebec, and at Quebec he accompanied the disguised Surratt from the Montreal steamer to the ocean steamer *Peruvian,* bound for Liverpool, which sailed September 15. Father Lapierre then introduced Surratt to Dr. McMillan, the physician of the steamer, as McCarty. Surratt wore spectacles and had his hair dyed. After the steamer started for the Old World Surratt appeared startled at the appearance of a certain man on board, and, turning around, said to McMillan: "That man is an American detective; he is after me." He put his hand in his pocket and drew out his revolver, remarking: "But this will fix him." McMillan inquired: "Why do you think this gentleman to whom you refer is an American detective; and if so, why do you care?" Said he: "I have done such things that, if you should know them, it would make you stare." The supposed detective turned out to be a lumber merchant from Toronto. There was a terrible burden weighing upon Surratt's heart, and there is no wonder that when he got out on the ocean, with only one man on board that he knew, that he unburdened his heavy conscience, as criminals often do. When the steamer approached Ireland, he hesitated whether he should land on the Irish coast or whether he should wait until he got to Liverpool; and he consulted Dr. McMillan as to which he had better do. Said Dr. McMillan, "I cannot tell you which you had better do; you can do just as you please." He replied: "I will go to Liverpool." Finally, as they neared the coast of Ireland, while coming into the bay, McMillan found him unexpectedly upon the deck, fully clad and a little satchel in his hand, ready to depart. He said: "I have changed my mind. It is now night, and dark, and I have concluded I will land here in Ireland."

On September 27 A. Wilding, vice-consul at Liverpool, cabled William H. Seward, Secretary of State, to the effect that John H. Surratt was either in Liverpool or expected there within a day or two. He again cabled on the 30th that Surratt had arrived in Liverpool on the 25th, and was staying at the oratory of the Roman Catholic Church of the Holy Cross. Americans of the Catholic faith had frequently lodged at the same oratory while visiting Liverpool, and the vice-consul believed that Surratt was really there.

All this information was given by the man whom Surratt made a confidant of on the voyage, who felt that it was his duty to give the information, that the fugitive might be arrested. Surratt manifested no signs of penitence, but justified his actions, and was bold and defiant when speaking of the assassination. Surratt said that he was obliged to remain in Liverpool until he could receive money from Montreal, stating that he had been in the employ of the Confederate Government, engaged in conveying intelligence between Washington and Richmond, and told his confidant that he had been concerned in a plan for carrying off President Lincoln from Washington, which was concocted entirely by J. Wilkes Booth and himself; that he went to Canada just before the assassination of President Lincoln took place; that while in Canada he received a letter from Booth, saying that it had become necessary to change their plans, and requested him to come to Washington immediately; that he did start immediately, but did not state to what part of the terrible affair he had been assigned. On his return to Canada, and while sitting at breakfast at St. Albans, a gentleman next to him spoke of the report of the assassination, and that he was surprised to see his name in the paper. Surratt being in Liverpool on the 26th, according to the evidence given by the person who accompanied him from Canada, and sworn to before a justice of the peace for the borough of Liverpool on the 26th, ought to have been, in my opinion, sufficient grounds for his arrest; but it was not made. On October 13 W. Hunter, Acting Secretary of State at Washington, cabled the vice-consul at Liverpool:

I have to inform you, that, upon a consultation with the Secretary of War and Judge-Advocate-General, it is thought advisable that no action be taken in regard to the arrest of the supposed John Surratt at present.

Surratt waited in Liverpool for the arrival of the steamer *Nova Scotian,* which sailed from Montreal Saturday, October 31, and on which he expected to receive money from parties in Montreal. At that time it was known in Montreal that it was Surratt's intention to go to Rome, and he did go, and upon his arrival there enlisted in the Papal Zouaves under the name of John Watson. When his company, No. 3, was stationed at Sezze, a friend who had known Surratt in America recognized him as soon as he saw him. He approached him, calling him by his proper name, and at that Surratt, taking him aside, admitted that he was right in the guess. Surratt acknowledged his participation in the plot against Mr. Lincoln's life, and declared that Jefferson Davis had incited, or was privy, to it. Surratt seemed to be well provided with money, and appealed to his acquaintance not to betray his secret. This friend was Henri Beaumont Ste. Marie, whom Weichmann introduced to John H. Surratt while on a visit to their old college in Maryland, April, 1863.

Ste. Marie, also serving under the Papal colors, communicated the intelligence that John H. Surratt was a
member of the Papal Zouaves, and was stationed at
Sezze, to Rufus King, minister resident at Rome, and
the usual long delay of correspondence took place between the minister and the authorities at Washington.
On June 21, 1866, this important witness made a written
statement as to his acquaintance with Surratt. He was
a Canadian, but was living in America when the War of
the Rebellion broke out. He was engaged as teacher in
a small village in Maryland, called Ellengowan. He
joined the Northern army as a substitute, and was soon
afterward captured by the Confederates and taken to
Castle Thunder, Richmond, but was early released
on account of having given some information relative to a plot of forgers that was being formed in the
prison. He went to England on board a vessel loaded
with cotton, on account of the Confederacy. Returning
to Canada, he remained there until he went abroad, and
recognized Surratt in Italy. He first met Surratt here
at a small town called Velletri. Surratt told Ste.
Marie when he first met him in Maryland that President
Lincoln would certainly pay for all the men that were
slain during the war. In Italy Surratt said to him: " We
have killed Lincoln, the nigger's friend." In speaking of
his mother, Surratt said: " Had it not been for me and
Weichmann, my mother would be living yet." Speaking
of the murder, he said the conspirators had acted under
orders of men who are not yet known. He said when he
left Canada he had but little money, but carried a letter
for a party in London. Surratt was asked whether he
knew Jefferson Davis. He said, No, but that he acted
under the instructions of persons under Davis' immediate orders.

Early in November, 1866, General Rufus King went to Cardinal Antonelli and told him who Surratt was, asking him whether, upon the authentic indictment or the usual preliminary proof, and at the request of the State Department at Washington, he would be willing to deliver up John H. Surratt. Antonelli frankly replied in the affirmative, and added that there was, indeed, no extradition treaty between the two countries, and that to surrender a criminal where capital punishment was likely to ensue was not exactly in accordance with the spirit of the Papal Government, but that in so grave and exceptional a case, and with the understanding that the United States Government under parallel circumstances would do as they desired to be done by, a departure would be made from the practice generally followed. General King requested, as a favor to the American Government, that Surratt should not be discharged from the Papal service until further communication from the State Department, and His Eminence promised to advise with the minister of war to that effect.

The cardinal went with the information to the Pope on the 9th of November. General King again called upon the cardinal, and was by him informed that John Watson, alias John H. Surratt, had been arrested by his orders, and while on the way to Rome had made his escape from the guard of six men in whose charge he had been placed. The following is the order for his arrest:

NOVEMBER 6, 1866.

COLONEL : Cause the arrest of the Zouave Watson, and have him conducted, under secure escort, to the military prison at Rome. It is of much importance that this order be executed with exactness.   The General, pro-minister,

KANZLEI

Lieutenant-Colonel ALLET,
    Commanding Zouave Battalion, Velletri.

Lieutenant-Colonel Allet telegraphed as follows:

PONTIFICAL ZOUAVES, BATTALION HEADQUARTERS,
VELLETRI, November 7, 1866.

GENERAL: I have the honor to inform you that the Zouave John Watson has been arrested at Veroli, and will be taken to-morrow morning, under good escort, to Rome. While he was searched for at Trisulti, which was his garrison, he was arrested by Captain De Lambilly, at Veroli, where he was on leave.

I have the honor to be, General, your Excellency's

Very humble and obedient servant,

LIEUT.-COL. ALLET.

His Excellency, the General-Minister of War, Rome.

PONTIFICAL TELEGRAPH.

VELLETRI, 8.35 A. M., November 8, 1866.

HIS EXCELLENCY, THE GENERAL-MINISTER OF WAR, ROME:

I received the following telegram from Captain Lambilly: At the moment of leaving the prison, surrounded by six men as guards, Watson plunged into the ravine, more than a hundred feet deep, which defends the prison. Fifty Zouaves are in pursuit.

LIEUT.-COLONEL ALLET.

At four o'clock on the morning of the 8th of November a sergeant and six men knocked at the gate of the Velletri prison, which opens on a platform which overlooks the country. A balustrade prevents promenaders from falling on the rocks, situated at least thirty-five feet below. After leaving the gate of the prison Surratt made a leap and cast himself into the void, landing on a ledge of rocks projecting from the face of the mountain, where he might have been seriously injured, but gained the depths of the valley. The refuse from the barracks accumulated on the rock, and in this manner his fall was broken. Had he leaped a little farther he would have fallen into an abyss. Patrols were immediately organized, but in vain. He was tracked from Velletri to Sora and Naples, stopping at the latter place for a few days, when he left on the steamer *Tripoli* for Alexandria, Egypt, under the name of Walters.

Surratt went to Naples on the 8th of November, dressed in the uniform of the Papal Zouaves, having no passport, but stating that he was an Englishman who had escaped from a Roman regiment. He said that he had no money, and the police, being somewhat suspicious of him, gave him (at his own request) lodgings for three days in prison. He stated that he had been in Rome two months; that being out of money he enlisted in the Roman Zouaves, and was put in prison for insubordination, from whence he had escaped by jumping from a high wall, in doing which he hurt his back and arm. On the third day he asked to be taken to the British consulate, to which place one of the police went with him. Here he complained of his confinement, stating that he was a Canadian, and the consul claimed his release as an English subject.

In the meantime the police had found that he had twelve scudi with him, and, on asking him why he went to prison, he replied that he wished to save his money. He remained in Naples until Saturday, the 18th, when, through the influence of the English consul, he obtained passage on the steamer *Tripoli* to Alexandria, at 9 o'clock P. M., some English gentlemen paying for his board during the voyage, and giving him a few francs. The United States consul at Malta, William Winthrop, was informed by the consul at Naples of Surratt's departure, but he was hampered by legal quibbles and the slowness of the proper authorities to act, and Surratt left Malta, in the steamer which brought him, at 4 P. M. on the 19th.

On board the steamer *Tripoli*, while coaling at Malta, Surratt gave his name to the superintendent of police as

John Agostina, a native of Canada. The steamer reached Alexandria, Egypt, on the 23d of November, and on the 27th Charles Hale, consul-general of the United States at that place, went on board and arrested Surratt, who was still dressed in the uniform of a Zouave. Mr. Hale found it easy to distinguish him among the

JOHN H. SURRATT.

In the uniform of the Papal Zouaves at Rome, Italy. He had it on when captured at Alexandria, Egypt.

seventy-eight of the third-class passengers by his Zouave uniform and his almost unmistakable American type of countenance. Mr. Hale at once said: " You are an American." Surratt said: " Yes, sir; I am." Mr. Hale said: "You doubtless know why I want you. What is your name?" He replied promptly, "Walters." Mr. Hale then said: "I believe your true name is Surratt," and in arresting him mentioned his official position as United States consul-general. Surratt and the other third-class passengers had been in quarantine four days, but when arrested the director of quarantine speedily arranged a sufficient escort of soldiers, by whom the prisoner was conducted to a safe place within the quarantine walls.

December 2 the following telegram was received at Washington:

To SEWARD, Washington.

Have arrested John Surratt, one of President Lincoln's assassins. No doubt of identity.

HALE, Alexandria.

The appearance of the prisoner at the time of his arrest answered well the description given of him by Weichmann in Pittman's report of the trial of the conspirators, and officially sent by the Government to the various consuls: "John H. Surratt is about six feet high, with very prominent forehead, a very large nose, and sunken eyes. He has a goatee, and very long hair of a light color." On the 29th Surratt was transferred, under a sufficient guard, from the quarantine grounds to the Government prison.

On December 4 Secretary Seward telegraphed Minister Hale at Alexandria, Egypt, that the Secretary of the Navy had instructed Admiral Goldsborough to send a proper national armed vessel to Alexandria to receive from him John H. Surratt, a citizen of the United States. Surratt remained in safe confinement until the 21st of December, when he was delivered by Mr. Hale on board the corvette *Swatara*, and taken to America, landing at Washington, D. C.

The criminal court for the District of Columbia, before which the trial of John H. Surratt took place, was opened at ten o'clock, June 10, 1867, and closed August 11, lasting sixty-two days. There were present the District Attorney, E. C. Carrington, his assistant, N. Wilson, and associate counsel, Messrs. Edwards Pierpont and A. G. Riddle, for the United States, and the prisoner and his counsel, Messrs. Joseph H. Bradley, R. T. Merrick, and Joseph R. Bradley, Jr.

During the trial there was a general impression that Surratt would be able to prove an alibi, but the testimony of several witnesses caused a sensation in the court, dispelling that impression. According to Sergeant Joseph M. Dye's statement, he, with a companion, was standing in front of Ford's Theater on the night of the assassination from the time of the arrival of the President's carriage until Booth stepped into the theater at ten minutes past ten. Dye's attention was first called to the low conversation held between two villainous-looking persons, after which they were joined by a third party, who was neatly dressed. The last one to join the trio stepped into the lobby of the theater, and, when he reappeared on the pavement, called the hour. This he repeated three times at different intervals, the third and last being ten minutes past ten. As he announced the time he looked at the two men, and seemed to be very much excited. He then walked briskly up Tenth toward H Street, and Booth (for it was he) went into the theater. The third party was lost sight of. Sergeant Dye's suspicions were aroused at the mysterious actions of these men, and he had his hand upon his revolver several times, not knowing what might happen. Sergeant Dye and his companion went into an adjoining saloon and ordered oysters, but before they were served the report came in that the President was shot. Dye immediately started for his battery at Camp Barry, junction of H Street and Bladensburg Pike. He was first sergeant, and felt sure the battery would be called out.

In walking out H Street a woman hoisted a window and asked what was wrong downtown, and he told her President Lincoln was shot. She asked who did it, and was told Wilkes Booth. She then asked the sergeant how he knew, and he said a man saw him do it. This woman was Mrs. Surratt, for Sergeant Dye remembered the number of the house, 541 H Street, and the appearance of it, as he had to stop and converse with her. He also swore during the trial that the man who called the hour was John H. Surratt.

David C. Reed, a tailor at 617 H Street N. W., testified before the Military Commission that he knew John H. Surratt since he was quite a boy, and that he saw him at half-past two o'clock on the day of the murder, on Pennsylvania Avenue below the National Hotel, and that they recognized each other as they passed. Reed noticed his fine new fitting suit of clothes, making him look unusually genteel.

Dr. Cleaver had no sympathy with this Government, but had a great deal for John H. Surratt. He testified to the court that he had not only met Surratt on H Street during the day of the assassination, but spoke to him. He told this in the strictest confidence to a friend, and would not have admitted it to the court had not this friend told a member of Congress. William E. Cleaver admitted that he wanted to shield Surratt.

A barber by the name of Charles H. M. Wood, who worked for Booker & Stewart, barbers, on E Street, near Grover's Theater, testified that he shaved John Surratt and dressed his hair between 9 and 10 o'clock A. M., on the 14th; that Surratt was dusty, as if he had just come in from a trip. Booth and O'Laughlin were in the barber shop at the same time.

Mr. John Lee, chief of the men employed by Major O'Beirne, the provost-marshal of the District of Columbia, swore that he saw John H. Surratt on Pennsylvania Avenue on the 14th.

Scipiano Grillo was with Herold in Willard's Hotel on the 14th, looking for General Robert E. Lee, whom they heard had arrived. While there Herold was engaged in conversation with a man, and Herold asked him if he was going to-night, and he said, Yes. Grillo did not know the man, but recognized him at the trial as being John H. Surratt.

A colored girl who had been a servant in the Surratt family for two weeks testified that when Mrs. Surratt returned from Surrattsville with Mr. Weichmann, about eight o'clock, she carried supper to Mr. Weichmann. Then Mrs. Surratt told her to bring a pot of tea to a gentleman. When it was taken to Mrs. Surratt, she said: " This is my son." The servant recognized the man at the trial as Surratt, confirming the statement of the witnesses who swore to having seen him at different hours during the day of the assassination, narrating minute circumstances, such as meeting him and having conversation with him. It does seem altogether probable that Surratt arrived in Washington on the morning of the assassination and left in the evening before or after the fatal shot was fired at Ford's Theater. Surratt claimed that he was in New York on the night of the assassination, and his statement had more weight with the jury than that of those testifying against him.

Over two hundred witnesses were examined. The jury disagreed, standing eight for acquittal and four for conviction. Of the four who were for conviction, none were born in the South; of the eight for acquittal, all except one were natives of Maryland, Virginia, or the District of Columbia.

Surratt was kept in the Old Capitol Prison for some months, but was finally liberated on twenty-five thousand dollars bail. His counsel were General Merrick and John G. Carlisle. He was again arraigned for trial. The prosecution declined to proceed upon the charge of murder of Mr. Lincoln, and proposed to try him upon the charges of conspiracy and treason. But his counsel showed that the law in such cases required that the indictment should be found within two years from the time of the alleged offense, unless the respondent was a " fugitive from justice." More than this time had intervened, and there was no averment in the indictment that he was a fugitive. The court thereupon discharged him.

From a lecture delivered by John H. Surratt a few years since, we quote a little from his story, which shows the work he did for the Southern cause, to which he was very much devoted:

" At the breaking out of the war I was a student at St. Charles College, in Maryland, but did not remain there long after that important event. I left in July, 1861, and, returning home, commenced to take an active part in the stirring events of that period. I was not more than eighteen years of age, and was mostly engaged in sending information regarding the movements of the United States army stationed in Washington and elsewhere, and carrying dispatches to the Confederate boats on the Potomac. We had a regularly established line from Washington to the Potomac, and I, being the only unmarried man on the route, had most of the hard riding

to do. I devised various ways to carry the dispatches—
sometimes in the heel of my boots; sometimes between
the planks of the buggy. I confess that never in my life
did I come across a more stupid set of detectives than
those generally employed by the United States Government. They seemed to have no idea whatever how to
search me. In 1864 my family left Maryland and moved
to Washington, *where I took a still more active part* in
the stirring events of that period. It was a fascinating
life to me. It seemed as if I could not do too much or
run too great a risk."

CHAPTER XIII.

NARRATIVE OF A WALK OF THE AUTHOR, MAY, 1901, OVER THE ROUTE OF FLIGHT AND CAPTURE.

HAVING had for a long time a great desire to walk over the route which Booth took when fleeing from Washington through Maryland to Virginia, and to talk with the people who were still living and who aided the assassin in that flight, I started, with a combination walking stick and umbrella, and a leather bag over my shoulder, from the back door of Ford's Theater at four o'clock on the morning of May 12, 1901.

It was a beautiful morning, and perfect quiet prevailed. For fear that my clumsy walking shoes might make an alarming noise over the alley cobblestones and raise some suspicion at that early hour, I had previously warned the night watchman of the building that I would be at his back door at that time the following morning, and not to be alarmed. My departure was unnoticed, except by a few cats that were winding up their night's carousal. One hundred feet brought me to the alley leading out on F Street, and the distance over that to the street was 150 feet. It is not known which streets Booth rode through after turning east on F Street, until he reached the hill on the south side of the Capitol Building, where he was seen by a man who was going to his work. My route led me along F to Seventh, down Seventh to the Avenue, down the Avenue to the Peace Monument, thence

EASTERN BRANCH BRIDGE.

Booth and Herold crossed this bridge into Maryland.

through the southern portion of the Capitol Grounds to Eighth Street, south on Eighth to G, east on G to Eleventh, and south on Eleventh to the Navy Yard bridge across the eastern branch of the Potomac. No one questioned my right to pass over this bridge, but when Booth reached this point his right to continue on his journey was challenged.

At half-past ten o'clock on the night of the assassination Sergeant Silas T. Cobb asked: " Who are you, sir? " He said: " My name is Booth." " Where are you from? " He answered, " From the city." " Where are you going? " He replied, " I am going home." " Where is your home? " He said it was in Charles. The sergeant understood the meaning of that to be Charles County, and asked him what town. Booth said he did not live in any town. " You must live in some town," said he. " I live close to Beantown, but do not live in the town." He was asked why he was out so late, and if he did not know the rule that persons were not allowed to pass after nine o'clock. He said it was new to him; that he had had somewhere to go in the city, and it was a dark night, and he thought he would have the moon to ride home by. The moon rose that night about that time. After this bit of quizzing the sergeant thought him a proper person to pass, and so passed him. The sensitive horse felt the nervousness and anxiety which Booth did not reveal by his voice or manner during the few minutes' stop. In less than ten minutes another person rode up and received the sentinel's challenge. He gave his name as Smith, and that he was going home; that he lived at White Plains. No doubt but what the sergeant had heard the name before, but not that of his home. His excuse for being late was that he had been in bad company. His horse did not

STREET IN SURRATTSVILLE.

Looking north from the front of the Surratt house toward Washington;
the road by which Booth and Herold entered the town.

show the uneasiness of its predecessor, and did not have
the appearance of being driven so fast as the first one.
The explanations of this man being entirely satisfactory
to the sentinel of the United States army, he was given a
clearance, and thus Herold followed Booth into Maryland. The war being at a close, the restrictions were
not so exacting at this bridge, and the sentinels were at
liberty to judge the proper persons to pass over. The
third horseman soon rode up, and inquired whether a
man riding a roan horse had passed. He was informed
that a horse answering that description had gone on.
The sergeant did not think the newcomer had business
of sufficient importance on the other side of the bridge,
so turned him back, although he finally consented to his
crossing, but told him he would not be permitted to re-

turn; so he did not cross. This man was John Fletcher, who had hired Herold a horse, which, not being returned at the proper time, he was out searching for, tracking it to the bridge. The distance from Ford's Theater to the south end of the bridge in Anacostia is three miles, and the first road turning to the left after crossing the bridge is the one taken by Booth and Herold. It leads up what is called Good Hope Hill. It was on this hill that Booth stopped a farmer and inquired the road, and asked whether a horseman had passed. He afterward passed a second man on a horse, but did not speak to him. Herold, upon being informed that a horseman had only a few moments preceded him, started off quite briskly, evidently anxious to overtake Booth.

At the top of the hill the road turns to the right, and then to the left, leading to Surrattsville. Silver Hill, six miles from Washington, was reached at six o'clock, and four miles farther brought me to Camp Springs. As I walked into Surrattsville, at a quarter to nine o'clock, the good people were flocking into the little Catholic Church that stood on the left side of the road. A short distance beyond, on the same side of the road, I recognized the historic Surratt House. It is nestled in a clump of beautiful trees, and I venture to say that the occupants of the house in war times would not recognize the place. The owner of it, Mr. J. W. Wheatley, was sitting on the front porch, and as I walked up and told him my business, stating that I wanted to stop with him until the next day, he at once made me feel at home. The sign at the corner of the house reads: " Village Hotel." The farm originally contained 168 acres. The Surratts sold it to John Hunter, and at his death it was left to Mrs. Addison, a relative, and she sold 117 acres to Mr. Wheatley ten years ago. At that time it was a perfect wilderness, grown over with pines and underbrush, but with liberal expenditure of money and time it now has no superior in southern Maryland. Every foot of ground, with the exception of a small piece of timber, is under cultivation. The house faces to the west, and a hall runs through the center. The room at the northwest corner is used as the barroom, and the one adjoining on the east for card-playing, etc. It was through the barroom door, leading out to the north end

HOME OF MRS. SURRATT, SURRATTSVILLE, MD.

Thirteen miles southeast of Washington. D. C. First stop made by Booth and Herold during their flight from the city. The carbine and field-glass that were left here by John H. Surratt, Herold, and Atzerodt were handed them by John M. Lloyd through the barroom door at the end of the house.

of the house, that Lloyd, the tenant, handed the carbine and whisky to Booth and Herold. The room in which Lloyd secreted them when John Surratt left them in his care, an unfinished one, was upstairs, but has been finished since Mr. Wheatley became possessor of the house. I obtained some good views with my kodak of the most interesting places around the house—the back door where Lloyd stopped on his return from Marlboro on the afternoon of the assassination, and handed his fish in the kitchen door, and where Mrs. Surratt met him and told him to be sure and be at home that night, for the guns that had been left with him would be called for.

Surrattsville during the War of the Rebellion was classed as a pretty hard town; but a reformation has since taken place, and the community is now very respectable. The Post-Office Department would not keep the name " Surrattsville " on their list, so changed it to Clinton. Two roads diverge here; the one to the east leads to Upper Marlboro and the one to the west to Piscataway. The latter is much nearer to the Potomac at Port Tobacco than the road Booth took to Bryantown; but he was compelled to go that route on account of having his leg dressed by Dr. Mudd.

After a good night's rest and a hearty breakfast I started on my walk, Monday the 13th. A bridge crosses Piscataway Creek about two and a half miles from Surrattsville, and swamps lined the road for some miles distance on both sides. T. B. stands right in the forks of the road, five miles from Surrattsville. Six roads branch out in as many directions. The first person that I met after entering the village of a dozen houses was Mrs. Margaret A. Thompson. She lives in a house that stands on the spot where J. C. Thompson lived when Booth and Herold rode through the village. Thompson was awake that night and heard the tramp of horses' feet, but did not know at the time who rode by, Mrs. Thompson said that John Surratt and Herold wanted to leave the guns at Mr. Thompson's house, but he would not allow it, as he was a Government mail-carrier at the time, and was afraid something was wrong in the work they were engaged in. Atzerodt joined Surratt and Herold here, and the three returned to Surrattsville and left the guns with Mr. Lloyd. Three miles from T. B. I crossed the Baltimore & Potomac and Pope's Creek Railroad, stepping from King George's into Charles County, and crossed near this point a small creek bearing the name of Mattawoman, and the Mattawoman swamps extended for some distance along the road. Beantown was passed, and I came to St. Peter's Catholic Church, beautifully situated to the left of the road. I drew my kodak on it, and next reached the graveyard in the forks of the road, a mile

T. B.

A small village five miles south of Surrattsville, through which Booth and Herold were heard riding very rapidly about 1 A. M., April 15.

distant from the church. The one to the right led to
Bryantown, but Booth kept on the straight one to Dr.
Mudd's. In this graveyard lies Edward Spangler, who
served Dr. Mudd so faithfully in Dry Tortugas while the
doctor was down with yellow fever, that he sheltered and
cared for him until he died, in 1881. Two miles from
the graveyard a gate on the right of the road leads into
a field, on the opposite side of which was the home of Dr.
Mudd. The road continues past this gate, probably for
half a mile, until it enters the road to Bryantown, so
that Dr. Mudd's house is situated in the forks of the
two roads, a quarter of a mile from each. It was one
o'clock when I knocked at the door, hungry, but not
tired, having walked only seventeen miles. It being past
the dinner hour, I did not like to ask for anything to
eat. This place is thirty miles from Washington, and
Booth rode the distance in six hours, while it took me
ten and three-quarters to walk it. Mrs. Dr. Mudd and
one of her daughters treated me very nicely. At the
same time Mrs. Mudd let me understand that she had
not become reconciled to the treatment and punishment
that her husband received, and felt very bitter toward the
men who composed the Commission that tried and condemned him to imprisonment. At the time Herold
knocked at the front door of Dr. Mudd's house, four
o'clock on Saturday morning, less than six hours after
the assassination, Doctor and Mrs. Mudd were sleeping
in a back room downstairs. When the doctor heard the
noise he called to a woman who was sleeping in an adjoining room to go to the door, but she did not answer
his call. He then asked Mrs. Mudd to go, as he was not
feeling well. Mrs. Mudd said she did not want to go,
so the doctor answered the call, and on opening the door
found Herold there, who said that the man on the horse

at the gate had broken his leg, and desired medical attendance. The injured man was assisted off his horse and into the house, and laid upon a sofa in the parlor

GATE LEADING FROM THE MAIN ROAD TO DR. MUDD'S HOUSE,

A quarter of a mile distant. A colored man met Booth and Herold at this gate near four o'clock, Saturday morning, and Booth offered him a drink of whisky if he would open the gate. He did so, but said Booth was so slow about giving him the whisky that he shut the gate and went on.

to the left of the hall. The doctor made an examination of the leg, and found that the small bone was broken nearly at right angles across the limb, about two inches above the instep. Dr. Mudd, with the assistance of his wife, who made her appearance, dressed the leg as well as circumstances would permit, after which the man was assisted upstairs to a room directly above the parlor.

One of the servants of the house made a rough crutch for the patient. Breakfast in Dr. Mudd's house was prepared early that morning, and Herold was invited to eat with the family. The breakfast of Booth was carried to his room. Herold talked quite freely at the breakfast table, not seeming at all worried at the sad plight that he and Booth were in. He talked in a familiar way about the people of the neighborhood, when Mrs. Mudd asked him if he lived in that section, and he said, " No." She remarked: " You seem to know a good many people around here," and he said: " I have been skylarking around this part of the country for about six months." Mrs. Mudd said: " Your father ought to put you to work." He replied, " My father is dead, and I'm ahead of the old woman." The breakfast sent to Booth was untouched, and Mrs. Mudd learning of this went to his room, and in entering it said to Booth: " I suppose you think I am not very hospitable." To this he made no reply. She then asked him if there was anything she could do for him, and he said: " Have you any brandy? " She said: " No; but we have some good whisky; " but he would have none of that. She sent him up some oranges and other delicacies, for they happened to have some extras on account of it being Easter time, but he ate nothing that she sent up. He was very pale and much debilitated.

In the forenoon of Tuesday, the 18th, Lieutenant Alex. Lovett, William Williams, Simon Gavacan, and Joshua Lloyd, detectives, with a squad of cavalry, reached Dr. Mudd's. The doctor was not in when they arrived, but made his appearance in a few minutes. The first question asked Dr. Mudd was whether there had been any strangers at his house, and he said there had not; but upon close questioning he admitted that there had. The doctor explained their arrival and the dressing of Booth's leg, and their departure about 4 o'clock P. M. next day; that they asked to be directed to Parson Wilmer's house and to Allen's Fresh, and that he accompanied them down to the swamps, showing them the road. On Friday, the 21st, the same officers ap-

HOME OF DOCTOR SAMUEL A. MUDD.

Thirty miles south of Washington. The two windows to the left of the door indicate the parlor in which Dr. Mudd dressed Booth's leg, and the two windows above, his bedroom.

peared at Dr. Mudd's for the purpose of arresting him. He was not in at this visit, but his wife sent for him, and when he came they told him the nature of their visit, and that they would have to search the house. The servant in cleaning up the room that Booth had used pushed a long riding boot under the bed, and, when the house was to be searched, Dr. Mudd went upstairs and

brought down the boot, with " J. Wilkes " and the name
of the makers, " Broadway, N. Y.," written inside. The
boot was cut some ten inches from the instep. A razor
that Herold had borrowed for Booth to shave off his
mustache was also brought from the room. Dr. Mudd
was asked if he thought his visitor was Booth, and he
said he thought not. He said the man had whiskers on,
but that his impression was he shaved off his mustache
upstairs. When they inquired of him if he knew Booth,
he said that he was introduced to him at church in that
neighborhood about six months before, by a man named
Thompson, and that Booth wanted to buy a farm, but
he believed the man who had been there was not Booth.

The officers did not search the house, as they considered the boot and razor were satisfactory evidence that
Booth and Herold had been there. When a photograph
of Booth was shown to Dr. Mudd, he said he did not
recognize it, but there was something about the forehead
or the eyes that resembled one of the parties. Mrs.
Mudd said that the whiskers became detached and
dropped off at the foot of the stairs, which surely proved
that they were artificial. If Booth wore them, it was only
while at Dr. Mudd's; for nowhere else were they seen
on him. Dr. Mudd finally admitted on the 21st, after
the boot had been found, that he recognized as Booth
the man whose leg he dressed. Dr. Mudd was taken
to Washington on the day of his arrest.

Mrs. Mudd told me that when she applied to President
Johnson for her husband's pardon, after he had been in
prison several years, Johnson promised her it should be
granted before he went out of office, but the pressure
would be too strong against such an action at that time.
She finally received a message from Johnson in 1869,
stating her husband's pardon had been granted, and she

THE HOME OF DR. MUDD'S FATHER.

This house is two miles from Dr. Mudd's, on the Bryantown road. To this house Dr. Mudd and Herold came on Saturday afternoon, to hire a buggy to convey the fugitives on their journey, but they could not procure it.

immediately went to Washington to receive it. When she obtained the paper, she inquired how she could get it to her husband, when President Johnson said he had nothing more to do with it. She determined to take it to Dr. Mudd in person, so went to Baltimore to take a boat for Dry Tortugas, but upon her arrival there found the vessel had gone. She then expressed the document to her brother in New Orleans, but it cost him five hundred dollars to get it to the doctor.

After spending a pleasant hour in conversation with Mrs. Mudd, and taking several snapshots of the house, I left, and, after getting on the Bryantown road, I walked off toward that town, and two miles distant came to the home of Dr. Mudd's father, a large house to the left of the road, surrounded by a forest of trees. Two miles farther brought me to within one mile of Bryantown and the spot where Dr. Mudd directed Booth and Herold to leave the main road, Saturday, 4 P. M., and go around to the west of Bryantown, as the soldiers had already taken possession of the town, and would soon have scouts upon all the avenues leading into the country.

Booth and Herold's long stay at Dr. Mudd's house has been somewhat of a mystery, for they surely knew that delay was dangerous to them on the Maryland side of the river. It was after dinner on Saturday when Dr. Mudd and Herold started on horseback toward Bryantown in search of a vehicle with which to more speedily expedite their flight. Frank Washington, a colored man working for Dr. Mudd, took care of the two horses, one a bay and the other a large roan, that Booth and Herold rode to Dr. Mudd's. At noon on the day they arrived he brought out of the stable the bay one and Dr. Mudd's gray, and Herold and Dr. Mudd rode off. The colored man then went to the field to work, and on his return to the house in the evening the bay and the roan horses were gone. Journeying on horseback with a broken leg was to Booth slow and painful. Another reason for changing their means of locomotion was that they would not be as readily recognized in a carriage as on horseback. Dr. Mudd left Herold some little distance from town while he went on to see whether or not the coast was clear. He did not stay long in town when he found it occupied with soldiers, who were on the hunt for the very two men that he was harboring at his home. Lieutenant David D. Dana reached

Bryantown the day after the assassination, about 1
o'clock P. M., communicating the intelligence of it,
and naming the assassin to the citizens, and in less
than a quarter of an hour everyone in the village
knew it. The lieutenant had sent a squad of four men
ahead of him, and they reached Bryantown half an
hour earlier. After Dr. Mudd returned to Herold, the
latter lost no time in going back to the house for Booth.
It is not certain that Dr. Mudd returned to his home
with Herold, but it is generally believed that he stood
as a sentinel between the soldiers in Bryantown and the
assassins at his home, and must have felt uneasy until
he had them well started through the Zekiah swamps
west of Bryantown. There was a cart road leading west
from Dr. Mudd's, passing the farm of his brother, Henry
L. Mudd. Within three-quarters of a mile from the
Beantown and Bryantown road they passed the farm of
Mrs. W. J. Middleton, and then followed the road leading from Bryantown to Beantown for a mile, when they
turned south, passing St. Paul's, or Piney, Episcopal
Church, presided over by Parson Wilmer. It will be
remembered that Booth inquired for Parson Wilmer's,
but this was only a blind, as the good old parson was
a staunch Union man all through war times, and did
good service by furnishing the Government with information regarding the movements of the Confederates
in that section of the country.

When Booth and Herold reached Brice Chapel (a colored church) they lost their way, and Herold went a
mile and a half toward Bryantown to the negro cabin
of Oswald Swann, who lived on the La Plata road, half
a mile from the Bryantown road. Swann accompanied
Herold back to Brice's, where Booth hired him to conduct them to the house of Colonel Cox, to which place

they had been directed by Dr. Mudd. With a good
guide they experienced no further trouble on their way.
They passed through the little village of Newtown,
reaching Colonel Cox's house early Sunday morning,
after which Swann was dismissed, Booth paying him ten
dollars for his work.

I registered my name at the Bryantown Hotel, and
after completing my toilet I started at half-past four
to walk out a mile south to the St. Mary's Catholic

BRYANTOWN HOTEL.

Booth made this his stopping place upon several occasions, and a number
of citizens of the community who were suspected of being implicated in the
conspiracy were confined here for a while.

Church, presided over by Rev. Edward Southgate, to
whom I carried a letter of introduction from his sister
at Falls Church, Va. I found Rev. Mr. Southgate a very
pleasant gentleman, and heard from his lips the interesting story of his trip through a cold, blustering winter
night to the deathbed of Dr. Mudd.

Dr. Mudd stood for half an hour in front of St. Mary's

Church on January 1, 1883, without an overcoat, and, it being a very cold day, he took a severe cold, from the effects of which he died on the 10th of the same month. Upon his return in 1869 from the Dry Tortugas he resumed the practice of medicine, and was very successful up to the time of his last sickness. His grave was pointed out to me, and from the tombstone I copied:

SAMUEL A. MUDD.   Died Jan. 10, 1883.

Rev. Mr. Southgate has been connected with this church for the past twenty years, and is held in high esteem by all who know him. It was here that J. Wilkes Booth attended service on a Sunday in November, 1864. He occupied a seat in the pew of Dr. Queen, who lives four miles south of the church, and after the service was introduced to Dr. Mudd. Booth carried a letter of introduction from a Mr. Martin, of Canada, to Dr. Queen. Booth's excuse for being in that part of the country was the purchase of some land. Of others he inquired for horses, for he wanted to buy a couple, and of still another he made particular inquiry about the roads through southern Maryland, their conditions and directions. The land purchase was a sham, but he did want to buy a horse or two, and did want to gain some knowledge of the roads, for horses and roads were to play prominent parts in his contemplated scheme.

John Surratt's, Herold's, and Atzerodt's acquaintance in the lower part of Maryland no doubt suggested to Booth the route to take the President in case of his capture, or Booth's road to escape if murder had to be resorted to. Booth's visit, as far south as Leonardtown, in St. Mary's County, for the alleged purpose of buying land, made him also well informed in that section. He tried to affiliate with the people whom he met upon his several visits, and no doubt intrusted to some of his newly made acquaintances the true object of his visits. Booth again visited this church in December of the same year, and on both trips stopped a night or two with Dr. Mudd. Dr. Mudd and his family were members of this church, and the doctor was much esteemed in the community.

I was so pleasantly entertained in and around this church that I detained Mr. Southgate from answering the supper bell, and the second call was made in the person of his charming sister, who appeared upon the scene and kindly invited me to accompany them to tea. I wanted to accept, but thought of the disappointment the young man at the hotel would experience when I failed to eat the meal that he would have prepared for me. He had complained of dull business, and said I was the only arrival of the day. After my return to the hotel, and supper over, I engaged in conversation with Mr. Peter Trotter, a resident of Bryantown for the past forty-seven years. He told me that when Thomas L. Gardiner, a nephew of Squire Gardiner, from whom Booth purchased a horse in November, 1864, brought it to Bryantown the following day, Booth took it to Trotter's blacksmith shop to have it shod. Mr. Trotter's blacksmith shop remains to-day on the same spot. Booth purchased a saddle and bridle from Mr. Henry A. Turner, who had a store there at that time. Mr. Trotter said that while he was shoeing the horse Booth was in conversation with a number of persons who had collected around him in the shop, all being charmed with his fascinating manner. Dr. Mudd accompanied Booth on this visit to Bryantown, and when the horse was shod, Booth mounted it, and the two rode away together.

I have it from unquestionable authority that Dr. Mudd acknowledged a short time before his death that he was connected with the original plan of kidnaping the President. The plan was to take Lincoln across the Potomac at Port Tobacco Creek, and Mudd was in readiness at any time to assist the work. Various plans were talked over at his own house. My informant feels very positive that the doctor would not have entered into any plot to murder the President, and was horrified at the deed done by Booth; but as Booth came to his house a wounded man, he felt it to be his duty to dress his broken leg and get him out of the way as quickly as possible.

Before the two railroads penetrated southern Maryland considerable business was done at Bryantown, and a number of wealthy people lived in the town. The shipping to and from this section of the country was done on the Patuxent River, about ten miles east, and the town of Benedict was the port of entry. White Plains and Waldorf are the two stations on the Pope Creek Railroad for Bryantown. I left Bryantown at seven o'clock on the morning of the 14th. The road, leading out one mile to the Catholic Church, which is situated in a beautiful grove to the left of it, is a very pleasant one to walk over. Six miles from Bryantown is Dentsville, and upon inquiring if there was anyone in the place that lived there when Booth rode through, I was informed that there was not, but a blacksmith by the name of Jones might know something, although he had only been in the place a comparatively short time. I called upon the gentleman, and found him to be John J. Jones, a son of Thomas A. Jones, the man who secreted Booth in the thicket. He could not tell me anything new of that eventful period, but I did learn from him something that pleased me very much. I

had been informed that Henry Woodland, the colored
slave who assisted Thomas Jones in getting Booth
across the river, was dead; but Mr. Jones informed me
that he was living twenty miles distant on the farm of
William McK. Burroughs, on Cobb Neck, near Tompkinsville, Charles County. I then and there made up
my mind that I would go and see the old man, and get
him up to show me the ground, from the spot in the
woods where the assassins were secreted to the point on
the river where Jones and he shoved them off in the very
boat that Woodland had used during the day fishing for
shad. I remarked to Jones, in the presence of several men
who were waiting for work to be done, that I would go
on to Cox's Station, six miles farther, where I intended

STREET IN BRYANTOWN, MD., LOOKING NORTH.

staying all night, and next day get a team and go after
Woodland. I could not spare the time to walk, and if
I took a buggy I could bring him up. With this I bade
the occupants of the shop good-by, and, when about a
square away, heard a voice calling me. Turning around,
I saw coming one of the men who was in the shop.
When he came up he asked me what I would give him to
take me down to where Woodland lived, and I said anything that was right. He fixed the price at three
dollars, and promised to land me at Cox's Station on the
return, bringing Woodland back with us, providing he
would come. I accepted his offer, which I thought was
liberal, and we walked a few feet farther, and came to a
yoke of young oxen hitched to a cart. He said: " Get
in," and I got on, for it was simply a flat bed with a
sack of ground corn in the middle. I wondered if that
was the vehicle in which I was to see forty miles of the
country, but my wonderment ceased when he said we
would go home and hitch up the team. He lived two
and a half miles from Dentville, and when about halfway
he turned the oxen to the side of the road to nibble the
foliage of the trees while he went into the woods to look
after his tobacco bed. He soon returned with his wife,
who had been pulling the weeds out of the patch. She
made the third passenger on the cart, and away we
started through the woods, bumping over the roots and
rough places, until it looked and felt as if we would be
dumped by the roadside. We reached his home, and the
good wife went to work and prepared our dinner, while
a message was sent out to the cornfield for his son to
bring in the horses. My mind was again disturbed, for I
thought of going the distance that we were to make behind a pair of hard-worked plow horses. I did not
worry, but took out my kodak and photographed the

old house, which is one hundred and six years old, and presided over by Mr. and Mrs. Millard Thompson. Dinner over, I took a back seat in a strong spring wagon, and behind two young horses that could travel as fast as I cared to go. We passed through Allen's Fresh, Newburg, Wayside, Harris Lot, and Tompkinsville, reaching the farm of William McK. Burroughs, on the Wicomico River, at 4.45. We were not very long on the beautiful farm, called in war times a first-class plantation, until we found Henry Woodland, pulling weeds out of a tobacco patch. I stated to him the object of my visit, and that I wanted him to go back to his old stamping grounds and pilot me over the territory the next day. He looked wonderfully pleased with the idea of again meeting old friends and old places, but he would have to gain the consent of Mr. Burroughs, as it was a pretty busy time and weeds were growing " mighty fast." We lost but little time until we were in the presence of the genial proprietor, and, after stating the object of my visit, he at once said: " Henry, you can't go with these gentlemen to-day, for you will have to hunt someone to take your place in the tobacco beds; you can put up the best horse I have on the farm and start by daylight in the morning, and you can reach Cox's Station by nine o'clock." Well, to say that I was pleased is putting it very mildly. We bade them good-by, and left on our return trip at 5.30, and reached Cox's Station at 7.40, just twenty miles in two hours and ten minutes. After a good supper at the Wills Hotel, for ourselves and horses, Mr. Thompson started home. The next morning a little before nine o'clock Henry Woodland rode into Cox's Station, perfectly bewildered at the improvements that had been made since he was last in that vicinity. A railroad had been built, and the steam horse plowed through the dense forest, letting sunshine into its darkest recesses. No wonder that he was confused when he attempted to tell where his master hid Booth. The ground on which

HENRY WOODLAND.

The faithful and honest slave of Thomas A. Jones. He assisted Jones while caring for Booth in the thicket, and during the journey to the river.

the assassin lay for five days has since brought forth good crops. Mr. Woodland and I walked one mile east of the station to the old farmhouse of Samuel Cox. We were met by Samuel Cox, Jr., the adopted son, and at once made to feel welcome. And this is the place to which the colored man Swann brought Booth and Herold from where he found them lost in the swamps west of Bryantown soon after they left Dr. Mudd's. I asked Mr. Cox to give me his recollections of the coming and going of Booth and Herold, and he cheerfully gave me the following reminiscence:

" On February 8, 1865, I was eighteen years of age,
and going to Charlotte Hall Academy, in St. Mary's
County, Maryland. When Lee's army fell back before
the overwhelming forces of Grant, about the last stand
they made was at Hatcher's Run, in which engagement
General A. P. Hill was killed. In Hill's corps I had a
very dear brother, who joined the Southern army in the
summer of 1862, and had served with it through all its
vicissitudes, and was in the engagement at Hatcher's
Run on the 2d of April, 1865, and up to that time had
never received a scratch. After Hill's corps fell back
from Hatcher's Run, brother Harry and some of his
comrades were annoying the Federal troops by their
sharp-shooting, when he received his first wound—a bullet through his right lung. His comrades removed him
to a private house in the vicinity, and my adopted father,
Colonel Samuel Cox, was written to, notifying us of his
wound. On or about the 12th of April I was called
from Charlotte Hall to go to Virginia to nurse my
wounded brother. The surrender of Appomattox had
taken place, and my adopted father and myself were to
have started for Washington on Tuesday, April 18, on
our way to near Petersburg, where brother Harry lay
wounded. On Saturday evening, April 15, when we received the mail, we were shocked to learn of the assassination of President Lincoln. It was peculiarly
shocking to us, for besides the deed itself, in which none
of us sympathized, we realized that it would prevent our
rendering such aid to my stricken brother as his condition required, as we would not be permitted to leave the
vicinity of Washington, which naturally had been thrown
into great excitement by the insane act of John Wilkes
Booth. Our fears were realized, for we were denied passage into Virginia, and, worse still, my brother, who

had sufficiently recovered to be able to sit up and write to us on the morning of April 18, was that evening removed by Federal troops from the private residence where he had been so tenderly cared for to a hospital, which removal started his wound afresh, and he died on the 22d of April, 1865, a victim to the harshness of foes maddened by the crime of Booth, and who had so soon forgotten the noble sentiment of Grant, uttered a few days before—' Let us have peace.'

"On Sunday morning, April 16, at one o'clock our household was startled by loud rapping on the old brass knocker that adorns our front door. Colonel Cox opened the door, and was confronted by a man who sought admittance for himself and his crippled companion, who was standing in the yard. Colonel Cox demanded their names, which they declined to give, and he thereupon refused them admittance, and in a short time they left, incensed at his want of hospitality. He had told them he had just heard of the killing of President Lincoln, and could not entertain strangers while the country was overrun with soldiers. It was Herold and Booth who were seeking admittance, but he did not know either of them. Herold, who had visited in the county, knew Colonel Cox when he saw him, but had never been introduced. Booth Colonel Cox had never even seen on the stage. They had been piloted to our place by a negro named Oswald Swann, who came with them from the vicinity of Dr. Samuel A. Mudd's, who lived about fourteen miles east from us. Dr. Mudd was a personal friend of Colonel Cox, and Booth and Herold said they came from Dr. Mudd and were assured Colonel Cox would take care of them. When they were dismissed from our door, they discharged the negro Swann, and during the morning while riding out on his farm Colonel

Cox came upon them secreted in a gully about half a mile southeast from his house. The crippled and suffering condition of Booth appealed to his humanity, and he then carried them into the pines, some two miles from his house, where they were secreted by him and Thomas A. Jones until Friday night, April 21, when they were put in a boat by Jones and his trusty servant, Henry Woodland, and left to their fate upon the stormy bosom of the Potomac. On Monday the 18th of April I was dispatched by Colonel Cox to Jones. Jones responded to the appeal of Colonel Cox, who besought him to aid him in getting them across the Potomac. Jones, who had had many adventures the preceding four years, in going back and forth across the Potomac, was very reluctant to engage in this undertaking; and, I am convinced, would not have done so but to aid his friend Colonel Cox, who had gone into it without reflection and without realizing the full meaning of what he was doing until it was too late, and then the only thing left for him to do was to escape the consequences of his impulsive act. To deliver them up after having accepted their confidence never for a moment entered his brain. Treachery was no part of the composition of either Samuel Cox or Thomas A. Jones. But neither Cox nor Jones was actuated for one moment by any sympathy for the act of John Wilkes Booth, and both earnestly expressed their condemnation of it, as being fraught with more evil consequences to the South and the Southern people, with whom they did sympathize, than anything that had occurred during the war.

" I have heard my adopted father, Colonel Cox, speak of a plan to abduct President Lincoln and carry him to Richmond to be held as a hostage, and also heard him mention the names of prominent gentle-

men, who then lived in Charles County, who were
cognizant of this plan, some of whom held boats at
different points upon the Potomac and its tributaries
to convey Lincoln and his captors across whenever
they should appear. In 1877 Dr. Samuel A. Mudd
and myself were the Democratic candidates for the
legislature from Charles County, and on frequent occasions during the campaign, when we were alone together, Mudd would talk about the assassination and the
part for which he was tried and convicted and sent to
the Dry Tortugas. He had been pardoned by President
Andrew Johnson, and had been at home several years
when these conversations took place. He told me that
he had never admired Booth, who had forced himself
upon him twice before he came to his house the morning
after the assassination; that several years before he had
refused to be introduced to Booth in Washington, and
that, after his refusal, Booth had introduced himself to
him on Pennsylvania Avenue; that some months afterward Booth came to the Roman Catholic Church at
Bryantown, of which Dr. Mudd was a member; that seeing Booth there he had spoken to him, and studiously
avoided inviting him to his house, but that when
going home from church Booth had followed him un-
invited; that he never saw him again until the morning
of the 15th of April, 1865, when Booth came to him with
a broken leg, and told him he and Herold had just come
from across the Potomac, and that soon after leaving the
river his horse had fallen and broken his rider's leg; that
he believed the statement, and knew nothing different
while he was ministering to Booth's sufferings; that after
he had made Booth as comfortable as he could, he left
him and rode to Bryantown to mail some letters, and
when he arrived within half a mile of the village he found

the place surrounded by soldiers, and was stopped by a sentry, by whom he was told of the assassination of the President the night before, and that Booth was the assassin. He then said his first impulse was to say, ' Come with me and I will deliver him to you.' But instead he rode back home with the full determination to warn Booth and upbraid him for his treachery and the danger he had placed him in; that he felt outraged at the treatment he had received at the hands of Booth, and that he did threaten to deliver him up. He then said Booth, in a tragic manner, had appealed to him in the name of his mother not to do so, and he yielded to the appeal, but made them leave his premises forthwith. This statement was made to me by Dr. Samuel A. Mudd several years after he had been released from the Dry Tortugas, when he could have had no motive in telling me what was untrue as to his part in assisting Booth. From statements made to me I believe Mudd was aware of the intention to abduct President Lincoln, but am confident he knew nothing of the plan of assassination. I am now the only living white person who knew of the whereabouts of Booth and Herold after they left Colonel Cox's on Sunday morning, April 16, 1865, and were launched upon the Potomac by Thomas A. Jones and Henry Woodland, Friday night, April 21, 1865. I am the only person living who knows where the horses ridden by Booth and Herold were taken and shot by Franklin A. Roby, who lived upon one of Colonel Cox's farms, and I can truthfully testify that, from what I knew of those of whom I have spoken, and their connection with harboring Booth and Herold during those five days, they were not actuated by any sympathy they felt for Booth for his mad act of assassinating President Lincoln."

Mr. Cox then ordered his buggy to the door, and Woodland and I were invited to take a seat. The buggy was left at the station while Mr. Cox took me down the railroad a mile, and pointed out a clear piece of ground to the right of the road as the tobacco bed on which Booth and Herold lay, surrounded by a dense forest. The public road runs close to this spot, the railroad within fifty feet of it. Mr. Cox saw a historic stump dug up near this spot when the railroad was being built. The stump had three large roots that ran down into the ground, and the cavity in them was used as a deposit for the Confederate mail. The mail that was going to Richmond and Southern points during the war, and from the South to the North, was deposited in this stump, and called for by the properly assigned agents. The letters from the South were then dropped into the United States post offices, after placing the proper stamps upon them; then they were delivered to their destination. Mr. Cox says he remembered his father getting the mail from the stump a number of times. Northern papers were sent through this way, and were read in Richmond twenty-four hours after they were printed. To avoid suspicion, the letters intended for the North were deposited by different persons, at various offices. I asked Mr. Cox why he didn't save the stump, and he said he did not think of it at the time, but has regretted it many times since. The tobacco bed where Booth and Herold were secreted, and near which the stump grew, was on the property of Captain Michael Stone Robertson, and when Colonel Cox sent the fugitives to this spot he well knew that the surrounding thicket would completely shield them from discovery. We returned to the station, where I hired a buggy, and with Henry Woodland started over the road just traveled with Mr. Cox, passing the historic spot, and continuing along the public road leading to Pope's Creek. After a three-mile ride we turned into the " Huckleberry " farm, the former home of Thomas A. Jones, and now owned by George Dent. The one-story-and-a-half house is about three hundred feet from the road, and three-quarters of a mile from the Potomac River. Woodland was very much gratified at seeing once again the little house that was a home to him for so many years. It pleased him very much when I took his photograph standing, with the house in the background. He took a position where he could in imagination see his master coming to the house from the public road. We returned to the road and drove to Pope's Creek, a mile distant, as I desired to make arrangements with a fisherman to take me across the Potomac the following day. After engaging a sailboat, we returned over the same road for a short distance, when we entered the farm of a Mr. Dent, whose house was the last that Jones passed when escorting Booth and Herold to the river.

Mr. A. I. Lyons lives in the old Colonial house, which the British partially destroyed by fire. We drove down to the river, on the same road over which Jones piloted Booth and Herold from " Huckleberry " farm. It was difficult descending the winding road through the woods with a buggy, and Jones probably experienced as much trouble in getting Booth down the road on horseback. After tying our horse near the water's edge, Woodland took a position near a large oak tree, saying: " Here is where I tied the boat up after fishing all day for shad, and that night Master Jones shoved it out in the river with Booth and Herold in it. Now let us walk up the river a short distance until I explain how I saved my life and that of my master." We walked up the beach probably a hundred yards, when we came to a little stream that backed in from the river and overflowed a flat space called Dent's Meadows. Woodland continued: "I was arrested a few days after Booth started across the river, and was asked what I did with the boat I used in fishing on the 21st. I replied that I sunk it in the river. I was taken to this spot, and I pointed up this little stream, and said that I bored a hole in the bottom of the boat and sunk it. I was asked to give my reasons, and I told the detectives that the soldiers were destroying all the boats along the river, and I could not

DENT'S MEADOW.

Henry Woodland standing near the spot where he told the detectives who arrested him that he sank the boat in which he was fishing during the day that he and Jones put Booth and Herold in it to cross the river. He did not sink the boat, but told that story in order to shield his master.

afford to lose mine, so sunk it until the excitement was over. This explanation seemed to satisfy them, for I was taken to Port Tobacco and confined in jail but one day, then released. Had they known that the very boat that they were inquiring for had carried the assassins across the river, the life of Thomas A. Jones and myself would not have been worth very much. I was determined to shield my master at the risk of my own life, and I did it, although I was pained to hear of the assassination of the man that had made me a freeman; but I could not prove false to the man that had been kind to me while I was his slave, and at all times since."

We returned to Cox's Station at half-past two o'clock, and after dinner I compensated Henry Woodland, my escort of the day, for the time and trouble it cost him in coming so long a distance from his quiet home. It was a task in every sense of the word, for he was sixty-four years of age, and it tired him very much to ride such a long distance on horseback. He had frequently to walk, in order to rest himself. I took the three o'clock train for La Plata, three miles north, and then walked three miles west to Port Tobacco. This is a quaint old place. Almost every person of energy has left it, and the doors of the old jail, the scene of murder and lynching, swing open, and the birds were nesting within. The court house is in ruins, as a new one has been built at La Plata. A very creditable Episcopal church has been spared, but for how long no one can tell, for rumor says it too must go to the more enterprising town of La Plata. There is one thing in Port Tobacco that is likely to stay, and that is the ever-flowing artesian well that stands in the heart of the town. I made some inquiry about George Atzerodt, one of the conspirators. The people of Port Tobacco have been too much blamed for harboring a class of worthless fellows during and after the war, but they ought not to have been so severely censured as they were, for objectionable characters came and lingered there, as it was one of the points selected for the transfer of contraband material across the Potomac. John Atzerodt, and his brother, George A., came to this town and started a carriage repair shop. John did the wood and iron work and George did the painting, and both were good workmen. I was told by an old gentleman that during the war J. Alexander Brawner, proprietor of the "Brawner Hotel," was the strongest sympathizer with the Southern cause, and annoyed the Union men very much. Port Tobacco and Pope's Creek were two ports of entry for the smuggling of mail and supplies to the Confederacy. From Chapel Point the Potomac backs up the Port Tobacco River. Some of the most prominent men who lived in this section, and also Surrattsville and Pope's Creek, were implicated in the scheme to kidnap President Lincoln. The party who gave me the names did not think for a moment that one of them was ever connected with the plot of assassination, nor did he believe one of them could have been induced to enter into any such scheme. Herold visited this place three weeks before the assassination, and while in company with some boys said that the next time they heard from him he would be in Spain, and that he would have a barrel of money. He frequently visited this neighborhood, for, being an expert sportsman, he hunted this section over, and had friends and acquaintances at almost every farmhouse. At the last visit that Atzerodt made to his former home he told his companions that if he ever came back to Port Tobacco he would be rich enough to buy the whole place.

The people in southern Maryland believe that the failure to abduct the President during the fall of 1864 and spring of 1865 was due to the condition of the roads during these periods. They believe the scheme would have been successfully carried out but for the mild winter and frequent rains. Relays of fast horses were in readiness at proper places between Washington and Port Tobacco Creek, where boats were hired and everything in preparation to transport the President across the Potomac, but they did not know of the difficulties that the conspirators met with at the Washington end of the line. Mr. Eddy Martin, a commercial broker of New York, came down to this place about the 10th of January, 1865, with the intention of crossing the river to Virginia, and remained here for ten days waiting a favorable opportunity to do so. He secured the services of George A. Atzerodt, who at that time was living here, to take him over, but Atzerodt failed him. While waiting here Martin made the acquaintance of John H. Surratt, who said he had to return to Washington, as he was employed by the Adams Express Company, and was on three days' leave. When this conversation took place, Surratt came to the supper table with his leggings on, and immediately after left on his horse for Washington. The same night at eleven o'clock Mr. Martin told Atzerodt that he believed that he was playing false with him, and that he intended crossing the river that night with another party. Atzerodt assured Martin he should cross in the first boat; that no one would cross that night, but on Wednesday night a large party of ten or twelve persons would cross; that he had been engaged that day buying boats; that they were going to have relays of horses on the road between Port Tobacco and Washington. Mr. Martin said: "What does this mean?" Atzerodt said: "I can't tell, but I am going to get well paid for it." John H. Surratt no doubt came down with instructions to Atzerodt that the President would be abducted at a certain time, and to have everything in readiness. Surratt had lately gone into the service of the Adams Express Company in Washington. Booth wanting him at a certain time, Surratt asked for leave of absence, and as it was denied him he left his place. It was for this work along this line that he resigned his position.

Instead of returning to La Plata over the same road, I took the one to Port Tobacco Station. On leaving the town a long hill had to be climbed, but the scenery to the station was quite romantic, which fully compensated for the uphill walk. The farms on this route were not under as good a state of cultivation as along the other one. I reached the station, situated in the heart of dense woods, where I sat for half an hour on a big pile of railroad ties, watching the lizards play " hide-and-go-seek " through the many holes in the ties. The train was on time, and landed me at Cox's Station a few minutes past seven; but not too late for a supper at the hotel. After staying at Cox's Station Tuesday night, Mr. Wills, the genial proprietor of the hotel, kindly offered to take me in his buggy to Pope's Creek. I had intended to walk down, but accepted his kind invitation; so we started immediately after breakfast Thursday morning, and the distance seemed very short behind a three-minute horse.

Pope's Creek is a small stream emptying into the Potomac about sixty miles from Washington. This is the southern terminus of the Pope's Creek Railroad. The point where Booth and Herold left the Maryland shore, at Dent's Meadows, is one and a half miles above this place. If they had gone according to the direction given them by Jones, they would have reached Machodoc Creek within five miles; but when their boat reached the heavy tide that was then coming in, in the darkness of the night they lost their bearings, and were carried twelve miles out of their way, reaching some time in the night Avon Creek, a tributary of Nanjemoy Creek. During the early morning Herold made his way to the house of

POPE'S CREEK, MD.

This point is sixty miles south of Washington, and was the popular ferry for transporting fugitives and contraband mail across the Potomac River into Virginia during the war, and here Thomas A. Jones conducted the work for the Confederate Government.

Colonel J. J. Hughes, a short distance from where they landed, and there secured something to eat and correct information as to their route back to Machodoc Creek. They remained in concealment Saturday the 22d, and during the night made their way to the mouth of Machodoc Creek. During the war Thomas A. Jones lived two miles south of this place, on a farm of nearly five hundred acres. The Potomac River bordered it on the west and Pope's Creek on the north. His small house stood on a bluff seventy-five feet high. A beautiful view was had from his house up and down the river for six or seven miles. It was just such a place as the Confederates wanted for a signal station, and Jones was just the man to carry on the secret transportation of the mail and also the people wishing to go south, and was connected with the mail service for the Confederates from the second year of the war to the close of it. It was his part of the work to transport the mail across the river, and he told me that he took over passengers many times when he feared they would be captured by the gunboats that were patrolling the river. Benjamin Grimes, who lived opposite to Pope's Creek, in King George's County, Virginia, two and three-quarter miles distant, attended to the business on that side of the river. Jones said it required great vigilance to carry out the work successfully. He was well qualified for just such dangerous operations. No one could detect anything in his appearance that indicated the business that he was engaged in. Grimes generally came across to Jones' farm and deposited the mail in the fork of a dead tree, and returned with the mail from the North that Jones had gathered up. Jones then delivered the mail to the three-pronged stump near Cox's Station.

Mr. Charles Drinks, the fisherman, announced his dory in readiness, so I stepped in, taking a reclining position in the stern, when the sails were hoisted, and the little fishing boat darted out into the river, pointing toward Machodoc Creek, five miles distant. There was a stiff breeze when we started, and I flattered myself I would have a short voyage, but the wind suddenly went

down, and the two boys in charge were compelled to
tack. The change was made so suddenly that it scarcely
gave me time to lower my head for the boom to pass
over. We now faced the Maryland shore for a short
time, when the course of the boat was changed. The
wind ceased entirely, and down came the sails. The boys
took hold of the oars and worked like old sailors. Two
hours' sailing, tacking, and rowing landed us half a mile
short of Machodoc Creek, but in front of the residence
of James A. Arnold. I had been directed to this place
as a proper one to gain such information as I desired
to obtain of that section. When I knocked at the door
it was opened by a bright young lady, and I inquired
for her mother. I was invited in, and when the mother
appeared I felt satisfied there must be a mistake, for she
looked entirely too young to know much of the early
scenes of the Civil War and the assassination of President Lincoln; but I ventured to tell her that I had been
directed to her for certain information concerning
Booth's stay for twenty-four hours in that section of the
country. A smile crept over her face, and she said
the lady to whom I was directed must be her husband's
mother, and I said perhaps that was true. She kindly
informed me that her husband was out at the light-house,
which we could see from the front room, and that she
was expecting to see him raise the sail of his boat at any
moment and come to shore. She made me feel at home
at once, and, while I was anxious to be going, I contented myself, patiently waiting for the sails to rise.

Mrs. Arnold has a very interesting family of girls, five
in number, and the mother seemed to be one among
them, making a cheerful, domestic home. An hour and
a half passed away pleasantly, and dinner was announced.
I did full justice to the meal, and felt thankful I had been

GAMBO CREEK.

A small stream running inland from the Potomac, into which Booth and Herold guided their boat, instead of the Machodoc Creek, as directed by Jones. The spot where they tied their boat was near a black-walnut tree. The tree has since been cut down, but a ten-foot section of it still lies upon the bank (1901).

detained at so pleasant a place. Mr. Thomas G. Ireland of Baltimore, a relative of the family, was spending some time here nursing a broken leg. He proved to be a good companion, so we chatted away until three o'clock, when Mr. Arnold, a jolly good fellow, landed with his faithful dog from the light-house. I said: " I have been waiting here since eleven o'clock to see you; " and he replied: " This is a pretty good place to wait." I at once told him the places that I wished to see, and if he would give me directions how to reach them I would start out, for I wanted to proceed on my way to Port Conway, twenty-two miles distant. He said: " I will show you these places, but you will have to stay here all night, for it will take the balance of the afternoon to visit these points." Well, as I had enjoyed the hospitality of the other side of the house, I concluded to accept his kind offer. I took my kodak, and we walked across his farm to a creek. " Now," said he, " this is Gambo Creek, and Booth and Herold came up to this point. There was a walnut tree standing upon the opposite shore, and it was under that tree that Booth rested while Herold went over to Mrs. Quesenberry's, a mile distant." The spot where they landed was on the farm of Dr. Hooe. The walnut tree was cut down lately, but the butt of it, probably twelve feet long, still remains by the stump. It will be remembered that Booth and Herold were directed to Machodoc Creek, on the banks of which Mrs. Quesenberry lived, but there was too much commotion among the small vessels that were in this creek, so they guided their boat up Gambo Creek. Mrs. Quesenberry sent Booth something to eat, and Mr. Thomas H. Harbin, brother-in-law of Thomas A. Jones, assisted Booth and Herold farther up the creek, and to Bryan's house.

We returned to the house, when Mr. Arnold had a horse hitched to a buggy, and Mr. Ireland was helped in, while Mr. Arnold and I walked. After passing through several gates of the farm, we came to a bridge over Gambo Creek. This was the end of navigation, as far as Booth and Herold were concerned, for here they were piloted to the house of Mr. Bryan. We passed over the bridge and continued for some distance, when we reached faint marks of a road leading into the woods to the right. The buggy could not follow, so Mr. Arnold and I continued to walk, stumbling over logs and dodging the low branches, until we reached a clearing on which once stood the log cabin of Mr. Bryan, in which Booth was entertained until the start was made for Dr.

Stuart's. The trees and shrubbery had grown up so thriftily around Bryan's cabin that a stranger going through the woods would never suspect that it was once inhabited. Bryan had for a housekeeper a colored woman by the name of Susan McGee, and Susan told the neighbors that she tried to cook some good things for Booth, but he would not eat anything. Booth left under the pillow that he rested upon a very neat little handkerchief, and Mrs. McGee kept it as a great trophy, after learning the name of the notorious person she had entertained. We retraced our steps to the buggy, Mr. Arnold returning on foot to his house after giving us the proper directions to get to Mrs. Quesenberry's. We drove on through fields and gates until

BRIDGE OVER GAMBO CREEK.

To this point Booth and Herold came in their boat, then left it as a gift to Mrs. Quesenberry for favors received. They were taken to the log cabin to Bryan's, a mile and a quarter distant.

we reached the house. It is beautifully situated in
a grove of trees, within fifty yards of Machodoc Creek,
the lawn sloping down to the water's edge. The
house and farm are now owned by L. N. Hoag, Sr.
On this farm the Confederate government established
a signal station to communicate with the one on
the Maryland side, located on a high hill south of Pope's
Creek. These two stations were successfully operated
for nearly two years—on the Maryland side right over
the heads of the Union soldiers who were encamped
there. Mr. Rously P. Quesenberry, a son of Mrs.
Quesenberry, lives on an adjoining farm. He was quite
young at the time Booth visited the neighborhood, consequently knows but little about those stirring times. He
says his mother was of a retiring nature, and did not say
much about the affair. Booth made Mrs. Quesenberry a
present of the boat in which he arrived, and it is said that
the Government took it in charge, but upon inquiring
at the National Museum I was informed it was not in
the possession of the Government. After spending half
an hour very pleasantly around this historic house, we
turned our horse toward Mr. Arnold's home, reaching
it just in time for supper. A social evening was spent,
with playing and singing by the young ladies. Mr.
Arnold, keeper of the Lower Cedar Point light-house,
left us, to remain at his station all night, but before going gave me proper directions to continue my walk to
Port Conway, which point I expected to make the next
day. Benjamin B. Arnold, the father of Mr. James A.
Arnold, my genial host, died some years ago. Mr.
Arnold, Sr., was engaged in the plot to abduct the President, and the part assigned him was to take charge of
Mr. Lincoln on the Virginia side of the river and hurry
him to Richmond. When the news of the President's

assassination reached the home of Mr. Arnold, which was at that time a few miles farther up the river, he expressed his regrets, saying: " I am very sorry the President was shot, but very glad they never succeeded in kidnaping him, for it let me out of a very dirty job."

On Friday morning, after breakfast, I bade this hospitable family good-by, and started on my day's journey as

HOME OF MRS. QUESENBERRY.

On Machodoc Creek, Va. To this house Booth was directed by Thomas A. Jones. Booth and Herold landed in Gambo Creek, three-quarters of a mile distant, and the latter made his way to the house for food and assistance, both of which were freely given.

the clock struck seven. I was a little fearful that I would get confused and lose my road, as the direction in which Bryan conveyed Booth was through woods and byways for some distance; but by inquiring frequently I succeeded very well. The only mistake I made I learned when I inquired at a neat little log cabin, with a colored portrait of President McKinley hanging in the window, where I was told I had walked half a mile past the summer home of Dr. Richard Stuart; so I retraced my steps until I came to a road leading to the right through rather a dense wood. The gate at this entrance was covered with wire, which tallied with the description that I received. The house is about half a mile from the road, facing to the east, over about ten acres of a lawn, and woods on three sides of it. I reached this place at eleven o'clock, ten miles from the river. Booth reached this place about 5 P. M. Sunday, and there is little doubt but that he expected a royal welcome; but in this he was keenly disappointed. Dr. Stuart had been under arrest several times for his complicity in the Southern cause, and, the war being over, he did not care to jeopardize his interest at that late date, so he absolutely refused to do more for Booth than give him something to eat and direct him half a mile farther on his journey to the house of William Lucas, a colored hired man living on Stuart's farm. To Booth this was a cutting disappointment, as the following note that he wrote and sent back to the doctor will prove:

Dea [piece torn out] Forgive me, but I have some little pride. I cannot blame you for want of hospitality; you know your own affairs. I was sick, tired, with a broken limb, and in need of medical assistance. I would not have turned a dog away from my door in such a plight. However, you were kind enough to give us something to eat, for which I not only thank you ; not for the rebuke and manner in which to [piece torn out]. It is not the substance, but the way in which kindness is extended, that makes one happy in the acceptance thereof. The *sauce* to meat is ceremony ; meeting were bare without it. Be kind enough to accept the enclosed five dollars, although hard to spare, for what we have had.

On my return to the road I inquired at the same little log cabin for the home of William Lucas, and was directed to it, which was almost opposite. I crossed a field and found the cabin unoccupied, except for various things stored there. A new house had been built within

ENTRANCE TO DR. STUART'S HOME.

Gate of lane leading to the residence of Dr. Richard Stuart, from the main Port Conway road.

thirty feet of it, owned by David Jett, a colored man. There ended the responsibility of Mr. Bryan, and he returned to his home. Booth remained in this cabin on Sunday night, the 23d, and early next morning William Lucas took them in a spring wagon to Port Conway, on the Rappahannock River.

After photographing the house I made my way to the road, and walked on two miles, which brought me to Weedenville, and I stepped into Mr. Weeden's general store and told him that I was a stranger, and hungry.

He said: " You shall not be hungry long." So he took three eggs from behind the counter, gave them to a colored man, saying: " Take these to the house and tell Mrs. Weeden to cook a dinner for a stranger." The house stood back of the store, and when I sat down to the table I felt that I could do justice to the good things Mrs. Weeden had prepared. I laid a silver coin upon the table, and gave thanks beside, but the good lady did not want to take the money. A few miles from this place I came to Edge Hill. A road turns here to King George's Court House, and at the forks of the road stands a large store building, and on the steps was a group of men engaged in exchange of opinions upon the prospects of the coming year's crops. They all ceased talking when I told of my errand through the country, and one of the number, R. H. Page, said that he was sitting on the steps of another store, that stood long ago where this one now stands, when he saw a two-horse spring wagon coming along. He only recognized the driver, William Lucas, and he asked him where he was going, and Lucas said: " Down the country." They did not stop. This was about 2 P. M. on the 24th. The last place that I stopped was in the country store of A. B. Golman, within two miles of Port Conway. The first question asked by him after he learned that I was from Washington was: " You must know my son, on the police force in Washington." I said, No, I did not know him, as I had avoided the police as much as possible in Washington, but I would look him up, and tell him that I had seen his father. I walked into Port Conway at 5 P. M., having covered the twenty-two miles since seven in the morning. The road the greater part of the way was sandy, making the walking difficult, and the day was quite warm. However, I did not feel fatigued. I stopped at the house of R. V. Turner, postmaster and storekeeper, with whom I had had some correspondence. Port Conway was at one time a busy little place, but it has gone into decay, and but little business is now transacted there. At this point the river is three-quarters of a mile wide.

At half-past nine on Monday the 24th Booth and Herold were driven into Port Conway on the Rappahannock River in a wagon. Booth paid William Lucas ten dollars for bringing them from his cabin, and

SUMMER HOME OF DR. RICHARD STUART.

This house is ten miles from the Potomac River. Booth expected aid and approbation from Dr. Stuart, but was repulsed instead. He was sent on to William Lucas, a colored tenant of Dr. Hughes.

then dismissed him. In half an hour after their arrival three Confederate soldiers, Captain William M. Jett, Lieutenant A. R. Bainbridge, and Captain Ruggles, made their appearance at the ferry. When the three officers stopped, Herold got out of the wagon and approached them, saying: " What command do you belong to? " Ruggles replied: " Mosby's command. Where are you going? " Herold replied: " It is a secret. Where are you going? " Herold then said his brother had been wounded below Petersburg, and asked if they could take him down to their lines. Herold then inquired of Captain Jett if they were raising a command, and, if they were, he would like to go with them south. When he was informed that they were not on recruiting service, he seemed to be disappointed, and then said: " We are the assassinators of President Lincoln." This bit of news seemed to shock the Confederates, and they scarcely knew what to say. Booth soon hobbled up to the party, when Herold introduced him as Booth, and Booth's first remark was: " I didn't intend telling that." After a short conversation the five were ferried across the river to Port Royal. Port Conway and Port Royal are two small villages directly opposite each other on the banks of the Rappahannock.

Saturday morning after breakfast I started in a buggy to the home of William Rollins, five miles north of Port Conway, to interview him, as he was the man whom the detectives pressed into service to conduct them and the cavalry to Bowling Green, the supposed destination of Booth and Herold. Rollins had heard the fugitives say upon their arrival at the ferry, in the presence of the three Confederate officers, that they wanted to go to that place. Rollins was at the time of my visit quite an old man, and very feeble,* but gave me a very clear account of his connection with the case. Said he: " While I was engaged at work on my fish nets at my house in Port Conway, someone called at my front door, and, upon

* Mr. Rollins has died since my visit to him.

my meeting him, he asked for a drink of water, which I handed him. He then asked for some more to take to his brother, who was lame, over on the other side of the street, thirty or forty yards distant. As soon as he returned from taking his ' brother ' the water, he began to ask some questions in regard to crossing the ferry, and

THE HOME OF WILLIAM LUCAS.

A mile from the country home of Dr. Stuart, now owned by David Jett (colored), whose family are seen in the picture. Booth was not refused admittance into this simple little home. He spent the night of the 23d of April in it, and the following morning William Lucas aided the fugitives on their journey.

what to do to get over. I told him that the boat was then aground, and they would have to wait until the tide rose before they could get over. Herold said they belonged to the Confederate service, had been over in Maryland, and wanted to get back to the army. I was asked which route would be the best, and I could not inform them, as they did not want to encounter any Union soldiers. While they were waiting for the tide to rise, so they could cross, three Confederate officers came down the road to cross, and they all crossed together. Next day in the afternoon a squad of Union soldiers came down and ordered my arrest as a guide to Bowling Green. The same night we crossed the ferry, just before sundown, and did not reach Bowling Green until between twelve and one o'clock. I was discharged about daylight, and returned to my home."

After my return from Mr. Rollins I went to the ferry to cross the river, but could not see the boat, and a man standing near said I should halloo; but my voice evidently did not reach the other side of the river, for I could see no stir. The gentleman standing near cried out in a stentorian voice: ".Ferry boat, ahoy!" The ferryman soon appeared, and rowed me across. Port Royal, in Caroline County, Virginia, is seventy-eight miles from Washington and twenty-two from Fredericksburg. It was created a town by the House of Burgesses in 1744. It was formerly one of the principal markets of the South for tobacco, but has long since lost its important trade. A boat stops here every other day from Baltimore to Fredericksburg, and the return is made on the alternate day. The harbor at one time admitted vessels drawing eleven feet of water. Some fine old houses still stand as monuments of past prosperity. The people at that period were intelligent, wealthy, hospitable, and aristocratic.

When Captain Jett with his companions and escort reached this side of the river he tried to leave Booth and Herold with a lady, who at first consented to receive them, but afterward declined: so the party started on toward Bowling Green, Booth riding behind Captain Jett and Herold behind Ruggles. Booth while crossing the river requested that he should pass thereafter under the name of Boyd.

As soon as I landed I started for Garrett's farm, three miles distant. When over half distance a young man from King George Court House drove up, and shared with me his seat in the buggy. He was looking up the faithful voters, and cautioning them to carefully look out for the doubtful ones. We soon reached the road that

PORT CONWAY, VA.

On the Rappahannock River. Booth and Herold were driven in a wagon to this place, Monday, April 24.

leads into the house, about three hundred yards distant. Captain Jett came this same road, and here unloaded his burden, which was surely a great relief to him. I had a pleasant conversation with Mr. Garrett, who at the time Booth made his visit was a young man. The house

stands just as it did at that time, with the exception of
the usual repairs. Several of the boards of the porch
floor, stained with the assassin's blood, have been taken
up and sold as relics. We walked out to the spot where
stood the tobacco house. The place had just been
plowed over for a crop of corn, and the plow struck the
end of one of the cedar posts of the barn and pulled up
at least a quarter of a peck of decayed cedar wood,
the remains of one of the posts of the house. Mr.
Garrett gave me a diagram of the barn, or rather
tobacco house. During the day (25th) Booth lounged
around the yard and was very little in the house.
While sitting on the porch the boys brought out a six-
barreled revolver, and were going to shoot at a mark,
when Booth said: "I'm a good marksman; let me
try my hand. Do you see the hole in the gate post?
I can put every ball in it." The pistol was an old one,
and frequently hung fire, and when he had snapped six
times one of the boys examined the hole and not one
of the bullets had entered it, but upon examination
were all found in the revolver. Booth felt somewhat
chagrined over the matter. It is to be regretted that the
last previous revolver he used had not hung fire as did
this one. Booth was very anxious to examine a large
map that hung on the wall, and asked one of the boys
to take it down. Booth spread it on the floor, and the
two sat down upon it, and Booth traced out a route,
and Garrett noticed that it led to Mexico. Now, the
great mystery is, Why did he keep the secret of his deed
from the Garrett's? They were sympathizers with the
South, two of the boys having just returned from the
Confederate army, and yet they say they did not know
why Booth was there. Booth felt free to tell Lloyd at
Surrattsville, Dr. Mudd at Bryantown, Colonel Cox, Mrs.

Quesenberry, and everyone along the route, and why did he keep it from the Garretts?

The capture of Booth was as follows:

William Garrett said that he and his brother John were ordered by the United States officers to carry brush and

HOUSE OF WILLIAM ROLLINS, PORT CONWAY.

The house with fish nets stretched in front was the home of William Rollins when the officers pressed him into service as a guide to Bowling Green, where Booth was supposed to have gone.

pile it against the south corner of the barn, and when Booth learned what they were doing, said: " Boys, stop that, or you will have to suffer the consequences." They suddenly ceased their operations, reported Booth's threat to the officers, and did not carry any more brush. The officers then placed William at the southeast corner and John at the northeast corner of the barn, and told Booth that if he fired upon any of the officers or soldiers these boys would be shot. Booth said that he did not want to shed innocent blood; that the two boys were innocent. William Garrett said that when the officer had set the barn on fire, and the flames encroached on the position that Booth took, near the middle of the barn, he could see him in the act of picking up a washstand that stood near him, for the purpose, he thought, of fighting the flames that were creeping toward him.

Miss L. K. B. Holloway, a school teacher, boarded at Garrett's at the time Booth visited the family, and tells some very interesting reminiscences of the occasion. She was at the house when the three Confederate soldiers rode up to it, Jett having Booth behind him on his horse. Herold had been left at the gate at the road. Jett dismounted and approached Mr. Richard H. Garrett, saying: "This is Mr. Garrett, I presume." On receiving an affirmative answer he introduced Booth to him as his friend John William Boyd, a Confederate soldier, who had been wounded in the battles around Richmond, at the same time requesting Mr. Garrett to take care of him until Wednesday morning, at which time he would call for him. Mr. Garrett consented to receive the so-called friend and entertain him. It was now about three o'clock in the afternoon of Monday the 24th of April. Jett and the two others returned to the gate where Herold was waiting. Herold was conveyed on the horse behind Ruggles to the house of a Mrs. Clark, who lived in the neighborhood of Bowling Green, where they spent the night, Jett going on to Bowling Green. On the following afternoon Jett and Bainbridge rode up to Garrett's, and Herold was seen to dismount from behind

PORT ROYAL, VA.

Opposite Port Conway. When Booth reached this side of the river he
was taken to Garrett's, three miles distant.

Jett and walk toward the house, while Jett and Bainbridge rode off. It was then that Booth asked Jack
Garrett to go upstairs and get his revolver. When asked
why he wanted it, he replied he always felt safer when
armed. Then he was asked who was approaching, to
which he replied: " Oh! that is one of our men."
" What do you mean? " asked Jack. " Why, one of
those who crossed over with us," he said, and, walking
off, he met Herold midway between the gate and the
house, where they remained in close conversation for
fully half an hour, after which they both came to the
house. Not long afterward Jett and Bainbridge rode up
hastily to the house to see, as Jett said, how his friend
Boyd was getting along, at the same time telling him
that he and Herold had better make good their escape,

for he had understood that the Federal troops were crossing over from Port Conway to Port Royal. They then galloped off.

It was about an hour before sundown, while Booth, Herold, and the family were seated on the porch, that the Federal cavalry was seen dashing along the road to Bowling Green. This somewhat alarmed Booth, and he and Herold repaired to a thicket back of the barn, remaining there until supper time. The action of Booth caused some little suspicion in the minds of the Garretts, and when Booth came from the timber he was asked why they, as ex-Confederate soldiers, should hide themselves now that the war was over? Booth replied that he did not care about meeting any Federal soldiers. Failing to comprehend the action of these two men, Jack Garrett resolved to institute some investigation. Upon inquiry, he learned that the Federal troops were in pursuit of two Confederate soldiers, one of whom was wounded; and the description which they gave corresponded exactly with those of the two men at his house. Upon returning home he asked Booth whether they had gotten into any trouble, saying: " You know what you have done; now if you have gotten into any difficulty, you must leave at once, for I do not want you to bring any trouble upon my aged father." Booth replied that they had gotten into a little brush over in Maryland, but it was all over.

Miss Holloway said that Booth was very cautious in his remarks while there. He would join in the conversation and make himself very agreeable, but said little. He never introduced a subject, but let others take the lead and then he would join in. A great many soldiers in going through that part of the country would stop at Garrett's for something to eat or drink, and

Miss Holloway said that as a general thing they were very talkative, ever ready to tell of what they did, and to express their opinion as to the final results of the war. Booth's ways were so different from these that it was noticeable by the family. When Jack Garrett brought Booth's revolver downstairs and handed it to him, Miss Holloway was sitting on the front porch. As Booth buckled the revolver on, she noticed that he had two others. There is no doubt that he could have done as he said he could—pick off a number of men around the tobacco shed.

Booth, being anxious to proceed on his journey, offered Jack Garrett one hundred and fifty dollars for his horse; but Garrett no doubt valued it far above that figure, for it was a present from General Grant at Appomattox. This was an illustration of the value of General Grant's magnanimous order, allowing the Confederate paroled prisoners to take to their homes their horses, and this order gave to the two Garrett boys two horses with which to commence life anew on the farm. Booth then offered Jack ten dollars to take him to Guinea Station, eighteen miles distant, and he agreed to take him early the next-morning. Booth paid Garrett the money in advance. The next morning came, but Booth was not alive to take the trip. Jack Garrett refunded the money to Lieutenant Baker. Booth had no money on his person when taken from the barn, and the Garretts supposed that when he found he could not escape he threw it into the flames. Jack Garrett asked Booth why he wanted to go to Guinea Station. He replied that he had heard that there was a Confederate Maryland Battery near Louisa Court House, which had not as yet disbanded, and if he could reach that he would be safe. When the hour came for their last night's retirement upon earth, Booth asked if there was an outhouse in which he could sleep that night, in order that he need not go upstairs. Being asked why he wished to sleep out, he replied: "I had rather not go upstairs." On being told that there was no place in which he could be made comfortable, he replied that anywhere would do rather than go upstairs. Booth proposed sleeping on the porch, but the elder Garrett objected, saying: "The dogs will bite; you can't sleep there." They were then conducted to a large tobacco house, in which was stored a lot of valuable furniture belonging to the people at Port Royal, who had placed it there for safe-keeping, as depredations were being committed by soldiers, and this furniture was principally old family pieces. After they had entered, Jack Garrett locked the door and gave the key to Miss Holloway, saying that he would leave it in her hands, and cautioned her not to let anyone have it, as it was his opinion their visitors intended trying to steal the horses and escape. After the strangers had been safely locked up, Jack and his brother William armed themselves and went out into a shed near the tobacco house to spend the night and keep watch on their neighbors.

About two o'clock the next morning (Wednesday) the family was aroused from sleep by the loud barking of dogs, the clanking of arms, and the heavy tread of soldiers pacing up and down the porch. Soon the inmates discovered that a sentinel had been placed at every door and window, and that the whole yard was full of soldiers. All at once there was heard a rush for the porch at the end of the house, followed by a violent battering against the kitchen door, with frequent demand that it be opened. When the senior Mr. Garrett heard the racket he arose, partially dressed himself, and hastened to the door to inquire the cause of the trouble. As soon as he made his appearance he was roughly seized and asked what he meant by harboring Booth, the murderer of the President. He answered that he was not harboring the murderer of the President. Instantly, notwithstanding the entreaties of his wife and little two-year-old daughter, he was taken by force from the house, half clad, threatened with handcuffs and the rope, and a pistol was placed at his breast. He was taken into the yard and set upon a block, where he remained until eight o'clock the next morning, with two soldiers guarding him. When Mr. Garrett learned that the officers and men had come to his place to arrest Booth, the assassin of the President, it suddenly dawned upon him that this Boyd must be Booth, and also that the officers had been directed to his place by Jett, who, when brought forward in the morning, was accused by Mr. Garrett of piloting the soldiers there and bringing all this trouble upon him. Jett made no reply to this accusation. Miss Holloway informed me that after Booth was shot and carried to the porch by the soldiers she moistened his lips and tongue three times, as he lay upon the porch, by dipping her handkerchief in some water. His tongue protruded each time that he made an effort to speak, and by this moistening he was enabled to faintly whisper his message to his mother, and the declaration that he thought he did what was right. Miss Holloway placed a pillow under his head and was rubbing his forehead, when he gave three gasps and died. A stray curl fell over her hand, and she requested Dr. Urquhart to cut it off and give it to her, which he did. After the departure of the body from the farm Miss Holloway said: " I went to the bookcase for some books, when the first thing that greeted my eyes was a pair of opera glasses, which I knew did not belong to any of the family. I concluded they must be Booth's, so I took them to Mr. Garrett and asked him what I should do with them. He replied: 'Take them out of my sight; I do not want to see anything that will remind me of this dreadful affair.' I told him I would send them up to my mother in a day or two. I then took a pin and marked J. W. B. under the buckle on the strap. During the day my brother, Robert G. Holloway, came to Mr. Garrett's, and I gave them to him to take up to my mother, thinking they were too valuable to be destroyed in the way of burning, as Mr. Garrett had directed. I thought of sending them to a friend of mine who lived in Richmond, Va. The next evening Lieutenant Baker, in company with Jack Garrett, came to Mr. Garrett's in quest of them. They did not really know they were there, but simply supposed Booth had them and thought they might be at Garrett's. Lieutenant Baker asked Mr. Garrett if they were not in his possession, and without any hesitancy he told the lieutenant that I had them. Baker then came to me and asked where they were. I very reluctantly told him. He and Jack Garrett went up to my mother's, about eight miles, and got them. They returned to Mr. Garrett's about four o'clock in the evening, and remained all night, returning to Washington the next morning."

The two boys, Jack and Willie, were taken prisoners to Washington by the soldiers and confined in Old Capitol Prison, and on the return of Lieutenant Baker to Garrett's he took Jack with him as a guide. Booth's stopping here has made a landmark of Garrett's farm. The family is of a retired nature, and do not enjoy the notoriety that has come to them.

I returned to Port Royal in time to dine at a new

boarding-house, politely presided over by Mrs. Arthur L. Garrett—not any way related to the family of the same name which I had just visited. Here I met Dr. Robert S. Holloway, a physician of many years' practice, and Mr. Champ Thompson, owner of the ferry. He is eighty years of age, and has always lived in Port Royal. In 1852 he purchased the ferry for two thousand dollars, and it was a fine investment, paying six per cent.

JAMES THORNTON.

The colored ferryman who ferried Booth and Herold across the Rappahannock on the 24th April, and the detectives and cavalry the following day.

Mr. Thompson let his son run the ferry for several years, making all out of it that he could. He hired a colored man, James Thornton, to run it, giving him half the proceeds. I was informed that the colored ferryman was still living in the place, so I looked him up. He is an old man now, but his memory of the crossing of Booth alive and Booth dead is very vivid. He was on the Port Conway side when Booth and Herold came to the river. They did not converse much with him, but were quite confidential with William Rollins and the three Confederate officers. When they were ready to be taken across, and rode up on the boat, Thornton asked Booth to dismount, as it was against the rules to allow anyone to ride a horse on the boat. Booth would not obey his command, so he was permitted to keep his seat. There was nothing in the actions of the party that created any suspicion in the mind of the ferryman, except the whisperings between the parties. The next day in the afternoon the cavalry came, and, as they stopped at the ferry, one of the officers asked the ferryman if two men had crossed the river recently. Mr. Thornton said that three men with horses and two men brought there in a spring wagon were all that passed over the day before. He said the wind blew very strong that day, and he only made one trip. The officers inquired their destination, and Mr. Thornton replied that he understood they wanted to go to Bowling Green. The officers wanted to compel Mr. Thornton to go with them to Bowling Green as a guide, but he told them that he had a "rising" on his finger, and it was very painful, but he directed them to William Rollins as having been present and engaged in conversation with the party, who, if the cavalry would go across the river, would show them the road. They crossed, and Mr. Rollins was pressed into service, much to the relief of Thornton. As soon as the order was given, the whole party, thirty men with horses, dashed on, crowding the "horse ferryboat" to its utmost capacity, the ferryman protesting, and saying that the boat leaked, and would not carry such a load; but the soldiers were not to be frightened at this announcement, and the load went over in safety, although a few worked hard bailing out the water. Mr. Thornton has been waiting all these years for the toll due from the two crossings of the officers and cavalry, and I think he ought to have been paid. Early on the morning of the 26th an officer rode into Port Royal and roused up Mr. Thornton, and told him to be in readiness to take a party across the river. When the procession came along the citizens turned out, surprised at the rude funeral car surrounded by an escort of cavalry. When a stop was made at the wharf the curiosity of some led them to peer into the vehicle, but they were soon ordered back. All they could see was a pair of feet protruding from under a blanket.

It was not long after the passage over the river until every inhabitant of Port Royal knew that the mysterious person was the assassin of the President.

The end of my journey had been reached, all the information relating to the flight, pursuit, and capture of Booth gained that could be, and I was ready to take the boat for Fredericksburg. The arrival of the boat from Baltimore depends upon the amount of freight to be loaded and unloaded at the numerous wharfs along the river. The Saturday previous it arrived twenty minutes past five, and I was ready at the wharf at the time, but, after waiting an hour, I walked back to the town and loitered around the street corners until Mr. Thornton invited me to accompany him home, there to remain until the boat whistled, which would give me sufficient time to reach the wharf by the time it made fast. I accepted his kind invitation, and was sitting in his spacious residence when I heard the boat whistle at half-past eight o'clock. I bade Mr. Thornton good-by, walked out to the gate, then turned to the left on a path leading along the fence. I had left my leather bag down at the wharf with the many views that I had taken, and was fearful that someone might purloin it, so started to run. I had not gone far when I thought I would step into the road, which I could see to my right, although it was quite dark. I had forgotten that the road had been cut through an embankment and was at least five feet below the path I stepped from. I fell, and lit on my right shoulder in the road. Lying stunned for a moment or two, I arose and proceeded to the boat, which had tied up at the wharf. I reached Fredericksburg a little after midnight, remained there until morning, and took the early train for Washington, where I arrived at a quarter of nine o'clock. I did not recover from my fall for four weeks, and a part of the time I suffered great pain. Aside from this accident there was no occurrence to mar my tramp of eighty miles.

I shall ever have pleasant recollections of the kind hospitality that I received from the people along the route. This is only characteristic of the Southern people.

307

BRYAN, 281 282 284 Mr 286
BUCKINGHAM, John E 16
BURNETT, 190 192 General 193
   H L 119 Henry L 116 117 189
BURNS, David 58
BURROUGHS, Joseph 15 21 55
   William McK 261 263
BUTLER, Rev Dr 204
BYRNE, William 87
CALLAHAN, 66
CALVERT, Mr 180 182
CANTLIN, John 218
CARLISLE, John G 238
CARRINGTON, E C 235
CHASE, Salmon P 40 Mr 173
CLARK, Charles 146 Clara 37 38
   Henry A 146 Mrs 295 Nannie
   37 P M 88 William T 37 38 39
CLARVOE, John 185
CLAY, 221 222 Clement C 219
   220
CLEARY, 221 W C 219 220
CLEAVER, Dr 236 William E
   144 236
CLENDENIN, D R 117 David R
   116
COBB, Silas T 243
COLFAX, Mr 4 5 Schuyler 3
   Speaker 217
CONGER, 69 Colonel 74 87 E J
   87 Everton J 68 86 Lieuten-
   ant-Colonel 78 79
CONOVER, 222 Sanford 221
CORBETT, 99 100 Boston 77 87
   98 99 Sergeant 74
COTTINGHAM, George 86
COX, 102 103 Captain 103 Colo-
   nel 101 256 257 266 267 269
   270 293 Harry 265 Mr 270
   Samuel 101 264 266 Samuel
   Jr 264 Walter 127
CRANE, Charles H 31 Dr 40
CURTIS, Dr 40
D'ANGELIS, 66
DANA, David D 255
DAVENPORT, E L 173
DAVIS, Jefferson 221 228 229
   Mrs 15
DAWSON, 164 Charles 79
DEAN, Appollonia 159 Miss 169
DELAMBILLY, Captain 231

DENIS, Father 157
DENT, Mr 271
DESAINTMARIE, Henri B 157
DEVORE, Eli 88
DIETZ, Frederick 87
DODD, L A 200
DOHERTY, E P 98 Edward 68
   Edward P 86 87
DOSTER, W E 127
DRINKS, Charles 278
DUNN, Mr 164
DUTILLY, Joseph T 224
DUTTON, George W 144 163
DYE, 236 Joseph M 235
EARLY, Bernard T 53 Mr 52 54
ECKHERT, Major 79
EDMONDS, J W 95
EDWARDS, Mr 235
EKIN, 191 James A 116 117
EWING, General 162 Thomas 127
FARRELL, Francis R 145
FITZPATRICK, Honora 65 159
   Miss 165 168 169 176 184
FLETCHER, John 46 245 Mr 47
   48
FORD, H Clay 8 Harry 10 15
   Henry Clay 11 James R 11 12
   John T 7 55
FOSTER, Robert S 116 117 Vice-
   President 217
FRANTZ, David 38
FREDERICK, G W 200
FREEMAN, Edward 78
FRENCH, B B 217
FULLER, John H 54
GALDMAN, Henry 69
GARDINER, George 45 142 Mr
   143 Squire 259 Thomas L 143
   146 Mr 79
GARRETT, 69 77 79 93 96 157
   222 292-297 299 Jack 71 296
   297 299 301 John 294 295 298
   Miss 96 Mr 292 293 299-301
   Mrs Arthur L 302 Richard H
   295 Richard Henry 70 William
   294 295 299 Willie 301
GAVACAN, Simon 251
GAYLE, G W 218
GEISSINGER, G W 200
GEMMILL, Z W 50 87
GENAY, Abraham 87

GILLETTE, Dr 204 Rev Mr 201
GLEASON, D H 172
GLYNN, Mr 222
GOLDSBOROUGH, Admiral 234
GOLMAN, A B 287
GRANT, 219 265 266 General 2 3
5 11 12 15 50 53 220 298 Mrs
5 11 53 Ulysses 189
GREENLEAF, Mr 124
GREENWALT, John 51 Mr 49
GRIFFIN, Mary Ann 88
GRILLO, Scipiano 237
GRIMES, Benjamin 278
GURLEY, Phineas D 31 Rev Dr
35
GWYNN, Bennett 179
HALE, Charles 233 Mr 234
HALLECK, W H 38
HANCOCK, General 84 205 W S
68
HARBIN, Thomas H 281
HARBORN, 135
HARRIS, Clara 5 97 General 127
Ira 97 Miss 23 98 T M xvii
116 117
HARRISON, John 224
HARROVER, 66
HART, May 28
HARTRANFT, General 132 198
200 201 John F 116 200 205
Major-General 124
HARVEY, Mr 209
HATTER, John C 53
HAWK, Harry 27 28 Henry 96 Mr
28
HENDERSON, James B 52
HEROLD, 47 48 66 69 71 73 78
79 84 86 91 100-102 106-108
110 120 134 135 144 162 163
172 174 176 196-198 200 205
206 210 211 237 241 244-251
253-256 258 264 266 268-272
274 276 277 280-282 284 288-
292 295-297 302 Dave 170
David E 46 79 127 135 136 157
195 204
HESS, C D 27
HILL, A P 265 Rich 102
HISS, Hanson 163
HOAG, L N Sr 283
HOEY, 66

HOLAHAN, John T 91
HOLCOMB, Professor 219
HOLLOWAY, L K B 295 Miss
297 298 300 Robert G 301
Robert S 302
HOLOHAN, 174 George 188 John
T 187 Mr 159 178 197 Mrs 174
HOLT, 192 J 84 Joseph 116 117
Judge 132 194 Judge-Advo-
cate-General 79 119
HOOE, Dr 281
HORMSBEY, Michael 87
HORNER, Eaton G 61
HOTCHKISS, George W 86
HOWE, A P 117 158 Alvin P 116
HOWELL, Spencer 166
HOYT, Philip 87
HUGHES, J J 277
HUNTER, David 116 117 General
119 John 245 W 228
HURON, George A 100
INGRAHAM, T 188
IRELAND, Mr 281 Thomas G 280
JACKSON, Susan 88
JENKINS, Mr 177 Olivia 65 184
JETT, 295 296 300 Captain 69
289'291 292 David 286 290
William M 288
JOHNSON, 135 Andrew 13 39 83
115 147 148 218 268 Hon
Reverdy 127 Mr 40 127 Presi-
dent 40 116 124 127 132 151
209 211 253 254 Reverdy 191
Vice-President 46 48 133
JONES, 105 106 108 260 272 276
278 John J 260 Thomas 261
Thomas A 100 101 107 109
260 264 267 269 271 273 277
281 284
JUDD, Norman B 213
KANZLEI, General 230
KAUTZ, A V 117 August V 116
KEENE, Laura 9 10 21
KELEHER, 46
KELLEY, Martin 87
KEY, 43
KIMBALL, J H 88
KING, Rufus 229 230
KIRBY, Mr 61 62
KLOMAN, Mr 174
KNOX, Kilburn 53

SURRATT (continued)
129 155 156 158 159 163 182
185 194 195 198 206 211 224
225 227–230 234–238 246 275
John Harrison 155 M E 182
Mary E 58 127 129 130 Miss
168 Mr 158 166 168 Mrs 59 61–
63 65 83 91 119 120 127–129
131 132 135 138 145 154 156–
159 161 163 165–171 175–182
184–187 190–192 195–198 200
204–206 210 211 236 237 246
247 Zouave 158
SWANN, 264 Oswald 256 266
TAFT, Charles 29 Dr 40
TAYLOR, Tom 10
THOMAS, Sam 108
THOMPSON, 46 221 223 253
Champ 302 J C 247 Jacob 219
222 James 221 John C 142
Margaret A 247 Millard 263 Mr
163 220 248 Mrs Millard 263
W S 137
THORNTON, James 302 Mr 303
304
TOFFEY, John F 44 Lieutenant
45
TOMPKINS, C H 116 117
TOWNSEND, E D 84 George
Alfred 198 S 50
TROTTER, Peter 259
TUCKER, 221 Beverly 219 220
TURNER, Henry A 259 R V 288
UNIAC, Michael 87
URQUHART, Dr 300
VANALEN, James H 3
VANNESS, 58
VANTYNE, Mary 51
VERDI, Dr 42
VEROT, Augustine 155
VEVINS, 66
WAITE, John M 67
WALDRON, Dr 155 E Q S 153
Rev Mr 155
WALKER, James 49
WALLACE, Lew 116 117 127
William 54
WALLACK, Lester 173
WALSH, Francis S 137
WALTER, Father 200
WALTERS, 234

WALZ, John 87
WARD, Anna 175 178 183
WARE, John 108
WASHINGTON, Frank 255 George
124
WATSON, John 228 230 231
WATTS, A R 200
WEAVER, J H 209 John C 38 Mr
210
WEEDEN, Mr 286 Mrs 287
WEICHMANN, 58 144 154 155
157–159 161 163–166 168–171
174–176 178–182 184–186 189
190 192 193 228 229 234 L J
153 Louis J 154 159 188 Mr
156 160 162 163 164 165 166
167 172 177 183 187 194 237
WELLS, H H 86 87
WENDELL, Andrew 87
WERMERSKIRCH, Captain 62 W
M 88
WESTFALL, J W 217 John W
216 Mr 217
WHARTON, John W 61 173
WHEATLEY, J W 245 Mr 247
WHITE, Charles I 155 Dr 180
WIGETT, Father 200
WILDING, A 227
WILKES, 89 Jim 89
WILLIAMS, Captain 105 Samuel
J 87 William 105 251
WILLS, Mr 276
WILMER, Parson 252 256
WILSON, N 235
WINTER, John 87
WIRZ, Captain 211
WITHERS, William Jr 20
WOOD, 175 Charles H M 236
Louis 167 Mr 168
WOODLAND, 262 270–272 Henry
109 261 263 264 267 269 270
272 273
WOODWARD, Assistant-Surgeon
206 Dr 40
WRIGHT, H Estes 37 J P 20 Mr
21
YATES, Richard 3
YOUNG, Bennett H 220 George W
87
ZIMMER, Charles 87
ZISGEN, Joseph 87